Accolades

"For years I've known Floyd Forsberg as a reliable source whose every news tip panned out. Now Forsberg has written the best personal indictment of America's horrific prison system that I've read since Ted Conover's 2000 classic, "Newjack: Guarding Sing Sing." Forsberg's plainspoken prose tells a soul-searching tale of survival and transformation that will touch readers from all walks of life. The angry young man determined to be the country's best bank robber has emerged as the sage author of a life story that reads like a thriller and traces his daring escape *from The Toughest Prison of All.*"

— **Richard Read,** two-time Pulitzer Prize winner, *the Oregonian/Oregonlive*

"After 35 years in law enforcement, I have worked with many professional cops and encountered many professional thieves. Floyd Forsberg was one of the best career thieves around and created thousands of headaches for my peers. *The Toughest Prison of All* is a great read with a twist ending that doesn't happen very often. The insider view of crime taught me things that I had never considered. I'm already looking forward to his next book."

— **Tom Allman,** Sheriff-Coroner of Mendocino County (California) and co-author of *Out There in the Woods*

"As a recently retired police sergeant, having served nearly 29 years, I can relate to Frosty's desire to escape prison. Transporting many prisoners to jail, I was always well aware when the gates allowing our vehicle to enter would slam shut, the steel bars to the doors clanging hard and loud as they closed, locking us in with the prisoners and the sign on one prison wall saying, "This is not a country club." I, too, couldn't wait to leave. Forsberg will take you from the edge of your couch to a small prison cell to a life on the run and keep you guessing every step of the way."

— **Angelo LaManna**

"As someone who has helplessly watched the horror of the criminal justice system from the outside, I can understand how incredibly frustrating it must have been for Floyd to be thrust into that nightmare from such an early age. A healthy society needs a healthy justice system, but as Floyd points out, that's not what we have here in America. Floyd's story of how he came to understand the trap he set for himself, and how he managed to get out of it, is an inspiration."

— **Jocelyn G.**

"When I started reading this book two things became clear: Floyd Forsberg is a very likable guy; and after hearing about his childhood, it was clear he didn't stand a chance to have a normal or easy life. Throughout the entire book I found myself rooting for Floyd to succeed or just to get out of his own way. The part I had the most trouble with was the behavior of the FBI. I think some of us have a hard-enough time walking a straight line without people that are supposed to enforce our laws and set an example for the rest of society behaving in questionable and sometimes utterly illegal ways. Hearing about the behavior of those agents doesn't just punish people like Floyd, it also leaves a mark on all of us. It sure left a mark on me."

— **Tony Onorato**

Half Title

THE TOUGHEST PRISON OF ALL
The true story of a career bank robber and
how he broke his addiction to criminal thinking
Floyd C. Forsberg

THE TOUGHEST PRISON OF ALL

The true story of a career bank robber and how he broke his addiction to criminal thinking

FLOYD C. FORSBERG

THE TOUGHEST PRISON OF ALL:

The true story of a career bank robber and how he broke his addiction to criminal thinking

Floyd C. Forsberg

The events described in this book are true, and many are part of public record. Some names and identifying details have been changed to protect the privacy of individuals involved.

ISBN: 978-1-952043-12-3

Library of Congress Control Number: 2020944483

Second Edition: 2020 by Carlisle Legacy Books, LLC

First Edition: 2015 by Genius Book Publishing

Edited by Manny

Back Cover Photograph from FBI files. Used under Creative Commons License.

Photo of McNeil Island photograph used under Creative Commons License.

Cover Design by C. Lindsay Carlisle

Published by Carlisle Legacy Books, LLC
https://www.carlislelegacybooks.com

Created with Vellum

Acknowledgments

As the reader will see, there are many people who played a role in my escape from the Toughest Prison of All.

Some who played the largest roles need to be mentioned here with special gratitude:

Nancy
Delores
Dr. John Akin
Manolo
Jane Fields
Dr. Rex Newton
My friends at IRC (Insulation Removal Corp.)
The Prison Ashram Project

An extra special thanks to my former editor and publisher, Steven W. Booth, who believed I had something worth sharing with the public. I would also like to thank Dr. Al Carlisle, who has supported this project from the beginning, and Ron Witkowsky, who has been my biggest fan and most dedicated champion throughout the publishing process.

Last but not least, I must thank my sister Sharon who never gave up hope that someday I would "grow up."

To Paula

Contents

Foreword

By Dr. Al Carlisle, Ph.D.

Crime is a popular topic in America. Television series such as *CSI, Criminal Minds, NCIS,* and a host of other crime-related programs are a large part of the weekly viewing schedule for millions of people. Nightly news reports often begin with "breaking" stories of homicides, police chases, and scandals. If there is an ongoing violent crime taking place now, a moment-by-moment account of it may crowd out other pre-scheduled network shows for several hours. America is fascinated by crime.

Crime novels and true crime histories are also extremely popular. These books are usually written by authors who glean their information from news articles, court documents, and police reports. It's relatively rare that we have an account of criminal activity which comes directly from the criminal himself.

The public often asks why a person chose that lifestyle.

Is he mentally ill?

Did he come from a bad family?

Is he a psychopath?

Is it possible for him to ever change?

The Toughest Prison of All is a personal account of Floyd Forsberg's life of crime, beginning when he was a teenager and continuing until he was released from federal prison in 1992. His criminal activity began with burglary in 1956 and it advanced to purse snatching, car theft, forging of stolen money orders, assault, attempted bank robbery, bank robbery, and finally murder. On September 24, 1974, he and three others pulled off a one-million-dollar heist at the First National Bank of Nevada in Reno, which was the most famous bank robbery up to that time.

Floyd has now been out of prison for 22 years. He and his wife are living in the Pacific Northwest. His full-time job as a truck driver provides a modest but comfortable income for the two of them. If you drove by his home you would not sense that at one time Floyd was one of the most famous bank robbers in history.

I first came in contact with Floyd when a friend told me about this book, which was written by Floyd while he was in prison. As much as it is an account of his life of crime, more importantly it is a diary of the emptiness he still experienced following years of robberies and other criminal activities. My career as a psychologist in the Utah state prison system allowed me to interview inmates who had engaged in homicide, robbery, sex offenses, and white-collar crime. I was intrigued by the challenge of understanding the man who wrote this book. He sent me a copy of his manuscript, all handwritten. My typist transformed his manuscript into text and I brought the book to my publisher, Stephen Booth at Genius Book Publishing, and the book was accepted for publication.

The reader is taken on a journey with Floyd from the time he began making adult decisions about his life, although still being too young to understand what life was all about, to the point he began to seriously ask the questions he should have asked as a child.

In *The Toughest Prison of All,* Floyd allows you to listen in on the planning of several bank robberies. He takes you into the bank with him and his friends and he allows you to watch from the sidelines while they attempt to pull off several heists. He delineates the obstacles they encountered and how they were pursued, and often caught, by the police.

He tells you about the difficulty he had relating to women. One moment he is unable to feel love and he believes it will never be possible for him to do so. But then he finds his "true love" and falls madly in love with her. He tells you of his struggle when having to choose between love and crime.

Floyd didn't start out wanting to be a master criminal, but even before age 10, Floyd's life was dysfunctional and challenging. It wasn't until he lost his father that his mind turned to criminal activity. Greed and revenge were primary driving forces in his life; his one goal for his future was to become an expert bank robber. An analysis of his personality at that time would likely have concluded that he met the criteria for the beginning stages of becoming a sociopath. The diagnosis has since been changed in the mental health field and what diagnostically began as *psychopath* became *sociopath*, and then the psychological community finally settled on the term *Antisocial Personality Disorder*. However, since Antisocial Personality Disorder is so broad and is based primarily on behavior, the initial term of psychopath remains popular.

Although Floyd was not a violent person per se throughout the years, he placed himself in the arena of violent activities. Floyd does not show the characteristics of a psychopath now, but when I spoke to him recently, he acknowledged that the definition fit him throughout his years of criminal activity. Floyd doesn't attempt to justify his actions. He details his crimes in a very personal way, and his time in a number of institutions and his criminal beliefs are laid bare. One comes away with an understanding of the various aspects of the life of a criminal. His discussion of his friends and his life in prison is particularly interesting.

As much as this book reveals criminal behavior and the particulars about living in a penal institution, this book is not about prison walls or institutional systems. It's about what Floyd discovered about himself that caused him to give up his life of crime. It's about why he decided to give up his psychopathic thinking and become a normal citizen. It's about how he has been able to remain out of prison for the past 22 years.

This book is a good read. Once you start into it, you will have a hard time putting it down.

Al Carlisle, Ph.D.
June, 2015
Price, Utah

Dr. Carlisle retired as the head of the psychology department at Utah State Prison in 1989, shortly after interviewing Ted Bundy for the last time. He is the author of *The Development of the Violent Mind* series: *I'm Not Guilty: The Case of Ted Bundy*, *Mind of the Devil: The Case of Westley Allan Dodd and Arthur Gary Bishop*, *Broken Samurai: One Marine's Journey from Hero to Hitman,* and *The 1976 Psychological Assessment of Ted Bundy.*

Prologue

Seeking El Dorado

September 27, 1974. We had planned long and very carefully for this day. *True Magazine* would later call what we were about to do "Reno's most perfect robbery." It was the biggest bank heist in American history.

Each of the members of our team knew that there were several million dollars locked inside the vault of the bank we had targeted. Ten months had been spent on the planning stage of this one Big-Time robbery which, like Aladdin's Lamp, would make all of our wishes come true. We'd left nothing to chance.

Collectively, we'd served a total of 22 years behind bars for our past bank robbery convictions. Time enough to review past blunders and learn from all our previous mistakes. Time enough, too, to grow bitter and plot revenge upon an "unjust society" that was simply too blind to see the nobility of our chosen profession. Thousands of days spent justifying the evil that resided inside each of us.

I was working with one of the nation's premier bank robbers:

Curtis Ray Michelson. Two years earlier, I'd helped him escape from McNeil Island, the nation's only remaining island penitentiary. Since then, his little band of revolutionaries had pulled off several lucrative bank robberies, including Oregon's largest heist —but nothing like the one we were planning—to finance the movement that was his war on society.

This was war, and we were its soldiers. Each of us had our rank. Curtis was our General. Ed Malone was Captain. This was my first robbery as a full member of the Michelson organization. As such, my rank was Lieutenant.

Ever since I'd begun stealing when I was 12 or 13 years old, I had always dreamed of being part of a highly sophisticated robbery gang. The petty burglaries and small-time stickups were all behind me now. In addition to the multimillion-dollar heist that was planned for this day, there was also an armored car robbery still on the drawing board. Before long, plans would also have to be finalized for the assassination of a federal judge who had stirred up the wrath of the General. At long last I was in the big time!

The bank had been closed for hours. The only people still remaining inside the building were a handful of tellers, some assistant vice presidents, and a single guard who watched over the counting of the huge cash volume handled by Reno's largest bank, which was situated on the corner of Second and Virginia Streets, right behind Harrah's Reno Hotel and Casino in the heart of Casino Row. The area was filled day and night with tourists who by and large were all seeking their own El Dorado. Like the early Spanish explorers who sought their fortunes, most of the tourists would go home empty handed. *We* planned to leave the City of Reno, Nevada as winners. We would do exactly that—with over a million in cash. Yet, like the majority of the city's gamblers who sometimes managed to hit it big, we would eventually lose our winnings in ways we could never imagine. If I could have foreseen the future on that September day, I'd have thrown down the million dollars I would carry out in my duffel bag and I'd have run off in the opposite direction.

In the moments before the robbery, everything seemed perfect. The street was empty of cars, which added a curious aura of unreality to what would unfold as the pinnacle of my criminal career. Even without the usual Reno traffic, the city was more crowded than usual. Eight hundred Shriners in their silly little hats would soon be marching down Virginia Street. It was for this reason that the police had stopped all traffic just past the bank we were about to hit.

Even gamblers love a parade, and many of them had swarmed out of the casinos to line both sides of Virginia Street. The bank, the only building on the entire block that was not an establishment for games of chance, held for us the highest stakes we'd ever faced in the game of FBI roulette. As professionals, the odds were in our favor, or so we believed. The General, for example, was a master locksmith and an expert at disabling alarms. He carried a .223 AR-15 in a specially-designed break-away duffel bag, ready for quick use in the event we became trapped inside the bank and had to shoot our way out. He also carried in his pocket a police scanner with an earphone attachment resembling a hearing aid. The scanner was tuned to the frequencies used by the Reno City Police and the Washoe County Sheriff's Department. It automatically ran across all four of their channels, stopping at any band actively in use.

Of greater concern to us was the matter of the casino's security forces. Each casino had its own uniformed and plain clothed guards. Harrah's security people were frequently in this bank, entering through their own private entrance into the basement. They represented just another one of the many obstacles that Curtis Michelson's genius had neutralized. I found it simply uncanny how the General could figure out and overcome anything.

Curtis assigned each of us our own primary objective. Mine was to restrain the bank employees and the guards. In my duffel bag, I carried a dozen pairs of handcuffs along with a bundle of rawhide boot lacings to bind my captives' feet. Each one of us also knew everyone else's job and we were assigned a secondary objective as an alternative plan of action in the event anything went wrong at any stage of the operation.

"Objective," "Maneuver," "Operation," "Rear-guard action." These and many other military terms are what I learned and memorized as a member of the Michelson band. Curtis *was* our General, and he demanded discipline and military precision from all who served him. I learned this the hard way. Years earlier, while helping to break him out of Federal prison, I deviated from the original plan and spoiled his early morning departure from the almost escape proof McNeil Island Penitentiary in Washington's Puget Sound. My lack of attention threw off the timing of the entire operation, and I literally had to smuggle him back inside the institution before he missed the morning head count. Later that same day, we tried the escape again, but this time I followed his instructions to the letter and he made it off the island.

On another occasion, Curtis was questioned by the police after a job we had just pulled off. He blamed me for this unwanted scrutiny, claiming that I had failed to follow the exact orders he'd given to me. He could have killed me for the blunder —which really wasn't my fault—but I was lucky, and he gave me another chance. The two officers who questioned him were also incredibly lucky for not having had any idea who it was they'd been questioning. Had they stumbled upon his true identity at the time they were speaking to him, they would have been dead before they knew they were in danger. Curtis Michelson was not a man to be trifled with.

More than a year would pass after the Reno job before I began to realize how much Curtis Michelson actually needed me as part of his overall plan. But on this day, as we pushed though the throngs of people that filled the sidewalk in front of the bank, I was convinced that I was the one who needed him.

Curtis was looking directly at me when we stopped to review our plan a final time. "Floyd, have you decided where we can leave the van so it will take the longest possible time for the cops to find it after we dump it?"

Curtis had asked me this same question several weeks before. As he waited for my answer, I couldn't help but feel somewhat embarrassed. No matter how hard I tried, it seemed I could never equal his criminal brilliance. Even when I came up with an idea I thought I could be proud of, he would tear it down and belittle me. Then, a week or two later, he would wind up using my suggestion—after tweaking it just enough to pass it off as his own.

In any case, I said we could leave the van at the airport or in one of the crowded casino parking lots. I believed this was the tactic most professionals would follow.

Curtis gave me a look of contempt. I wasn't surprised, but it still hurt coming from a man I admired so much. He was never satisfied with any idea unless we ended up doing things in some unique or different way, which is to say, *his way.*

"Don't be ridiculous! That's the first place they'll look." Then he smiled at his own brilliance. "We're going to leave the van parked right across the street from the damn Sheriff's office!" His eyes were bright with a kind of gleeful criminal arrogance. "Just imagine the sight of all those pigs pouring out of the station and jumping into their cars to search for the van—and it will be sitting there right under their noses the whole time!"

No doubt about it, I really did admire him in those days. I admired his genius, his artistry, his confidence, and the seeming touch of class with which he carried himself, all so reminiscent of the legendary bank robber Willie Sutton. Yet he could also be quite cutting.

"I guess some people are just destined to remain in the ranks," he snorted, his derisive laughter flicking like a serpent's tongue.

In the years I had known Curtis, he had often said I would never make it as a successful criminal.

While we were imprisoned together at McNeil Island, he had just as often disparaged my plan to work as a meat cutter when I was released from prison. Curtis had never been interested in any trade other than bank robbery. Perhaps he assumed that the same was true of me. Hence, in his mind, all my intentions to go straight would always and inevitably come to naught. I could never change, he told me time and time again. "The system" was designed to cause ex-cons to fail.

"So you might as well join my group," he had said to me, "and maybe you just might make something of yourself."

During the five years I worked in the prison butcher shop, I genuinely believed I could change. Some prisoners, at least initially, really *do* hope for some form of personal transformation. Like caterpillars imprisoned in a cocoon of concrete and steel, we dream of stopping the cycle of pain and despair that people in the penal system so bureaucratically refer to as "recidivism." We yearn for a rebirth of sorts, a fresh new nature that might allow us to soar away with butterfly wings to an unspoiled life, never to return to the agony of repeated incarceration. But, in my case, the only lesson I ever learned from all that time and pain was that Curtis Michelson was right: For me, transformation was a virtual impossibility.

Chapter One

A BUDDING CRIMINAL MIND

Community—as defined by Webster:

A)All the people living in a particular district, city, etc.

B)A group of people living together as a smaller social unit within a larger one and having interests in common.

How strange the circumstances that led to my enlistment in Curtis's little army. Looking back, it's hard to remember a time when I wasn't in trouble, either committing crimes or locked up behind bars. Even as a kid, I had been wild, no doubt about it. Ironically, my first stint behind bars was a six month stretch for the *crime* of being a runaway, even though my mother was just as happy to be rid of me. I had even told her that I was leaving.

In those days, disposable children were routinely incarcerated for no other reason than they had no parents or legal guardians willing to watch over them. It certainly seemed unfair to me at the time. I was the victim of an unjust society. I've since learned that being a victim was much easier than playing by the rules. Victims have no responsibility for their actions or the compromising situations in which they find themselves. The truth is that this "victimhood" was just an excuse to do whatever

I damn well wanted to do. Throughout my entire life as a criminal it was this mindset that characterized and ruled me from my earliest days as a runaway to my later years as a hardened felon.

∽

I was born on November 25, 1941 to the working class, the alcoholic class, and the hit-your-wife-if-she-gets-out-of-line class. Smoking was cool and done in the theaters, restaurants, and hospital waiting rooms. All the adult men I knew as a child worked and drank and screwed around and hit their wives and kids. It was *normal,* and society did not interfere into "family matters" like domestic abuse. I was whipped with a belt for bad behavior and felt lucky about it. Some of my friends got a parental fist.

As with most people, early memories of youth don't come with a calendar. I remember moments of joy or pain, or sometimes feeling nothing. Living in the country around Ridgefield, Washington, I was always in the woods near the Columbia River, shooting birds, frogs, rabbits; anything that moved. Such disregard for living creatures was a part of my emptiness. Those feelings of isolation are the foundation for many types of antisocial behaviors, and I guess I wasn't spared.

One of my earliest memories was of long hours spent waiting in our 1948 Dodge for my father to come out of the local tavern. Every hour or two he would emerge and give me a couple of candy bars as payment for my patience. I did not like to wait, not in front of the bar nor in front of the house where his ex-wife lived. It took me a while to figure out why I was bribed to not mention these stops to my mom. Despite drinking and other faults, I was saddened by his death when I was ten years old.

At such an age, death is not real, not a fact. I had lost pets, of course, but these animal friends were always quickly replaced, continuing the illusion of permanence. It was a Sunday and life had been moving along at a happy pace. My dad had been sober for a couple months. School would soon end and the prospect of spending the summer with my dad on his commercial fishing boat was the highlight of my life. It was my bedtime and I was in bed listening to the radio. Radio was the medium of the day. You listened and the story unfolded in your mind.

I heard car doors slamming, and I looked out the window. I saw five or six cars, a couple I recognized as belonging to my uncles, which surprised me because it was the spring salmon run, and they did their gillnet fishing at night. I heard a commotion downstairs but could not hear clearly enough to know what was going on. My curiosity led me to make up a story that I thought would give me a reason to break my bedtime curfew. I decided to ask if my shirt for the next day had been washed. I knew it had been, but I hoped my mother would forget she had told me.

Upon reaching the first floor, I could hear my mother sobbing. I entered the kitchen and saw her seated at the table, her head on folded arms. My aunts and uncles all looked upset. Someone told me my dad had fallen overboard and was presumed drowned. They had searched but not found the body. Since I had formulated a lie to excuse myself for being downstairs, it was still in my mind and had to come out. I asked if my shirt was ready for school. I was told I didn't have to go to school the next day.

Even children can enter into denial. I went back upstairs, not realizing how completely my life had changed that night. The next morning, I awoke and wondered if my experience of the night before had been a dream. I turned my radio on and heard the news of my missing and presumed drowned father. It seemed even more unreal because my father and I shared a name, and they kept repeating that Floyd Clayton Forsberg was dead.

As I listened to the events unfold on the radio, it occurred to me that this was all a made-up story. My father, I decided, hadn't died. Obviously, he had gone undercover for the FBI, as happened all the time on the radio shows I listened to. In 1952, the United States was in a cold war against the Red Menace. And just a few months earlier, the leader of my Cub Scouts pack had been labeled a communist and run out of town. My dad and everyone I knew hated "the Commies," and I just knew my dad had gone undercover to help the FBI seek out those traitors who wanted to destroy our democracy. As the days passed and no body was found, I believed my denial fantasy even more. His brother was in Korea fighting the Reds and now my dad was doing his part. I was proud of my dad even as I missed him.

About ten days went by before the body was recovered. The funeral was a closed casket ceremony, so for a while I thought that even the funeral was just part of the cover story. Eventually, however, the denial turned into emptiness and my childhood ended.

∽

While my dad lived, he provided for his family. His death left my 25-year-old uneducated mother with my sister and me and no way to support us. My dad and his brothers owned a fishing business together. After my dad's death by drowning, my uncle gave my mother $5,000 towards my dad's share of the family business, promising the other $20,000 at a later date, which not surprisingly never came. My mother being cheated by my father's family led us to leave our small town and began a series of moves that continued for years. We were lucky if we only moved *once* in a school year. The only sense of community I ever had was with my classmates in Ridgefield, Washington. Leaving them to move to Arizona after the sixth grade was a great emotional loss for me.

When I was 12 years old, I was introduced to shoplifting by a neighbor. It was a hobby I continued on my own as we moved from town to town and state to state. It wasn't long before I graduated to burglary. I felt alive during a burglary. I felt unique, not bound by any laws. At the same time, I found myself feeling alone.

In 1956, I ran away from home with a neighborhood friend. Or, as the authorities put it, I "left home without my mother's permission." At this point I really didn't need her permission. I was big enough that she could no longer physically control me. We had had our showdown about six months earlier, when I was 14. She had started to take the belt to me and I grabbed it from her hand and shoved it at her and said that there would be no more of that, in a voice that made an instant believer out of her. She never tried to whip me again.

When the neighbor boy returned home, his dad whipped him and he confessed that we had stolen a purse to get money for bus tickets. Not long after the showdown and my unauthorized absence, my mother found some guns under my bed and figured that was good enough to get the authorities involved. She turned me in to the police. I would hardly ever speak to her after that. She was a "rat," at least under the code I believed in.

Being locked up in the Luther Burbank School for Boys should have been a strong indicator to me that I'd gone too far. Even before this, I should have learned from all those times I'd already had to face the fear of getting caught. All those times I lay hidden in the grass of some abandoned lot, too afraid to breathe as the cop searched only inches away from me, close enough that he might step on my arm—and then it would be all over.

I had always been ready to give up criminal behavior any

time I was hotly pursued by a man wearing a uniform and badge. Desperately, I would swear to God that I would clean up my act, if only He would help me evade my pursuer. Then, after getting away safely, I would sometimes quit prowling the streets and stay home for a few days. But I was never one to honor my prayers or commitments to God, I'm afraid. Really, the reason I'd stay home was only because those near captures were physically and emotionally draining. Inevitably, as my strength returned, so would my sense of superiority over the society—over "the herd," as I saw everyone who lived outside and beyond my mother's front door. Without any doubt, mine was a predator mentality.

ᔓ

The Luther Burbank School for Boys, located on Mercer Island near Seattle, was a reform school, a place of detention with heavy prison style mesh wire screens covering all of its windows. Daily dress at Luther Burbank consisted of a short-sleeved shirt, jeans, and work boots. We could wear jackets when it was cold —which, being near Seattle, was most of the time. At the end of the day the work boots were locked up and we wore slip on laceless shoes which were only enough to keep our feet warm indoors—and which were intentionally inadequate for running through the nearby woods in the dead of night. Those young detainees who had yet to complete the eighth grade were required to attend classes all day long. The older boys were expected to work half of each day and then attend classes the other half.

Even then, our budding criminal minds embraced the notion that work of any kind was beneath us. All new arrivals were expected to run off at least one time. This would prove that they were "regulars," and also make a token show of defiance against what we considered to be forced labor.

I was no exception. After a week of picking vegetables half the day and then lying awake at night with my mind ever fearful of homosexual attacks, I was ready to leave. When I left, I went with two fellow delinquents, Ralph and Tom, who were equally prepared to flee.

It should surprise no one that when it comes to youngsters breaking out of any kind of lockup facility, a complete lack of foresight or attention to detail inevitably leads to capture. Most escape attempts are rarely ever planned with anything more in mind than getting over the outside fence or wall. We had every reason in the world to go. It was common knowledge that escapees from Luther Burbank would never be charged with any crime committed while on the run. Ironically, the adults viewed us as "kids who'd just never had a chance. Society had failed them." If we were caught, our punishment would never be more severe than 60 days additional time for "failure to respond to treatment." It was an unspoken rule, and we all knew it.

Ralph and Tom had both escaped before, so they were familiar with the island, which was attached to the mainland by a floating bridge. They also knew where a car could easily be found and stolen. We left during the showing of the weekly Friday night movie.

It was wet and cold that night. My slippers were soaked the minute I squeezed out the window of the basement clothing room. As we disappeared into the darkness, which was filled with the sounds of crickets, frogs, and other creatures of the night, I was already wishing that I was back inside, warm and dry, watching the Friday night movie. Soon enough though we were well away from the school with our stolen transportation and financing our flight with a string of burglaries that we managed to pull off before our clothes were even dry.

The next day, I took my share of the loot and headed home to Ridgefield, far south of Seattle, to see my friends. Most of them had moved away by then, and I couldn't blame them. Ridgefield was a small town near Vancouver and anywhere else was better. Some of my friends had joined the military early, while others were in the Washington State Training School in Chehalis, another reform school. With all my friends gone, I quickly became bored. Remembering that I had only six months to serve, I decided to turn myself in. Tom and Ralph had been caught in the stolen car less than 24 hours after I'd left them and were already back at Luther Burbank. When I returned, I guess you could say that I was finally back among friends.

Chapter Two

DOGS AREN'T WELL VERSED IN PSYCHOLOGY

My six months passed quickly, and I was released at age 15 without fanfare and returned to my mother's care. Immediately, I started planning some new jobs with my next crime partner, Leon Baker. Our idols were John Dillinger, Baby Face Nelson, and Bonnie and Clyde—all the bad guys of the 1930s. It never once occurred to us that all of these colorful characters had all either been gunned down in police ambushes or died while serving incomprehensibly long prison sentences.

I'd heard a lot of bragging in reform school about how much money could be hustled by laying paper—passing bad checks—so Leon and I decided to give that a try. It didn't take long to find out that they had lied back in reform school. It should have come as no surprise to me. We had *always* lied to each other when it came to making our own exploits more worthy of attention and veneration. As it turned out, the fake identifications Leon and I made were spurious and amateurish. The store clerks were especially leery of our counter checks. We had considerably better luck at purse snatching and burglarizing smaller businesses with no alarm systems. None of this ever approached the really big action that we envisioned in our criminal fantasies.

"Too bad we couldn't witness a bus wreck or a plane crash," I remember saying early one afternoon as Leon and I were shuffling alongside the railroad tracks paralleling the Columbia River near town. "Everyone would be so busy saving themselves we could easily grab up a whole bunch of purses!"

As soon as that sentiment passed my lips, Leon stopped and grabbed my arm. By the look on his face, I could tell that he thought I'd just hit upon the world's greatest idea.

"Or a train wreck!" he said excitedly, his eyes all bright and wide with criminal glee.

We looked at each other and smiled. Within hours, we constructed a wall across the railroad tracks, four feet high and ten feet thick, from the material that we hauled from a nearby abandoned brickyard. Loose brick. Neatly stacked. No mortar.

It didn't occur to us until the passenger train came barreling around the bend that people could be hurt, maybe even killed, in a successful derailment. By then it was too late. When the train hit our wall, pieces of brick exploded in an ever-widening cloud of debris, with a noise that was utterly deafening. To our tremendous surprise, the train wasn't slowed in the least. We hadn't considered the awesome weight and sheer momentum of the speeding passenger train versus the relatively tiny mass of our pile of loose bricks. We were relieved that we had survived our spur of the moment attempt at train wreck mayhem with nothing more than a pair of embarrassed and slightly bruised egos. For us, the matter was over. We stuck our hands in our pockets, lowered our heads, and made our way home in silence.

The next day, Leon and I spent the entire morning and part of the afternoon at a favorite swimming hole several miles outside of town. When we returned, it seemed that our hometown was under siege. Dozens of police cars, marked and plain, were lined up all along Main Street. It didn't take long for us to discover that the authorities were conducting a house to house inquiry regarding the attempted train derailing. Even the FBI was involved. We panicked and fled that evening.

There was only one place in my hometown that sold new

cars, a Pontiac dealership not far from where I lived. I had never considered robbing the dealership before that particular night. True to my predatory nature, I'd already mentally sized up the place, just as I'd done with virtually every other business in my hometown. I knew that there was a sawdust chute that could provide us access into the furnace room in the basement of the dealership. That was all the information Leon and I needed before breaking in to provide ourselves with a brand-new car and roaring off on a new adventure in style. I never had had the opportunity to learn how to drive, and neither had Leon, but it wasn't much of an issue for us.

A few hours later, in the middle of nowhere in eastern Washington, I lost control of our sparkling new getaway car. It spun five times and crashed over an embankment, stopping by the side of the road where it could easily be seen by any passerby. Although we were unhurt, we quickly determined that the car was a total loss. We were afraid to be seen hitchhiking so near to the wreck, so we decided to hide out and wait in a big wheat field to see what might happen next.

We weren't exactly surprised when we saw a highway patrol car pull over and stop next to the crash site soon after we'd hidden ourselves in the field. Someone must have seen or heard the crash. We watched the patrolman go over the embankment to check out the Pontiac. Finding no one inside the wreck, he returned to his car to write a report. He drove off some ten or 15 minutes later. We remained watchful and on high alert throughout the night. Not until around 6AM did we feel safe enough to lie down, close our eyes, and sleep for a short while.

By 10:00, we were awake and arguing about what to do next. We could see a grain elevator off in the distance, and Leon suggested that we walk over to where the structure stood. There we could at least find shade and maybe some water. I didn't think this was a good idea, so I protested the move.

"I'm worried about the cop. Why didn't he stick around any longer than he did? It looks very suspicious to me."

"What did you *expect* him to do?" Leon asked impatiently, clearly annoyed at my paranoia.

"Well, if he felt the engine, he *knows* that it was a recent wreck, and he's probably wondering what happened to the driver. It won't take him long to find out it's stolen. When he finds out, he'll *know* we can't be far away."

"Man, they probably already towed the car away while we were asleep," Leon replied, exasperated. "And, besides, we can't stay here all day. Let's go!"

He stood to leave. Against my better judgment, I followed. We made it only halfway to the grain elevator before we noticed the patrol car that had been sitting there the whole time, hidden in the shade that had been beckoning us forward. With nowhere to hide, the jig was up and we surrendered.

Leon confessed to everything and received probation. I had a criminal record, so I was sent to the Diagnostic Center at Fort Warden, an old Army base that had been taken over by the State. When the headshrinkers were done "evaluating" me, I was transferred to the Washington State Training School.

The psychologist at Chehalis quickly determined that I had "not responded to treatment," but the State Reform School had a brand-new program that would soon help me "see the error of my thinking." He said all this with such sincerity and certainty I actually convinced myself to believe it—until I duped the kitchen guard into unlocking and opening the back door, ostensibly so I could empty a trash can, which afforded me the opportunity to run off yet again.

When I left it was about 9:00 AM. It was miles to the woods around the Army Base—which is now the site of Olympia National Park in northwestern Washington—and I knew I wouldn't make it. My plan was to hide out until night. I only went a quarter of a mile or so and randomly chose one of the dozens of empty base buildings. I found an attic entrance and hid for the night.

Only four hours later, I was tracked down by a trained

German shepherd who apparently didn't take into consideration that my escape and choice of hiding place were just more manifestations of my "erroneous thinking." German shepherds, it seems, are not all that well versed in psychology

A week later, I was taken to the Green Hill Academy for Boys back in Chehalis. For me it was like a class reunion as I was greeted by many of my old friends from my Luther Burbank days. Even my old psychologist was there. It seems that we were both working our way up through the system, albeit from opposite sides of the desk.

"I can see clearly where we failed you," he mused sympathetically as he looked through my file during my intake interview. "You should never have been placed back in your mother's custody. Obviously you subconsciously blame her for your father's death. Yet you still have conflicts about hating her, so you have transferred all of this internalized hatred toward society in the form of criminal acts."

Even as juvenile delinquents, we understood how important it was to let the caseworkers and psychologists think that they had you all figured out. Once they had you tagged and labeled, they pretty much felt their job was done and were far less apt to interfere with your life.

"Unfortunately," he said, continuing his spiel, "we have no academic program available here beyond the 10th grade. You'll have to repeat it."

"That doesn't make sense!" I exclaimed. "Why can't I just work all day?"

"It's our policy that every boy has to attend class half the day and then work half the day. That's the way the program is set up here."

Less than a week later, I escaped again. This time, I went by myself, with no one to mess up my plans. I was now 16, a year older and more capable—at least in my own eyes—than when I had escaped Luther Burbank. The system, however, had made provisions for that. Almost predictably, I was picked up for a curfew violation at the all-night theater where I was trying to catch some sleep. When I was captured, I was feeling so alone and lonely I was almost glad I'd been caught.

When I was returned to the Green Hill Academy, no one felt more badly about my escape than my psychologist. "I really blame myself for all of this," he lamented. "Do you know why?"

"No," I replied, my voice almost a whisper. Not for a moment could I imagine or understand why he would ever blame himself for *my* decision to escape.

"You are an overachiever, Floyd. You really resented my placing you back in the 10th grade, especially since you'd already successfully completed it. I've made arrangements for you to work full time," he announced with a big self-satisfied smile on his face. "That way, you'll be afforded the opportunity to find yourself."

After reporting to my job assignment the next day, I wondered how I would ever be able to "find" myself by shoveling cow shit. What I did manage to find was another inmate—a kid named Frank, if I remember correctly—who was willing to attempt another escape with me. Of course, we were soon arrested some 30 miles away from the academy, but we at least gave them a run for their money.

Clearly, the authorities had gotten wind of our escape. Escapes from the Green Hill Academy had become epidemic, so it wasn't long before we saw three Highway Patrol cars converging on our stolen vehicle, a 1940-something model that we could hotwire with a piece of tinfoil. There was no hope of outrunning their new high-powered Fords, but that didn't stop us from trying.

The highway was four lanes wide with a broad strip of grass and shrubs separating the northbound and southbound lanes. I wasn't about to give up easily, so I swung the car off the freeway, rumbled down the small embankment and up the other side, skidding sideways on the wet grass before landing on the northbound lane, the nose of our stolen vehicle barreling away from the roadblock that had been set up to stop us on the southbound lane. Two of the patrol cars continued speeding south toward the next overpass, where they would get off and double back after us. I had the gas pedal pushed all the way to the firewall, but our getaway car wouldn't go over ninety.

"Turn up that road!" Frank shouted, pointing to a freeway onramp.

I spun the steering wheel and started skidding over the crest of the hill. We briefly went airborne, but I managed to land the car on blacktop and shot up the steep incline that ran onto the freeway. Our vehicle began to lose power. I noticed that the tinfoil I'd used to hotwire the car had fallen off and was now lying at my feet. The patrol car was in hot pursuit and closing fast. There we were, rolling uphill without power.

"Jump!" I yelled, flinging my door open. I rolled out of the car, hit the ground, popped onto my feet, and darted toward the shoulder of the road—only to be disheartened by the sight of a huge dirt embankment rising steeply before me, maybe 40 feet to the top, nearly straight up. Desperately, I threw myself upwards and started digging my hands into the earth, trying to claw my way toward the top. The last few feet were almost vertical and, unable to gain a foothold, I kept slipping. Finally, my hand caught hold of a bush. Just as I was about to start pulling myself up and over the crest of the embankment, I heard the loud clicking sound of a revolver's hammer being pulled and cocked.

"Freeze or you're dead!" came the command from below. Once again, the jig was up.

I was so close! I let go of the branch and slid back down to the bottom of the embankment, where I was handcuffed and led to my pursuer's patrol car. Only then did I notice that there was no embankment on the opposite side of the road. Mentally, I kicked myself at the realization that I could have easily fled into the woods and escaped, if only I'd run the other way. Later, while reliving the whole experience in my mind, I cursed myself for not having gone over the top. It's what a professional would have done.

As the other patrol units arrived, Frank sheepishly walked out of the woods and gave himself up. Our only consolation was the sight of the patrol car that had been chasing us. It had been struck and damaged when our stolen vehicle eventually lost its forward momentum and rolled down the hill backwards, ramming into the cop car's front end. What a *mess*!

After that, the State began a new practice that drastically reduced the number of escapes by delinquents like myself who were over 16 years of age. The D.A. started prosecuting these escapees for any and all crimes that they committed during and after the act of getting away. To everyone's horror, they also started remanding all such cases to adult court. Judges began handing out five- to ten-year sentences in the State Reformatory, an adult institution with a wall and gun towers, fully intending to keep convicted juveniles locked up there for the bulk of their sentences. A lot of youngsters who previously had been unable to suppress the impulse to flee were now suddenly in possession of remarkable self-restraint.

I did not try to escape again!

After being returned to the Hill, I became interested in boxing and joined the boxing team. Our coach was a former Navy boxing champ by the name of Warren Brenning, a man who all of us admired and respected. The warden didn't think much of Coach Brenning's Christian beliefs, nor did he appreciate the way our coach would often preach to us during our training sessions regardless—or perhaps because of—his popularity and positive influence with the inmates. Not surprisingly, it wasn't long before Coach Brenning was dismissed.

My psychologist was still convinced that my foremost problem was my mother, so he decided against returning me to what he termed as "the unproductive environment" of my single-parent home. Instead, they kept me for another year.

When I was 17, in May, 1959, I applied for and was granted

a five-day furlough to spend with my sister. Naturally, when the five days were up, I didn't want to go back. If I didn't show up, they were going to issue a warrant. I called and requested another five days. I was advised that passes weren't issued that way. I had to return and request another pass in person.

"But I'm here now," I protested to one of the administrators at Green Hill Academy. They didn't seem to understand the absurdity of making a round trip. Something in my tone made the administrator ask, "Are you threatening to escape? Because if you don't come back, when the authorities catch up to you, and they will, they're going to treat you the same as if you went over the wall. Is that clear?"

The absurdity of his attempt at intimidation made me smile. I was 100 miles from the Hill. "Very clear. On the other hand, I am here and you are there. Is that clear? Is it?"

There was a long silence. I could just imagine the tightening of his jaw. I knew that I would take heat for something—anything—when I returned. But I had made up my mind to never go back to the State Training School. I wasn't sure how I would pull that off, but I knew I was done with their "training."

"Okay, Mr. Forsberg." It was always a bad sign when the administration stopped using my first name. This guy had reached the end of his patience, not that that bothered me. "I am granting you five more days. However, you will be back here at the end of your furlough, no exceptions. Do we understand each other?"

"Thank you, sir." I hung up.

I stared at the phone. I had no plan for how I was going to keep from going back to the Hill. I thought that if I could avoid capture until I was 18, six months away, I would be fine. The law said that no one 18 or older could be housed at the training school, and I doubted I would be remanded to adult camp just for being six months late for returning from a furlough. Of course, that raised the question, where could I hide out for six months?

I had one day left when I realized that I should start coming up with a real plan. I was in Downtown Vancouver and ran into Mitch, an acquaintance who had been out of the training school on parole for a few months. Mitch had just joined the U.S. Army, even though his record was about as long as mine.

"They took you?" I began wondering if this might be the answer to my problem.

Mitch nodded. "There's a recruiter in town who is trying to set some kind of recruiting record. He even took Jim!"

I was shocked. Jim was the most arrested juvenile offender I knew. He made me look like an altar boy.

"Come on, I'll introduce you to the recruiter, but I won't be able to stay. I have to go pack my stuff. I leave tomorrow early in the morning for basic training."

Mitch brought me to the recruiter and told him that I was interested in enlisting but that I had a juvenile record. Mitch wished me luck and left.

The recruiter had me sit down. "So, Floyd, what's on your record?" He looked me over as he waited for my answer.

"Well, I've got burglary."

"No problem."

"And a couple car thefts."

"That's fine."

I hesitated. "I escaped from reform school three times."

"You mean you were 'absent without leave.'" I watched as he cleverly changed the seriousness of the offense like a magician transforms a handkerchief into a rose.

"One of your parents will sign for you, right? I mean, give consent?"

"It's just my mother, but she'll sign." There were some other convictions to mention, but I decided this guy would give a pass to anything.

The recruiter handed me a piece of paper. "Take this consent form and have your mother sign. We have a flight leaving in the morning. Can you be back here by 5PM?" He was beaming like a shady car salesman.

I cleared my throat. "There's one other little problem we have to take care of."

His smile began to fade. "What's that?"

"I'm still serving time in reform school."

His mouth dropped. "You on escape?"

"No, I didn't escape. I'm on a five-day pass. Actually, it's my second one in a row. There won't be a third."

His smile broadened. "Okay, here's the plan. You go home and get your mother to sign that consent form. I'll call the training school and smooth things over."

I came back at 5PM with the consent form and my clothes. The recruiter put his arm around me as he explained that the administration at the Hill agreed to release me on the condition that I go immediately into the Army. I spent the night at the YMCA with 50 other recruits. The entire group was flying out at 0600 the next morning.

I was deemed "cured" of my criminal ways by the State of Washington and released to become a member of the United States Army. I had ended my "training" as a juvenile delinquent and headed to boot camp to train to become a soldier.

Chapter Three

"I'M NO RAT, SIR!"

Much to my surprise, I liked boot camp. Playing soldier appealed to me, the discipline being little worse than that of reform school. I became an expert marksman and was personally commended by the Company Commander for finishing at the head of my entire boot camp training class.

I had hoped to receive an assignment to Airborne School. Instead, because of my aptitude for math, I was picked out to become a forward observer in the Artillery. I had two weeks before having to report to Fort Sill, Oklahoma. Two weeks was time enough for a little robbery that I'd been planning inside my head during my off hours. I took my leave and immediately rounded up some old friends from Chehalis to help me organize and pull off the heist. It always takes money to make money, even illegally, so our first order of business was to steal and then pass off some payroll checks in order to finance our operation.

We spent a whole day cashing checks at local markets and managed to accumulate around $1,200. As midnight approached, it became harder and harder to find any stores that were still open. I decided to take a nap in the backseat while my buddies drove around. When I woke up, the car was not moving and there was an eerie quiet in the air.

"Where are we?" I asked, my gut instinctively sensing that something was amiss.

"Shh!" someone replied. "We're siphoning some gas."

I couldn't believe it! We had over $1,000 at our disposal from a full day of passing checks, and there we were *stealing* gas! These knuckleheads were likely to blow my entire $20,000 robbery plan over a measly $5 tank of fuel.

"Why didn't you just go to a gas station?" I growled out loud. "We don't need to be taking this kind of risk!"

I was so angry I had to get out of the car or explode. As I walked away from my idiotic comrades, I noticed we were behind some kind of lumber yard. I guess my friends figured it was secluded enough to pull off this petty theft.

I was leaning against the front of the car when I heard a crunching sound on the gravel. How that patrol car ever managed to get so close without me seeing or hearing its approach is still a mystery. There it was, a city police car, not ten yards away, with two cops looking directly at me. They turned on their lights and leapt out of their vehicle.

"Cops!" I hollered, sprinting between piles of lumber. The back of the lumber yard was enclosed by a large wooden fence, maybe ten or 12 feet high, the same size that I'd practiced going over in Advanced Training. My left foot hit the fence halfway up. Twisting my body upward, using the impact as I'd been taught, I caught the top and then threw myself up and over, landing in the huge patch of blackberry bushes that was growing on the other side of the fence. I ran several miles to a tavern then hailed a taxi to take me to our base of operations, the house of one of my friends. I was the first to arrive. Soon, the others came back as well. Amazingly, we had all managed to get away even if it was not exactly a clean escape.

The car we abandoned was registered to *me*, so there was no choice but to report it as stolen. Two of us went to report the car missing. The welts on my hands and face did little to make me appear like your average law-abiding citizen, and my colleague was known to the local police for his past criminal activity. We were promptly arrested on suspicion of theft for the siphoned gasoline. Neither of us budged from the cover story we had rehearsed before arriving at the police station, so they had no other choice but to release us.

The robbery we had worked so hard to set up would have to wait. Not only had we wasted too much time, but we simply could not risk continuing to arouse the suspicion of the local authorities, who undoubtedly had us on their radar. My buddies went home. I went on to Fort Sill, where my affection for the Army quickly waned.

The hours I spent figuring coordinates and azimuths to call in artillery barrages or airstrikes were excruciatingly boring, and I was soon longing for the action of the street. I stuck it out until payday. Then, after stealing $60 from a fellow soldier, I walked away from my post and went AWOL. I made it to Amarillo and bought a gun. Then, like a shark returning to its home waters, I headed for Seattle for what I hoped would be the Big Time.

Even as a kid, I always carried a gun during my burglaries. The sense of security and power it gave was false, of course, but I didn't like being unarmed. Only later did I learn that professional burglars, for some very good reasons, never carried a weapon during the commission of their crimes. If caught with a weapon, a burglar could expect a judge to set a higher bail, and the District Attorney would be harder to bargain with. He could pretty much expect a harsher sentence if—when, really—he was convicted of his crime. Younger criminals never consider all the angles. That's one reason they are so dangerous.

I finally wised up to the fact that I wouldn't get anywhere with my ex-reform school buddies, although the problems I encountered with them would continue to plague me throughout my criminal career. Once they had money in their pockets, most of them wanted to play the Big Spender, with no one really interested in stealing anything more until all the initial loot was gone. Worse yet, most of them had discovered girls, meaning they were much more preoccupied with chasing skirts than with chasing the kind of money that I sought to rake in. Suddenly none of my former buddies seemed the least bit interested in doing all the big jobs we had talked about in reform school.

In the midst of my discouragement over not being able to find a willing crime partner, I got word that the FBI was asking around for me. I was also wanted by the Army for desertion. I decided there was little point in planning or pulling off a heist when I was already wanted by the authorities. I returned to Fort Sill voluntarily to face the music with the U.S. Army, fully intending to say or do whatever it took to get myself kicked out of the military.

When I eventually stood before my commanding officer, he was not at all pleased about my having been AWOL for a month. When he was done berating me, he ordered me confined to the barracks.

"But I don't want the barracks," I responded defiantly. "I want the stockade!"

I thought—hoped, really—that being sent to the stockade meant an automatic discharge, like being fired from a job for stealing.

"Well, you may get that soon enough," he replied. "But, until your court-martial, I'm confining you to quarters."

"I want out!"

"You want *what?*" he asked, acting as if he hadn't caught the meaning of my words.

"I want out of the Army!"

He smiled contemptuously. "You don't get out *that* easy, soldier. You signed up for three years, and any time you end up spending in the stockade won't count toward that three years. I'd say you're losing ground real fast. If we discharged every enlistee who ever went AWOL, we wouldn't have much of an army, would we? If you thought that 30 days on the run without official leave would get you out, well let me just tell you, you were *wrong*!"

I was determined to push the issue. "But what about the $60 I stole?"

It was another miscalculation. In the Washington penal code, the only penal code with which I was familiar, theft of anything less than $75 was considered petty larceny. I had assumed this figure was a universally accepted definition. I was appointed an attorney who showed me my error. I would be facing a possible five-year sentence—and *that* was just for the theft alone.

"The best I can get you is two years," he said, his voice grim as he advised me of my very limited options. In the meantime, I was sent to the base stockade, which is the Army's equivalent of a county jail. Every Army base has one. I was held there awaiting court-martial.

❧

All Army sentences were at hard labor, and two years of *that* would seem like an eternity to me. I quickly became part of an escape plot.

The plan was simple enough. One of us would set our mattress on fire, forcing the guards to open all the cells and move everyone away from the smoke. During the commotion, we would all run. Since I was the new recruit, my bedding was selected to burn.

"But won't they just open my cell and pull the mattress out?" I asked nervously.

"Hey, you're pretty sharp, kid," replied one of the ringleaders of the escape plot as he thrust a box of toothpicks in my hand. "That's why you're gonna take these things and jam them into your lock. They won't have time to pry out the toothpicks, so they'll have no choice but to cut your lock open. By then, the place will be so full of smoke, they will *have* to move us to the day room."

The plan would then call for us to smash our way through an iron framed window in the day room and run across the yard to freedom. That we were smack dab in the middle of an army base, ten miles from the main gate, never occurred to me until much later, when I reflected upon the entire escape attempt while sitting inside a prison at Leavenworth.

Except for the unselfish dedication of the duty officer who was assigned to the unit on that day, I would have died. I later learned that the same plan had been tried before, after which they'd had to bury the unfortunate fool who'd been chosen to set his mattress on fire. Since that time, bolt cutters were kept on hand in the Sergeant's office for just such an emergency. But, as I myself witnessed firsthand, those bolt cutters couldn't and wouldn't save *anyone* unless someone cared enough to use them.

In those days, everyone smoked, including prisoners. I used the matches I had to set my mattress on fire. At the time it sounded like a good idea.

Smoke from my cell drifted out through the bars and engulfed the entire cell block. Everyone kept to the plan, and no one hollered for help. I knew *I* was in trouble when my eyes started swelling shut. The wet towel covering my nose and mouth was no longer filtering out the smoke. I started to panic, and cried out to the leader of our plot.

"I... I can't breathe!"

"Shut up or they'll hear you!" he growled. "We need more smoke."

"I can't breathe!" I repeated in a choked whisper.

"Lie down on the floor with your mouth to the bars. There's air on the floor."

The paint on the walls began to bubble and melt, adding yet another noxious odor to the air. Others were now choking, unable to control themselves. All at once, men started rattling the bars, crying out desperately for help. I tried holding my breath for as long as I could, but with each tortured gasp I found the air fouler.

"Are you still alive?" Someone asked from outside the front of my cell. I could hear the jingling of keys, followed by exasperated cursing. "You stupid son of a bitch. You plugged the lock!"

My would-be benefactor began choking and left. I could hear others being let out of their cells. I must have passed out briefly right about then. The next thing I remember was being dragged along the tier and dumped in the day room. Still unable to open my eyes, I immediately started calling out for our leader, a man named Charles.

"How you doin', kid?" he asked, kneeling down beside me where I lay sprawled on the floor.

"I'm okay, but I can't see. How am I gonna go when I can't see?"

"The escape is off, kid. Someone ratted. There's MPs all over the place."

Six weeks later, two days before my sentencing for the $60 theft, I slashed one of my wrists with my shaving razor. I left a note saying that I simply could not handle serving a long prison term. In order to avoid damage to my tendons, I had slashed only the side of my arm, not the vein. Unimpressed by my less than convincing suicide attempt, the judge still sentenced me to a year at hard labor. I was flown to the U.S. Disciplinary Barracks at Fort Leavenworth, Kansas.

Upon my arrival, it quickly became clear to me that these were no "barracks" to which I'd been sent. The place was a huge prison surrounded by 30-foot walls and gun towers. Discipline was severe, with every prisoner compelled to march in step everywhere he went, and to work all day long.

There were few teenagers inside this prison. I didn't have to wait long to see what *that* meant. The first time I was approached by several of the older sexual predators at Leavenworth, I thought my mind was playing tricks on me, that I was listening to some kind of joke that I'd somehow missed.

"What did you say?" I asked nervously. I stood there mute and afraid. I knew in my gut that I wasn't handling the situation correctly. Forced homosexuality had always been a part of reform school, but only against the weaker inmates. There, I was bigger than most kids my age and had rarely been considered easy prey. *Here,* I was much younger and less physically imposing than most of the other convicts. I was undeniably more intimidated and terrified when approached by these older, bigger inmates.

I was only 17 years old when I was beaten, raped, and left nearly unconscious in my cell by those brutes. I was already so enmeshed in the "prisoner's code of honor" that I refused to identify the men who assaulted me. "Thou shall not rat" was the ethical cornerstone of the criminal underworld, at least in theory. So it was with me.

I was thrown in the Hole for two weeks for refusing a direct order to name my assailants. At the end of these two weeks, I was given the same order. Again, I refused. I was sentenced to an additional 30 days in the Hole.

Today, most prisons allow inmates in the Hole at least some period of time outside of their cells for exercise. Many, like the prisons in California, which provide little or no exercise time for segregated inmates, *do* allow them to have everything necessary to combat and ease the monotony of prolonged idle inactivity: radio, television, books, magazines, and so on. These changes were hard won by inmates who fought for such basic considerations through the court system. During the 1950s and 1960s, however, the Hole in most prisons was simply designed to break a person's will. At 8PM, we were given a mattress, a pillow, and a blanket, which was taken from us promptly at 6AM. Other than that, there was nothing but four blank walls to occupy a prisoner's mind. Fortunately, they did leave the lights on for us during the day. As I sat in the Hole at Fort Leavenworth, I was determined not to let it break my will.

Talking or refusing to stand up when an officer entered the unit automatically meant time in The Box, a punishment reserved for those who broke a rule while in "segregation"—a fancy word for the Hole. Naturally, at one point I refused to stand up.

The Box was total darkness. Later in life, when I began to take a genuine interest in spiritual matters, especially concerning the light of self-awareness and human dignity, I finally understood why the last disciplinary threat they held over our heads was the removal of light. It was our last remaining privilege. As I awaited my release from The Box, my mind and spirit became numb from all those seemingly endless hours spent sitting there surrounded by total silence and complete darkness.

After 44 days of isolation, I was again taken to the Captain's office. Once more, I refused to name my attackers. For my failure to provide him with their names, Captain Olsen ordered his goons to throw me back in the Hole for another 30 days.

I would never know a tougher Hole than the one I was so unjustly forced to endure at Leavenworth. The Hole at Lompoc would come close, but the one at Leavenworth was definitely the worst. Isolation there was an oppressive weight that relentlessly ground down and crushed my very soul, thrusting me into and under the suffocating depths of sheer boredom. With nothing and no one in the cell but me, I turned inward for entertainment, activating my imagination to spin up plots to murder Captain Olsen. At the end of this additional 30-day stint in the Hole, the sadistic bastard actually came to my cell to see and speak with me, thus cheating me out of a walk to his office in the light of day.

"I don't understand you, Forsberg," he began, speaking to me through the small, unlatched opening through which my food tray was passed into my cell. "It's your assailants who should be in here, not you. Yet you won't help me punish them, which means that you're willing to let the same thing happen to the next kid who comes in here. I can't let you do that. I *won't* let you do that. I *order* you: Give me the description of the persons who assaulted you!"

I wondered how long a person could live on the Hole's diet of bread and lettuce and an occasional boiled potato. I had serious doubts as to whether my sanity could endure another 30 days of silence and darkness on that concrete slab. Even as those doubts crystallized in my mind, I hated myself for weakening, even momentarily. I knew that I would never be able to look myself in the mirror if I didn't stick to my guns. So, as the Captain waited for my answer, and telling myself that this *had* to be the last 30 days that he would force me to remain in the Hole, I resolved myself to more isolation.

"I'm no rat, sir," I replied through gritted teeth. Then I turned my face away, swearing to myself that I would not rest until I had the son of a bitch Olsen killed.

Although the Captain did in fact order 30 more days of isolation for me, I spent only ten more days in The Box—84 days total inside that pitch dark mini-dungeon—after which I was moved to Administrative Segregation to finish the last 20 days of my Hole time. There, for the first time in almost three months, I had a bed. I had regular food. I had library privileges and some earphones to listen to the radio. Most importantly, I still had my dignity. I had kept the code. I had maintained my silence to the end.

Chapter Four

FIFTY-STATE APB

I was 18 when I was kicked out of Leavenworth after serving a year. I had $30 in my pocket with which to begin a new life. They had discharged me dishonorably but I didn't care. A few months later, they migrated my discharge status to "undesirable" anyway. As I made my way back to Portland on a train, I didn't give Captain Olsen another thought. The only thing that mattered to me was that I was free and on my way to the Big Time again.

For the life of me, I just could not understand why anyone would be so foolish as to work for a living. During my Administrative Segregation time at Leavenworth, I ended up reading every single book I could find about crime and how to perfect it. Soon enough, I was clearing several thousand dollars a day with stolen postal money orders. I enlisted my younger sister to work with me, promising her $10 for every hundred dollars she cashed, plus allowing her to keep whatever items she purchased during the cashing process. We worked Washington and Oregon, and then we headed south to California, Nevada, and Arizona.

I also wanted to take my girlfriend, Karen, a pretty brunette

I'd met a few weeks before, but she was barely 16 at the time and still under parental control. We solved that problem by getting married. Then Karen, my sister, and I were on our way to becoming one of the most successful teenage forgery rings in the country. I spent my days exchanging shoeboxes full of money and change for hundred-dollar bills. When we finished working our way through Arizona, my sister left us and returned home. Karen and I headed for Miami to enjoy our newfound ill-gotten wealth.

Every Saturday night, I placed a prearranged call to my police connection in Portland, a friend of my mother's, asking for news about the weather in Oregon. This was our code for whether I was being sought out by the police for any reason. By agreement, my connection billed me $100 for each of these calls. I continued placing these weekly calls while working the Southwest and right on through my arrival in Miami.

One Saturday night in Florida I was feeling safe and smugly untouchable, half a continent away from the last place I'd cashed a money order. I decided to skip a call and save myself $100 by not checking in. Just in case, I did go ahead and follow up with a call a week later.

"How's the weather up there?" I inquired.

"Where the hell were you last week?" came the reply from my police connection.

"Hey, don't worry about your money," I responded dismissively, trying to play the big shot. "I'll send you two c-notes this week."

"Yeah, you do that," he snarled. "Send two and then get rid of my damn phone number, if you were stupid enough to write it down."

"What's your problem, man?" I asked, wondering why he was so uptight. "There's no reason to get upset."

"No reason, eh? I should have known better than to get involved with a dumb kid."

"Hey, I'm doing pretty damn good these days, pal!" I snapped back defensively.

"Well, you won't be if you try to draw any more money out of your bank accounts!"

"Bank accounts?" I repeated, my voice barely a whisper. I *had* been opening saving accounts all over the country. How could he possibly have known about them?

"I don't have time for games, kid. You've got accounts in Vegas, Phoenix, Denver, and who knows where the hell else. All in *your* name. That's real bright, kid. That's really, really bright."

He paused for a few seconds, perhaps waiting for me to respond. When I said nothing, he continued. "Let me tell you something, kid. If you want to live to see your 21st birthday, you'd better make damn well sure my phone number is not found on you when you're caught. There's a 50-state alarm out for you. Don't you dare call me again for any more information. You're just too damn careless. When they throw you back in prison, try to learn something—like some street smarts!"

He hung up. I stood in the phone booth, receiver in hand, my mind reeling over everything I'd just heard. I couldn't understand what had gone wrong. Now that I knew every state in the union had received an all-points bulletin about me and my activities, I had only one overriding thought. I *had* to get out of the country.

I found and spoke with a recruiting officer in Miami who was looking for ex-servicemen to fight as mercenaries against Fidel Castro. Unfortunately, he was only interested in men who had more than four months of active military duty under their belts. Even though I was a marksman with a rifle, I had only fired a machine gun twice in training, which may as well have been never. The time I had spent in the stockade didn't impress him in the least.

"But I *will* take on a few men who are willing to pay for their own training and living expenses until we're ready to go," he offered.

"When would we leave the country?" I asked impatiently.

"Who can say?" he replied, smiling knowingly. "But $2500 should cover everything."

My immediate problem was money. My wife and I had spent thousands of dollars setting up our apartment and generally living high on the hog. My plan to fly to various cities and withdraw my hefty cash reserves as needed was no longer an option. Each stolen money order that we'd passed represented a possible sentence of five years in prison, and I'd long since lost track of how many that was. For one desperate moment, I toyed with the idea of taking money at gunpoint, but then quickly decided I didn't possess the nerve to pull off an armed robbery, at least not yet. I opted instead for the known risk, cashing just enough money orders to send Karen home and enlist myself in the anti-Castro militia group.

As I was driving out of Orlando for good, I noticed the flashing red lights of a patrol car in my rearview mirror. I'd been driving a bit fast, so I assumed I was simply being pulled over to be ticketed for speeding. Out of nowhere, there were guns pointing at me and loud commands for me to show my hands. I'd started my crime spree in Portland, Oregon and traveled across the entire country, raking in tens of thousands of dollars along the way. Now, on a highway just outside the city lights of Orlando, Florida, it was all over for me yet again!

My lawyer ended up getting all my money, but he earned it. Karen got off with only three years' probation, and I never heard from her again. My sister, who hired her own attorney in Portland, was able to wrangle a deal for five years' probation. My attorney thought that he could get me off with a couple of years in prison if I would only play along with his request for a psychiatric evaluation at the Federal Correctional Institution in Lompoc, California. I didn't have much of a choice, so I agreed. I left for California with a few of his pointers on how to handle the doctors, as well as with his assurance that everything would be fixed by the time I was returned to Portland.

There was only one hitch. In order to qualify for the 120-day evaluation at Lompoc and receive the kind of psychiatric diagnosis that was needed to mitigate my sentence, I first had to accept the maximum sentence for my crimes: 35 years. At the end of the evaluation period, the judge would then review the sentence. *Review*—but not necessarily *revise.*

At first, I was excited about this new opportunity to speak with a psychiatrist. I had never really asked myself why I committed antisocial acts. Over the previous four months, I had begun to wonder. I quickly realized what I *wanted* to tell the psychiatrist and what I *had* to say to him was now separated by the harsh, brutal reality of a potential 35-year sentence. I would say what I knew *they* wanted to hear, just as I had always done in the absurd game that we'd all been playing since I was fifteen years of age.

ൾ

A ride to prison is unlike any other in the world. Unless one has experienced it, it defies the imagination. Something between a ride in your own funeral procession—while not actually being dead—and a ride on a Ferris wheel. You know that, for all practical purposes, you will soon be as good as dead to this world, buried in a judicial grave for a number of years, your sentence entombing and shutting you off from all that is living. This somehow expands the senses and allows for an enhanced level of perception as outside stimuli flood into the brain. One sees everything with increased clarity, as from the top of a Ferris wheel on the most sparklingly clear day of your life. Trees passed are not blurred objects that otherwise would go entirely unnoticed. Instead, they are individual entities. Even each leaf has a noticeable and uniquely recognizable shape, with its purpose and intricate relationship to the tree being perceptible all at once. For the law-abiding citizen riding in his sedan, the road is just a way to get from one place to another. For those en route to prison, however, it is a road that leads surrealistically from the world to the un-world.

It took three days to reach Lompoc. There were three of us chained together in the back of the U. S. Marshal's transport vehicle. At first, we were very talkative, exchanging the usual personal details with everything couched in the usual convict bravado. By the third day, however, as we approached our destination, all three of us had retreated into our own separate, somber cocoons of silence, each man lost in his private thoughts.

ꟹ

The tower greeted us, its imposing height and bulk overshadowing the parking area and lawns of the prison. As if there could possibly be any doubt as to where we were, a huge brass sign displaying the name of the prison in big block letters assured us that we were in fact at the Lompoc Federal Correctional Institution.

Once inside, our cuffs and leg irons were removed by the U.S. Marshals who had brought us there. When they left, the reality of our arrival and imprisonment suddenly felt all the more intense, as if they had been the umbilical cord connecting us to the free world—a connection now severed for who knew how long.

We were led through an endless series of doors. In the basement, the last remnants of the real world were stripped and taken away from me. Even washing away sweat and dirt seemed to symbolize the complete removal of all I had brought with me from the other world. When I stepped out from the shower, I emerged with a new identity: YE 18. "YE" stood for Youth Evaluation. As far as the other cons were concerned, I was "Frosty," a violent force to be reckoned with. At least, that's what I wanted them to see.

My focus was soon directed very sharply to the solid door that led into the dormitory to which I had been assigned. I knew I would find a large group of inmates on the other side of that door who, like myself, had all been stripped of everything upon which they had ever placed any value. All of them would hold the very same fears—although none of them, of course, would ever admit it. There would be no avoiding the usual phoniness, the usual bullshit macho games. It was simply understood that everyone *had* to become a part of the collective hate and despair.

Once inside the dorm, my fellow travelers started recounting to the others the mischief the three of us had caused the previous night at San Luis Obispo county lockup where the U.S. Marshals had lodged us for the night. We had set a big fire and raised a considerable amount of hell. Now, as the story was retold, it gave the three of us instant credibility. We were immediately established as regulars. Unfortunately, however, I couldn't help but notice that some of the lingering glances I was getting seemed to hold more than your typical criminal admiration.

Lompoc is a correctional institution for prisoners 30 years of age and under. There were always a considerable number of older convicts who were there for psychiatric evaluations, like me. When I noticed several of them gazing at me in that certain appraising manner, their eyes moving up and down my body, I knew exactly what they had in mind. Individual inmates and gangs both fought for possession of the willing homosexuals, the so-called "girls," but there were never enough to go around. Hence, the newer inmates who were too weak or powerless to resist were often threatened or beaten into submission, then traded and/or sold as sex slaves.

I had no intention of allowing myself to be raped again. When I stumbled into an old friend from my Luther Burbank days, I had him find me a weapon. Two days later, a knife was found on my person during the standard pat down and I was sent to the Hole for possession of contraband. As the date of the court's review of my final sentence drew near, I feared the judge would never understand why I'd felt the need to have a knife. In the event he gave me an unfair sentence after my 120-day evaluation, I had a set of handcuff keys made for use in a possible escape. I showed them off to three friends, bragging about how they just might not ever see me again at Lompoc after I was taken to my evaluation hearing. Only a few hours before I was to leave for court, I was abruptly strip searched and the keys were found. Naively, I just couldn't understand my "bad luck."

When I arrived at court, I felt certain that the judge didn't have any knowledge of the handcuff keys, so I didn't mention them to my attorney. He was already worried enough about the matter of the knife and the impact it would have on the judge's decision on my sentence.

"You fool!" he said to me when we spoke before my hearing. "I had probation in the bag for you. Now the judge is all pissed off about the knife. What am I going to say to him about *that* when I go in there and make my pitch for probation?"

"Tell him the truth," I replied without hesitation. "Tell him that I was protecting myself from being raped."

"Do you really think that a judge understands or even cares about that kind of talk?" he asked, throwing his hands in the air in total exasperation. "He'll say that you should have gone to the prison staff. Regardless of what he says, you blew it. The institution has recommended a minimum of two years behind bars, and you *will* get it!"

When the proceedings got under way, the Assistant U.S. Attorney reminded the judge about the significant amount of money represented by my little money order operation. Then he argued against a light sentence. Since I was underage, I was already being shown ample consideration by being charged with only seven counts.

My attorney countered those arguments by telling the judge about my father's untimely death, about how this resulted in my never having had a chance, and that I had at long last learned my lesson. The usual stuff.

Judge Solomon interrupted his spiel to ask about the knife. In response, my attorney explained my youthful appearance made me a target for Lompoc's sexual predators, and I'd felt compelled to obtain a weapon to protect myself. It was all sounding pretty good to me. Judge Solomon just looked bored.

"And just how do *these* things figure into all of this?" He asked from the bench, holding up my homemade handcuff keys for all to see.

My attorney stared at me blankly.

"They belonged to a friend of mine," I whispered miserably. "I was just holding them for him!"

My attorney shook his head in abject surrender and sat down without saying another word. The judge had no trouble finding *his* voice, however. When he spoke, he sentenced me to seven five-year terms. I was so stunned I couldn't breathe. Then I heard the word, "concurrent," and I was able to breathe again. Five years total. Still bad. If I played it straight, there was at least some chance I could make parole.

The trip back to Lompoc was noteworthy for the fact that, during a layover in Klamath Falls, Oregon, I had my first voluntary homosexual encounter. At 19 years of age and with no further hope of imminent release, I had a new master to serve: lust. The kid I selected was so pretty I thought about keeping him myself, but I didn't have the reputation or the backing to possess such a fleshly treasure. It was a given that the Indians would eventually end up with him. The kid actually begged me to help him stay alive by keeping him for myself. The simple reality of it was that I had enough of a problem keeping *myself* from being "turned out" by the older cons. I promised to give him to a powerful Indian who I believed would treat him well, and that is exactly what I ended up doing.

Federal prisoners are required to serve a third of their sentence—in my case, 20 months—before becoming eligible for parole. We all followed that carrot like a herd of starving donkeys. The sooner we made parole, the sooner we'd be out to pull off that proverbial Big One—the million-dollar robbery followed by yachts, sports cars, and women. In order to start building up a resume to impress the Parole Board after my return to Lompoc, I enrolled in a vocational training class. I was training to be a house painter. Without any question, however, *bank robbery* was the only vocational training in which I was ever truly interested.

Although escape from that cesspool was constantly on my mind, I made no attempts to break out of Lompoc, and I avoided all prisoner unrest. Even with a strong recommendation from the institution that I should be paroled, the Board refused to grant me an early conditional release.

The parole judge pointed to my juvenile record, noting that it showed an ongoing pattern of criminal behavior. I explained to him that my past antisocial behavior was only an outward manifestation of the inner frustration and anxieties that I simply had not known how to handle. I had never learned to deal with negative emotions in an appropriate manner. I also pointed out to him the apparent unfairness of my having been sentenced to an extra three years for contraband—the knife and handcuff keys. I didn't realize how presumptuous and ludicrous I must have sounded until it was too late. The judge actually screamed at me.

"Who in the hell do you think you are?" he shrieked, interrupting me in midsentence. "You come in here talking like some slick, oily psychologist about this and that. Well, I don't give a damn about what you think your problem was, or what you think is fair. You are a threat to society. If I let you out, you'll just cash more money orders. You know it and I know it. You are a parasite and you are right where you belong: in prison. As far as I'm concerned, you are going to *stay* in prison. Now get out!"

I was very upset. I knew that sometimes the Parole board still voted for a conditional release over a parole judge's histrionics. In this case, however, the full board turned me down cold.

Chapter Five

"NEEDLESS TO SAY, I WAS CONVICTED"

Almost immediately after learning I would have to serve my full sentence, a big Indian in the paint shop threatened to make me his girl. He was in prison for killing a sheriff, so he had a very intimidating reputation. When he approached me, goon-like and menacing, he spoke directly to the point.

"I think you're a girl and you just don't know it yet," he said.

In no way did I consider myself a girl—and I wasn't about to be made into one. It's hard to explain to someone who has never been in prison, but as long as you assumed only the masculine role in these prison liaisons, you were considered to maintain your straight male sexual identity. Rather than be passive, I returned his challenge, obscenity for obscenity. He didn't like it one bit.

"Do you know who you are talking to?" he blustered.

"Yeah!" I blustered right back at him. "I'm talking to a big dumb Indian who isn't gonna live long enough to finish his time if he doesn't back off *now*!"

"I've been watching you, punk. You're all bluff. You have until Friday. Then you're mine or you die. You'd better think it over."

He smiled coldly, entirely confident of his position. There

was no way I could physically fight this animal and he knew it. I weighed 165 pounds. He, on the other hand, was a solid 280 and built like a tank, one of the strongest weight lifters in the prison. Worse yet, he had a powerful political backing, followers who were always willing and eager to do his bidding just to gain his favor. Even if I did beat him in a fight, I'd *still* have all the other Indians to contend with.

Friday came. I went to work extremely worried, my guts twisting, hoping against hope that he'd back down. Right around 2:00PM, I saw him striding towards me.

"Well, punk, this is it. Either I screw you or I kill you. What's it gonna be?"

I looked at him, still very scared, but also having emptied myself of all human compassion. In the past, I had always feared the formless, violent entity that I sometimes felt rising inside me. Now, however, I welcomed it. I could feel a murderous rage filling and overtaking me—and it felt good.

The big Indian smiled, wolf-like, clearly having overlooked any third option. Feigning submission, I told him I'd already placed a blanket in the closet for us. We stepped inside, closing the door behind us. I could smell the sweaty beast as he drew close enough to touch me. It seemed as if the entire closet was filled by his massive bulk. As I stood there in that dimly lit space, I focused my mind, trying to control the pounding of my heart, the shaking of my knees, the trembling of my hands.

I wiped my hands several times on my pants, too scared at first to pull out my knife. He was looking right at me, his eyes shining bright with lust. What if he were to snatch the knife from my hand and kill me with the damn thing? Panicky, I thought about running out and fleeing to "the man" to plead with the administration to place me in protective custody. In the very next instant, I realized I'd have to face this situation sooner or later, here or elsewhere. Seeking protective custody was too much like being a rat, a loathsome label that I simply could not bear to hang upon myself. It was now or never.

I told him that the blanket was on the top shelf, which was stacked full of assorted boxes of junk. As he reached up for it, I pulled out my knife. Like it was a living thing, I could feel that the monster was out of the bottle, a formless upswell of violence ballooning inside of me, completely filling me and infusing every fiber of my being, *empowering* me as I plunged that cold steel blade into his back. He gasped and spun around, his face whiter than my own. His eyes were wide with surprise and shock, yet completely devoid of all lust.

"You son of a bitch!" he roared, reaching for my throat. I flashed the knife wildly, keeping him back. He grabbed a caulking gun off the shelf to use as a weapon. I couldn't understand why he was still on his feet! In the movies, whenever someone was stabbed, that person dropped dead, plain and simple. So much for the "reality" of the silver screen. In my own real-life situation, this monster, regardless of the serious stab wound I'd given him, was still going to kill me!

I kicked open the closet door and fled, sprinting through the shop area and back to the main institution. Realizing I still had the knife, I ducked into a mop closet to hide it, then scampered quickly to my cell to get an apple. By the time I started heading back to the shop, the prison "Goon Squad"—a group of corrections officers who were the equivalent of the local SWAT team—was already searching for me. Someone had seen the Indian collapse outside the closet door and me running from the shop.

Six officers took me aside and a lieutenant checked my pulse. When he asked why it was racing so fast, I told him I'd just run to and from my cell to fetch an apple. Wordlessly, I showed him the half-eaten apple in my hand.

"Don't you know it's against the rules to leave the shop and go to your cell during work hours?" he asked, apparently buying my story for the moment.

"That's why I ran, sir." I called upon all my will power to stay cool.

If I hadn't been so scared after delivering that first knife blow in the closet, I could have finished off the Indian. As it turned out, he lost a lung after being evacuated by helicopter to a hospital for emergency surgery, but managed to survive my attempt to kill him. Eventually, I was thrown in the Hole for the stabbing, and I settled myself in for another long stretch of mind-numbing isolation. This time around I was at least consoled by the fact that I had done what I had to do. The Indian had gotten exactly what he deserved.

As I sat in the Hole, I was confident that I would never be formally charged for assaulting the Indian. Few non-fatal prison stabbings ever ended up in a courtroom. Besides, there couldn't possibly be enough evidence to charge me. They never found the knife. There were no witnesses. With the big Indian supposedly being an old school "hardened" convict, I was certain he would never testify against me. I fully expected that I would serve out the first part of my sentence at Lompoc and then be transferred to the penitentiary at McNeil Island to finish off the rest.

I was looking forward to that. It seemed that I had developed a measure of mental clarity during this last round of isolation. I had come to see that the penal system was calculated to ensure recidivism. It was a numbers game. I saw how it controlled me by deliberately pulling on the emotional strings of my own inadequacies. The solution, as I saw it, was for me to recondition myself, to remove every human emotion from my person and transform myself into a Super Criminal—as deadly cold, as cunning, and as utterly ruthless as a tiger. This was war. Me against a world of sheep and goats. My prey would never know what hit them. Just as soon as I was delivered to McNeil Island, I would begin my training in earnest.

I was chained up and led out the same door through which I had entered nearly two years before. The outside world seemed exactly as I remembered it. Clearly, it had not suffered in the least by my absence. But *I* had changed. As I settled in for the long ride to McNeil Island, I resolved that I would make society suffer when I was freed.

Within half an hour, we reached Highway 101 and started heading south. Wait! McNeil was north! Why were we heading south? The Marshals advised me that I was being taken to Los Angeles to be charged with the stabbing of the big Indian!

The L.A. County Jail—where I was staying long enough to plead not guilty to stabbing the Indian—proved to be something of a hellhole. The cells were seven feet long and five feet wide. Six men were crammed like sardines into these tiny cubbyholes. Each cell had two narrow, one-man bunks, which left three to sleep on the floor and one unfortunate man to sleep sitting on the toilet. We were allowed one shower per week, so these cells, except on shower day, reeked with the stench of body odor. The Hole at Lompoc, by comparison, was paradise. It was there in Los Angeles, while sleeping on the floor of its filthy County Jail, that I marked the passing of my 21st birthday. It felt funny to be 21. Not that there was much feeling left inside me. Blessedly, though, ten days later, I was returned to the comforts of the Hole in Lompoc to await trial.

All inmates in isolation are provided with a Bible, if they ask for one. At first, as I sat there with nothing while awaiting my preliminary hearing in two months, I resisted asking for one. Eventually everyone in the Hole asks for a Bible, and I was no different. It was better than having nothing to read. Besides, it made for a good pillow during the day. I'd never held a Bible in my hands before. I started in the front, struggling through Genesis, Exodus, and Leviticus. In Numbers, I gave up. The whole thing was a jumbled mess as far as I was concerned.

Back in Los Angeles, the trial was unremarkable. I couldn't believe the big Indian had ratted on me. There had been eight stabbings that month. *He*, of all people, was the one person who'd they convinced to cooperate. Moreover, after he fingered me, it was *he* who begged and pleaded not to be returned to Lompoc, saying that *he* feared for *his* life.

"Do you mean you're afraid Forsberg's friends will get you for testifying against him?" asked the prosecutor.

"No," he replied, trembling from head to toe. "It's the *Indians* who will get me!"

For me, however, the highlight of my trial was when the assistant U.S. Attorney was caught bribing a federal witness. After secretly promising immediate parole for the testimony of an inmate who had seen me run out of the closet where I'd stabbed the big Indian, the prosecutor's witness took the stand and exposed the whole scam. I was found not guilty of attempted murder, but would be retried for assault.

The County Jail in Los Angeles was so intolerable that I, like many other inmates, attended chapel service just to get out of my cell. The services were lively, and they talked of the same Jesus about whom my old boxing coach preached. The part of the Bible they read from was much easier to understand than the part I'd tried to read while at Lompoc. It was called the New Testament and was located at the very back of the Bible. I took a copy back to my cell. This time I started reading at the Four Gospels, looking for the words of this Jesus. I found them at last.

My eyes brightened at the revelation that I could have anything I wanted if I asked for it in the name of Jesus. Well, the thing I wanted was OUT! I prayed very fervently that the second jury would find me not guilty of assault with a deadly weapon.

Needless to say, I was convicted. So much for asking Jesus for anything! I was angry at myself for being so weak as to ask a god—who could not possibly exist—for help.

Ultimately, the lesson I learned from all this was that, if ever I had to hit someone again in the future, I'd better make damn sure that they didn't live to testify against me. *That's* what went through my mind as I was sentenced to five years for the stabbing and shipped off to the Federal Penitentiary at McNeil Island.

Chapter Six

"PROFESSIONAL" CONS

I was transported to McNeil Island in the very same manner in which I'd been taken to Lompoc: chained to two other Federal prisoners in the back of a U.S. Marshal's transport van.

It was very early in the morning when we left Los Angeles. Already, the streets were alive with intoxicating scenes of humanity and movement. In a limited way, I—or at the very least, my *eyes*—were part of the free world. One of the first things I noticed while gazing out the windows of the van was just how beautiful women really were as a species. Having been in prison for the previous two years and four months, even the plainest of those females I saw walking along the street seemed to possess a grace I had never before recognized. Truly, they *were* man's better half. It was with this thought in my mind that I settled in for the three-day ride to McNeil, determined to absorb and enjoy all the sights that were part of a world now lost to me.

Seventy-two hours later, at Fort Lewis, Washington, we turned off the freeway and made our way to the prison's mainland dock. It was a clear day, and we were able to see McNeil Island Federal Penitentiary sticking out of the water approximately two miles in the distance. It was an island fortress just 20 minutes away by boat. After crossing the Sound, another quarter mile separated the island dock from the main institution, a distance we covered quickly by foot.

I did not have a long enough sentence to warrant escaping from McNeil, but this didn't stop me from contemplating how a successful escape might be effected. A single fence, ten feet high, topped with three strands of barbed wire, surrounded the compound and its gun towers. The real enclosure was the dark, cold forbidding waters of the Sound. It was, without any doubt, a formidable barrier.

Still in leg irons, we stood by the front gate as one of the Marshals approached the closest guard tower. A canvas bag was lowered by rope, into which the Marshals surrendered their weapons. These were quickly hoisted up, disappearing into the tower, and then the front gates yawned open to welcome us inside.

After passing through a heavy iron door that was slammed shut behind us, our chains and handcuffs were removed and the ritual of paper signing began. Next, one of the trustees, a "girl" named Bunny, led us up a flight of stairs into the main corridor, which was filled with inmates, all milling about and staring at us. Some sought a familiar face from happier times; others, a past lover to help erase the empty years of loneliness. We entered a cell block so large and depressing that I was immediately overcome with despair. I later learned that this area was actually two cell blocks that had been joined together to make one huge and insanely cavernous living space. At the moment, all I knew was that the vastness of the place seemed to swallow me whole, making me feel as insignificant as a grain of sand.

The cell block was five tiers high, as long as a football field, jam-packed with over 800 beds, and was always filled with a constant deafening cacophony. There were showers on each tier, from which extended a long snaking line of men waiting for their turn. We followed Bunny into a basement room that had a large sign nailed over its entrance that read BCR—meaning "Basement Clothing Room." I smiled humorlessly at the simplicity of the acronym. In a world of unlimited empty time, the need for abbreviations seemed ludicrously pointless. Even so, it was there that I was issued three sets of the standard prison denim blues and my new number: 30210.

I would spend only one night in the fish tank, the housing area for first timers in the Federal Prison System. As a transferee from Lompoc, there was no need to test me. I was already a known quantity. I was eager to get into the general population. There, I could devote myself to becoming the very best robber in the world—by interviewing every bank robber I could find and learning from their mistakes.

My arrival in the block caused quite a stir among the older queens, there being just two inmates younger than me at McNeil, and only nine others under the age of 25, the official minimum age for this institution. We were all violent rejects from Lompoc, transferred as a result of assaults and pipings, and no one bothered us. We were all housed together and were pretty much protected by our reputations against harassment or attack.

McNeil was different from Lompoc in ways somewhat difficult to explain. The violence, while still ever-present, was more subtle, somehow more subdued. At McNeil, the older convicts usually tried to resolve things peacefully rather than resorting to violence. There was also the fact that if you messed up at McNeil you were sent to Leavenworth or someplace just as bad. Overall, McNeil was a pretty nice place to spend time.

There was also self-inflicted violence that I witnessed on occasion. One day, for example, I saw a young Canadian man kill himself by leaping from the uppermost tier in the block, a fall of at least 50 feet. At first, I was shocked. He'd been serving an 18-month sentence. Then again, I understood his despair. Sometimes the mind could become so gloomy and black from the sheer coldness and emptiness of imprisonment that it really *did* seem better to die all at once, rather than one day at a time, regardless of how close one was to his eventual release date.

On another occasion, an inmate with a long history of

mental illness approached a guard saying he felt like killing someone. Instead of taking the nutcase seriously, the guard dismissively told the man to find someplace else to do it. Not surprisingly, he did. The man walked over to Cell Block Number 2 and killed the very first inmate he encountered—a guy who was doing two years for car theft. As it turned out, the deranged inmate had killed before in other institutions. If one dwelled too long on such seemingly random acts of violence, it could leave you feeling entirely helpless or paralyzed by constant fear and dread.

I concentrated my efforts instead on developing friendships with the more experienced "professional" cons. Unfortunately, there just weren't that many of them to befriend at McNeil. When I did find one, they generally avoided me. Prisons are *not* as full of dedicated, totally committed, well-disciplined criminals as I had always believed. On the contrary, they are mostly filled with uneducated, unskilled, undisciplined, poverty level types who steal to pay for the illegal—and hence expensive—drugs they use to escape from their wretched existence. In the entire prison there were probably no more than 20 really dedicated criminals to be found.

After asking around, I located a couple of guys who would prove to be very useful to me. One was a black man named Hank, who had forgotten more psychology than I could ever hope to learn, and the other was a Chicano named J.P., who was really the only true "intellectual" Chicano that I'd ever met up to this point in my life. J.P. was a genuine "heavy," the real thing, and it was he who provided me information that I was to save and use for my first Big Score. The plan was to use the money from that job for a boat to use in his escape—after which he and I would wage war together on the street.

Hank, a pimp by profession and an addict by conviction, was doing 20 years without parole for possessing just enough heroin to fix three times—his daily intake at the time of his arrest. His educational background was such that I was able to learn from him the kind of psychology that I could never learn from a textbook on my own. His keen intellect had earned him a very sensitive position in the Records Office. I was also able to use him to develop the kind of contacts I would need later on. Hank would check out the file of a likely candidate for recruitment and then would tell me what the institution had to say about that person. If that individual seemed to be serious about crime, I'd try to get close to him.

Hank thought I was stone cold crazy for wanting to take money at gunpoint when it was possible, as in his case, to get a woman to hand over her cash earnings just by controlling her mind. He didn't understand that it was a very personal war I was engaged in, and the matter of revenge was more important to me than the money alone.

Then there was Royale, another one of the "girls" at McNeil Island. Royale was a fascinating blend of bank robber, writer, and intellectual. Right from the start, she encouraged me to try my hand at writing down my thoughts, suggesting that it would be good therapy. When I asked her why she thought I needed therapy she just laughed and said that anyone who didn't smoke, drink, or use drugs—especially in prison—*had* to be in serious need of therapy. I didn't tell Royale that abstinence and self-discipline were the very things I depended upon to hold at bay the terrifying unmentionable entity that I knew lived somewhere deep inside my soul.

Taking her advice, I went ahead and wrote a novel while I was there. A "master criminal" novel that, at least at first, I intended to use as a blueprint for my war on society once I was out. It featured a professional armed robber whose career had begun by being sent to prison as a youth for a petty crime. Beset by anxiety and guilt after years of homosexual activity during his imprisonment, he is bent and twisted into a mass of hatred and frustration, eventually becoming not just an elite robber, but a ruthless killer whose victims always seemed to be women.

Royale cried when she read it. “Poor Frosty,” she whimpered as she flipped from one page to the next. “Poor Frosty.”

I told her that it was just a piece of fiction, *not* an expression of my own inner turmoil, which is apparently what she thought my words to be. She cried nonetheless, believing it contained much of my own troubled self.

Chapter Seven

WALT KEARNY

Christmas Day, 1963. I received the most fantastic gift. I finally got to see Walt again.

A genuine friend from my time at Lompoc, I'd known he was here at McNeil. He was being housed at the Camp, which was considered a separate institution on the island, so I never had a chance to find him. They'd called him "Wheat Germ" back at Lompoc. If ever there could be a genuine bright spot within a prison setting, Wheat Germ had been precisely that to me. I still remember the first time I met him.

Several other men and I had just been processed into Lompoc and led to our dorms. There were few empty beds. The bunks beneath the windows were already filled, so I took one halfway down the center row on the right. I was so tired from the night before that I lay down on my bed almost as soon as I finished tucking in the sheets.

My companions were already talking to the other inmates. Why, I remember thinking to myself, do these guys have to talk all the time? I always understood intuitively that silence is what most protected me. Words spilling out from my own mouth could give me away. But there they were, chattering away, recounting the story of the riot we had instigated the previous night in San Luis Obispo. At the time, I had enjoyed the chaos that we had caused in the County lockup. Tired as I was though, it all seemed very far away, unreal, as I drifted off to asleep. Laughter awakened me. More inmates were returning and gathering around to listen to what was being said about the fire we had started.

I opened my eyes—big mistake. The person on my left pounced on my wakefulness and immediately started telling me his entire life story. He had done this and had done that. He was 20 years old and, this time around, he was doing an eight-year number for theft and a weapons charge.

"I'm Frosty," I mumbled, barely looking at the guy. My attention was focused instead on a much older man, built like a Greek god, who was standing directly across from my bunk several beds away. Just to look at him was to be filled with a strange and utterly compelling longing to know him.

"His name is Walt Kearny but everyone calls him 'Wheat Germ' because he's such a health nut. He doesn't talk to many of the younger inmates, but he likes *me*," the blabber boasted. "Hey, Wheat Germ! Come over here!"

I felt embarrassed. What could I possibly say to this man? His body moved like a panther. His gait was fluid and graceful, a beautiful thing to behold. It was also inexplicably intimidating.

"Wheat Germ, this is Frosty."

"Frosty?" he asked, looking me square in the eye. "Is that your real name or a nickname?"

Apart from his piercing dark eyes, the simple straightforwardness of his question made me feel uncomfortable, vulnerable. Yet I also sensed a strange, mystical kinship with this unknown entity.

"It's a nickname," I replied, almost inaudibly.

He asked for my real name. When he did so, I felt trapped, nervous, irrationally afraid.

"Floyd Forsberg... Floyd Forsberg is my real name."

"Well, since that is your *real* name, I shall call you Floyd."

The emphasis tore at my gut, although I couldn't sort out exactly why I was feeling so intimidated. There was nothing unkind or menacing about his appearance or speech. Why did I want to turn and run? Then I remembered I had just arrived, and I *had* to survive. This meant having to project some sort of image.

"The name is Frosty," I said, a little louder this time. "Coolness is my game. Death and destruction my claim to fame."

I usually spoke these words with a practiced tone of confidence and ruthlessness. This time around, there was nothing about my delivery that inspired any kind of fear. I bit my lower lip to maintain the scowl I'd twisted onto my face. He just looked at me with an amused smile and walked away.

My neighbor was laughing. "Hey, man, you really put that old nut in his place. You're all right!"

As he continued jabbering away, my own internal radar remained pointed in Wheat Germ's direction. If he was broadcasting any unspoken vibes in my direction, I wasn't catching them. He lay on his bunk reading.

My second weekend at Lompoc, I decided not to go to the weekly Saturday night movie. I was worried about my upcoming meeting with the psychiatrist. I would be required to allow him to classify me, label me, explain me. I could not let him understand what was really going on. If he saw the real me, he would see the emptiness and that formless, awful something that lived within me. With all of this anxiety whirling inside my head, I was in no mood for a movie.

As for Wheat Germ, he never went to the Saturday night movie. When everyone else had gone to the movie room, he and I were the only two people left in the dormitory. After a short while, I felt him sit down at the foot of my bunk. I opened my eyes and explained I had a headache and I *didn't* feel like talking to *him*.

The moment I said this I was sorry. While I *did* have a headache, I really wanted to talk to him. I wanted to speak with this man more than I'd ever wanted to speak with anyone else in the whole world.

"Would you feel like talking if your headache was gone?" he asked.

"Of course," I answered, trying to sound indifferent.

"Sit up then."

Before I knew what was happening, he had his fingers on my temples, saying something in a language I'd never heard before. Moments later, the pain was gone. I was astonished!

"How did you do that?" I asked, incredulous.

"How does a man do anything? We can only function within the spectrum of our own accumulated knowledge. What we do is not always a reflection of what we are, but what we are is always the sum of what we know. That which we know is always changing, so that we can never truly be defined. It's like the old saying about how a man can never really step into the same river twice. The river, like our knowledge, is always as ever changing as the man himself."

His words seemed to lift me, filling me with a mystical energy.

"Wheat Germ..." I said, preparing to ask him a question. He interrupted me, telling me that "Wheat Germ," while amusing to him, was a nickname that *others* there at Lompoc had given to him. *I* was to call him Walt.

"Walt," I said, feeling a bit embarrassed. "Why are you so different from everyone else?"

He smiled. "Why are *you* so different, Floyd?"

I was taken aback by his question, alarmed over *what* he'd been able to see. I had always thought that if I *was* different from others, the difference was perceptible to *me alone*.

"I understand," he said reassuringly, noticing my reaction. "And I won't expose you. I have seen your torment from the start. You play a part that is not you to survive. Survival *is* the number one law of the jungle here. You are a very beautiful young man, Floyd. Your real beauty is not your physical youth; it is in the torment of your highly developed soul. This could be your last incarnation, if you will but follow your own light."

"Incarnation?" I asked, altogether confounded.

"Have you ever read the teachings of the Buddha?"

"No."

"You are a seeker, are you not?"

"What do you mean?"

"There are those who seek, those who do not seek, and those who reject. We are imprisoned with those who reject, while society as a whole is comprised of those who do not seek. There are few who truly seek, who lay themselves open to the ultimate reality that everything is an illusion, that everything one has ever valued and pursued is emptiness."

I began to perspire. All of this talk of seekers and rejecters made me feel as if he was somehow seeing inside of me and articulating my struggle. If *he* could see it, then surely the prison psychiatrist could and would be able to see it as well.

He continued, "You are reaching a spiritual age where you will no longer be able to deceive yourself, Floyd. You already know that you cannot accept the rubbish reality to which others are clinging, and yet you cannot escape it. You *must* learn to stand alone, to not grasp for anything. If you open yourself, everything needed will come. You must study and learn."

"Study and learn *what*?" I was so caught in his words and so hungry for awakening that I could not contain myself.

"Study and learn whatever comes to you, Floyd. I cannot say what your path is or what your karma is. You are not on the same primal, rudimentary level as the others here around you. First and foremost, you must free yourself from them. Then you must follow wherever your flow takes you."

"My flow?"

"Yes, your flow. That is, the currents and forces of the universe at work in your life. Flows of energy and matter. The material with which God—"

"God?" I hissed, interrupting him in mid-sentence. "I am an *atheist!* There is *no* God!"

"Do you know that for a fact?" he countered, smiling.

"Look around you!" I snarled. "Look in the newspaper! Do you really think that God would allow such misery and suffering if he actually existed? Show me your proof of God!"

"You will have to discover God for yourself, Floyd. Mark my words, there is nothing more meaningful to your existence, nothing more satisfying, than attaining the complete fulfillment of your spiritual appetite. We, all of us, are but an extension of God's own nature. The misery and suffering you see around you are just as much a part of God's plan as his miracles."

"Miracles?" I scoffed. "*What* miracles?"

"The miracles of love, and life, and death."

I had to stop him. I loved no one. I was certain I never would.

"You're just a bunch of shit like everyone says!" I growled, my insides twisted with a mixture of disappointment and anger. "I didn't believe it about you at first. Now I do. You think you're better than the rest of us just because you read a bunch of crap in a book!"

"Did I read in a book that you've been worrying yourself sick about next Monday's appointment with the psychiatrist?" he asked, his voice soft and sincere. "Did I read in a book how terrified you are that he'll see in you what you don't want him to see?"

My throat went dry. I tried to reply, but could not.

"Floyd, these people don't care one bit about who you are or what you do. Don't worry about it. Walk in there like anyone else. Be a little belligerent. Act confused about why you do the things you do. They'll label you. While that won't mean anything to you, it will mean a lot to *them*. They have their fears, and labeling yours is how they alleviate them."

"Their fears?" I asked, incredulous. "What in the world do *they* have to fear?"

"Psychiatry is a dangerous profession, Floyd. They analyze and dissect all human behavior down to certain basic fundamentals. At first, it's all very interesting and exciting to them. Then they realize that they're not so different from the people they study. They begin to see through the illusion, and this in turn leaves them feeling on the brink of irrevocable extinction."

"They reduce everything to its lowest denominator. Unless their lives are fitted with a complement of spirituality that few such men ever permit within their strict regimen of learning, they can no longer be the dedicated open-minded researchers that they started out wanting to be. There are too many pathways, too much cause and effect, too many explanations. Needing the comfort of illusion, they label everything and everyone, including themselves. You have nothing to fear. Nothing. Everything is going to be all right."

Although I couldn't grasp all he was saying, I wanted to hear more. Walt's words were very comforting, very reassuring. As soon as his own psychological evaluation was completed, he, too, would be transferred to McNeil Island to serve out a five-year sentence. On that late Saturday afternoon and evening at Lompoc we talked of many things, until the enchantment was finally broken by the noise of the others returning to the dorm after the Saturday movie.

Before he left Lompoc, he kissed me goodbye—a *real* kiss!—and then gave me a list of almost a hundred books, making me promise to read and study them all. I couldn't accept his beliefs and teachings about God, but I became fully committed to his secondary principle of self-realization: the finding of just one act to lift me beyond the mere trappings of physical existence. One act that would free me from the vanity of clinging to the mere quantity of life instead of to a higher qualitative integrity. I had no idea what that one act would be. Walt told me I would know it when it came. I believed him.

His list of books contained authors I'd never heard of before: Plato, Aristotle, Epicurus, and other Greek, Chinese, and Hindu names I could not pronounce. His list also included almost all of the important classic novels. A new world opened up to me. I became hungry for more knowledge and grew obsessed by the thought of going to college when I got out of prison.

I began to see why I had always been in so much trouble. I had acted out from a sense of worthlessness and a lack of personal dignity. I began to wonder what my life would have been like if my father hadn't died. He was no prince—he was a violent alcoholic with not much more to recommend him—but with only my mother to keep me in check there was nothing to keep me from crashing around, looking for a model of manliness to take for my own, and finding it among my criminal heroes. I was in rebellion against myself and had gotten myself entangled in a system of penal absurdity that only exacerbated the problem. With that budding self-awareness, I began to think I might really make it on the outside the next time around, if I could just make parole.

After the stabbing, and after being prosecuted for having defended myself, I began to see clearly that I was trapped in a system planned and calculated to ensure failure. Any first year psychology student could predict the end result of years of treating men like animals, of removing from them every degree of control over their lives and filling them with bitterness and frustration, of keeping them from their wives and loved ones for years on end with no natural sexual or emotional release, twisting them toward unnatural sexuality and violence. Consumed by rage after this regimen of incarceration, the released inmate was destined to fail and return to prison without ever knowing he was part of a giant conspiracy.

It was at this point that I determined to go my *own* way, the way and the path of the Tiger. Seven months later, Walt was before me yet again, and I told him I'd found my way. We had two magnificent hours to talk during the Christmas show inside the larger facility where I was being held. Walt was pleased to hear of my growth and progress, and his praise thrilled me immensely. I also couldn't help but cringe over his chastisement for my refusal to acknowledge a Supreme Deity. Moreover, he was clearly disturbed that I intended to use all my knowledge to make myself a more skilled and dedicated criminal, a "super criminal." He cautioned that one could not and ought not use good to achieve evil.

Like a practiced pitchman, I gave him my views on how the concept of evil was purely artificial, that "law" and "morality" were merely bolts across the doorway of hard reality, placed there by non-thinking, very superstitious men, and that my studies had removed all doubts about the rightness of my atheism. God, I told him, was merely man's artificial construct for dealing with his universal fear of death and the unknown.

"Floyd," he said, his voice filled with obvious concern, "it grieves me to hear you deny God, and to reject him so adamantly, with such intense animus. Better that you were completely indifferent. Your refusal to recognize a Higher Order will deprive you of spiritual grace. Whether you think so or not, it *will* put a damper on your growth and limit your other endeavors."

I confided to him that in fact I was not having much luck enlisting the aid of the more experienced professional convicts to mentor me. "Why won't they talk to me, Walt? Everyone knows that I'm no rat. I'm as tough as nails."

He smiled. "You just answered your own question, Floyd."

I didn't understand, and said as much.

"You younger guys in 3J5 believe that everyone leaves you alone because of your *reputation* for being 'tough as nails.' Have you ever noticed how most of the older cons are quiet all day long, doing their own time, always reading or studying, regardless of whether their goals are positive or negative? The truth is they don't *need* to swagger or strut around *acting* tough. They *are* tough!

"That's the difference that you have yet to perceive. You didn't even make it through your initial sentence without getting busted and collared with a new beef. Do you really think the same thing won't happen on the outside?"

"But I *had* to stab that fool! I had *no* choice!"

"Are you sure there was no other way?" he asked. "If nothing else, you could have piped him. Instead, you *chose* to go all the way and try to *kill* him. You didn't control yourself. You allowed your emotions to control you. The old pros can see that. Yes, they know that you're not a rat. They also know that a person who isn't in control of himself is just as dangerous to them as a snitch, if not more so. You'd be about as welcome to a real pro as some unstable, unreliable addict. *Control*, my young friend, is the name of the game."

To my great misfortune, Walt had just three months remaining to serve out his Federal prison sentence. He *cared* about me, and genuine love for another human being inside prison walls was a very rare commodity indeed. I saw him one more time after the Christmas show, and that was on the day of his release. His parting words encouraged me to remember that *all* things, especially *people*, were perpetually in a state of flux, and that I was to always be careful of them, seeing them as they *are*, not as I wanted or needed them to be.

"Man makes a poor God," he said as we shook hands and wished each other well. I wondered whether our paths would ever cross again.

ꕥ

Taking Walt's advice to heart, I quit trying to impress the older cons with my toughness and instead focused on developing myself mentally. I continued reading and learning. I also started lifting weights to develop my physical strength. After realizing that, as a professional criminal, I might one day find myself having to flee the country, I hooked up with a Mexican inmate, Tito, who agreed to teach me Spanish, and after getting the other Mexicans to agree to my request to change beds, I moved into his cell. A white guy living with nine Chicanos was considered a betrayal and an outrage by most of the Anglo population, and I was immediately ostracized by them. As I grew in physical stature and personal insight, I also became more self-assured and came to be accepted by one of the old timers who had been transferred to McNeil after the closure of Alcatraz. His name was Blackie.

To my great surprise, he eventually suggested to me that I should give up the idea of becoming a professional bank robber.

"But why?" I exclaimed. "I want the big money!"

"For starters, Frosty, you can't have any kind of a *real* personal life with that career choice. You cannot rob a bank and then expect to live like some honored or beloved king. You have to live like a bank robber *all* the time; ever-cautious, ever-suspicious, even when you aren't working. Just stop and think about it for a minute. Few robbers with any kind of sense ever actually get caught inside the bank itself. They usually end up getting busted a week, a month, or maybe even years later, and this happens because they all eventually get to thinking they're invisible. The FBI *never* takes a time out. In this game, they are after you 24 hours a day, playing man to man defense one minute and zone defense the next. Worst of all, they only have to score *once* and the game's over. *They* can make mistakes. *You* can't. Few people can take that kind of unrelenting pressure. Most just do *not* have that kind of discipline."

"What you're telling me is you don't think I have what it takes?"

Blackie shook his head. "No, you're not following me. You're certainly ahead of the game when compared to the average sucker in this place. You don't use dope. You don't drink. Most importantly, you have a better than average brain. Then again so does every FBI agent." He paused. "All right. If you really want to learn the ropes, I'll teach you."

By reputation, Blackie Audette was one of the best bank men around. During the '30s and '40s he had in fact been one mean machine. Simple mathematics should have told me that, at sixty-eight years of age and over 40 of those years spent behind bars, Blackie was not exactly the epitome of a bank robber success story. I couldn't see that. Blinded by my thirst for money and revenge, all I could see was that Blackie could teach me how to take what I wanted from the banks. Regardless of his past failures and many years behind bars, I embraced him as my mentor.

As time passed, I gave no thought to plotting any kind of escape and instead kept myself busy learning and perfecting what I considered to be the Ways of the Master Criminal. One afternoon, I got a piece of news that sent my head spinning. Hank discovered an ambiguity in my sentencing documents. One of my sentencing orders clearly indicated I was to serve two consecutive five-year terms, effectively a ten-year sentence. A second sentencing order had been computed erroneously and reflected a total sentence of seven years and 24 days. Hank felt certain that if he could pull the ten-year computation order from my file, the faulty commitment order with the shorter incorrect sentence would probably withstand scrutiny and I would be free before my time.

Ever opportunistic and a pimp at heart, Hank offered to fix my file for $1,000. I would not have to pay up until and unless the fix actually worked and resulted in my early release. I immediately accepted his offer, and he trusted me to send the money to his wife at a later time, after I was able to pull off my first robbery.

With so little time left before my earlier than expected release, I committed to memory every detail of the robberies that had been plotted out and given to me by J.P., my Chicano friend. Royale, on the other hand, counseled me to do *nothing* for at least one year, to give myself enough time for the poison of prison life to work its way out of my system. If I still wanted to wage my war on the world after that year of rest, she said, I would then at least be able to do so with a clear head.

Within one year of my release, I intended to be a living blissfully in Mexico, a retired self-made millionaire. Too much of life had already passed me by, and there was no way I would ever follow Royale's advice. There was no time to lose. As far as I was concerned, society *owed* me Big Time, and I intended to collect!

Chapter Eight

BACK IN THE REAL WORLD

If a baby during childbirth could somehow describe the newness and utter shock of the experience, I believe his description would not be too dissimilar from the emotions one feels when released after a long period of confinement. Anxiety enshrouds everything. One's new surroundings seem so solid, so permanent. You are in the realm of purpose and systematic order based on time. Everyone seems to be so conscious of and driven by some vague sense that each is allotted a very limited number of hours and minutes per day.

In a prison setting, time, of course, is the single measure of one's existence. But it is *different*. In prison, time gives the prisoner a bridge over despair, a direct line to a future, and he must try to endure. When that future finally becomes the present, however, we all end up scratching our heads, wondering where exactly all of that time went. We wonder how our lives could have been filled with such monotony that less than one percent of our prison existence actually stands out with any kind of discernible emotional detail in our memories.

My sister Sharon picked me up at the prison dock. She was married now, with three children, glaring proof that life had continued on without me. Even so, the psychological divide between prison and me grew wider and wider with each physical mile we drove away from that place. I had been *there*. There and here. I said it several times to myself.

Already, being *here* had changed some of the being *there*. Sexual desires I'd once allowed myself to feel about my sister suddenly vanished. The simple realization I was again in a two-gender world had reinstated her in her appropriate role as my little sister. She no longer represented to me the sole bridge of femininity spanning the here and the there.

Sharon asked me if I wanted to drive. The mere thought of doing something so normal so soon made my hands sweat. I declined. "Not on the freeway," I said to her.

As I looked at the faces of people driving alongside us, I wondered: What holds them together here? What demons do they resist and conquer daily in a world not surrounded by walls and gun towers? Against what common foe do they take such an uncompromising stand? I knew so little of their morality or their ways. In my heart of hearts, I did know this: *They* had given their stamp of approval to what had been done to me. For that, I hated them. I hated *all* of them.

Sheep and goats, I thought to myself. They were all nothing but a bunch of sheep and goats. I would shape the humiliations of my prison experience into a sword and cut them all down. Each would tumble into the abyss of their own apathy. Just as soon as I settled down and sharpened my mind into focus, I would release the monster *they* had unwittingly spawned inside me by way of their indifference as I'd sat caged inside reform school, Leavenworth, Lompoc, and McNeil.

One of the embittering aspects of the Federal parole system was that even if a man served out his full sentence in prison without benefit of an early release, he was still compelled to accept parole supervision and forced to obey the rules of a conditional release. While it was true I had quite literally stolen back three years of my life, I remained angry at this intrusion and continuous stranglehold on my life.

Not surprisingly, I resented my parole officer. Although he was nothing like the small-minded political game players about which I'd heard so much, it infuriated me that I had to report to him. After all, as far as the Feds were concerned, I had *not* been granted an early release, so it didn't seem fair that I had to accept *any* conditions to my freedom.

The first condition was that I had to get a job. I did not want a job! Predators hate to work. It's not that they're lazy, it's simply that the notion of working and then saving to achieve a certain goal strikes your average predator as being too quaint and time consuming. The reward is just too far off in the future, which doesn't cut it for someone who exists always in the world of *now.* Besides, I had no other skill but crime. Lest I be violated by my parole officer and thrown back into prison, I found a job working ten hours a day as a busboy.

☙

Three days after I got out of prison, Sharon's husband invited me out to the races. There, the noise and shouting of the crowd just added confusion to my sense of urgency to "make it" on the outside despite the odds. Then, from out of the blue, I heard a voice calling an old, familiar name.

"Frosty! Hey, Frosty!"

It must be a different man, a square who was part of this world. Frosty was my name in prison and since I was "here" and not "there," I ignored it. Then a strong hand tugged at my arm and spun me halfway around. When I looked to see who it was, I saw the smiling, alert face of an ex-con from my past, Matt Dillon.

"When did you get out?" he asked cheerfully.

"Three days ago," I said.

Matt was a bank robber, one of the best old school robbers of them all. He served five years of a 25-year sentence for bank robbery before the Supreme Court overturned his case in *Dillon v. United States of America* and ordered him set free.

"Jesus, you've gotten big!" he exclaimed, squeezing my bicep. "Come on over here with me, Frosty. I want you to meet my wife."

My sense of adventure was awakened by this chance encounter. Surely, Matt and I could hook up and do a job together. I was elated when, after the last race, he invited me to join him and his wife at their apartment. We talked for hours about who was still back on the island and who was doing what. He'd been out almost two years and was hungry for news. Finally, his wife excused herself and went to bed, and I could at long last ask him about what kind of action he had going on. When I saw his nice apartment, I could see he was doing well.

In response to my question, Matt smiled and walked to a closet, returning with a large black case. My heart raced when he set it down and reached for the latches. I envisioned stacks of hundred-dollar bills inside, along with an assortment of large caliber handguns. When he popped open the lid to show me his wares, I saw a vacuum cleaner and an array of accessories.

From my dumbfounded expression, Matt could see an explanation was very definitely in order.

"Frosty," he began, "I've done time for robbery in Washington, Oregon, and California. With each stint behind bars, I always came out more bitter than when I went in. Then I caught that 25-year federal sentence, and I thought for sure *that* was the end for me. With my record, I was going to be down for at least 15 years, and probably more. When the Supreme Court overturned my conviction and ordered my release, I managed to get out after serving just five years of what almost certainly would have been 15 years *minimum*. That made me a free man some ten years earlier than I had any right to expect. That's when I decided to quit while I was a winner. You already know how everyone always comes out of prison feeling like a loser. Well, my beating them out of those ten years made me feel like a winner. Besides, I was getting way too old for all of that stuff anyway."

ꟹ

One afternoon, while hanging out not far from Portland State College during my off-work hours, I noticed a pretty girl just as she was about to enter a shoe repair shop. Our eyes met and she smiled. I walked past her, seemingly incapable of a spontaneous reaction. Then I remembered Hank telling me that a pimp's success was in his outrageous flamboyance, his ornate loquacity, his ability to draw her out with verbal wizardry. I turned around and walked into the shop, where she smiled at me again.

"Excuse me," I said, speaking as grandly as a Prussian noble, "but your smile just so captivated me that to wander any further without inquiring as to its hidden meaning would forever condemn me to an unfulfillment beyond my capacity to bear."

Her high-spirited laugh told me she had been touched—or at the very least amused—by my pretentious spiel.

"Wow!" she said, still smiling. "Where did *you* come from?"

"From the deepest corners of your unrealized fantasies," I replied, trying my best to match her smile.

Her name was Beth, and she was a 19-year-old college student. She told me almost apologetically she already had a steady boyfriend. She added excitedly she had an older sister who would almost certainly flip for me. When she asked me to follow her several blocks to the nearest pay phone, I *went.*

Admittedly, I felt like an alien in her presence. In the past, whenever I walked the streets looking at women, I rarely ever saw flesh and blood, three dimensional shapes that I could reach out and touch. Instead I usually saw two dimensional figures as if in a movie, not entirely real. Now as I walked alongside this girl who actually knew my name, and who had shared with me *her* name, she somehow seemed more real to me.

Her sister Kay was a 23-year-old divorcee with three young sons. As Beth dialed her number, I stood by, amazed at just how completely casual she was about the whole thing. After telling her sister that she had a present for her, Beth handed me the phone. Within minutes, Kay and I agreed to meet. Beth then went her way and I left to put in another ten-hour shift at my job.

Eventually, after going out together several times, Kay suggested it was time I spend the night with her. Once inside her bedroom, I felt like a nervous teenager, my mind awash with adolescent fantasies of all I wanted to do, but my hands not having any idea where to begin. Fortunately, Kay sensed my awkwardness and sweetly took the lead, teaching me and forever etching in my mind the wondrous differences between a man and a woman.

"Not too experienced," she said afterwards, her voice playful, as if weighing whether or not to keep me. "But you'll do!"

After that night in her bedroom, she asked me to move in with her. Just like that, my war against society and my plans to break J.P. out of McNeil seemed like part of another world altogether. Now I understood what Blackie meant when he told me that women were the greatest threat to a successful criminal.

"Besides breaking your discipline and fogging your mind," he said, "women are also the main reason that most guys end up getting ratted out and busted. Nine times out of 10, when a partner betrays you, it's because some woman behind the scenes is influencing his decision to tell on you. It takes a eunuch to be a successful bank robber!"

After a few days of living with Kay, I knew I could never be a eunuch. I also began to doubt whether I wanted to lead the life of a bank robber. After a few weeks, as the novelty of daily sex wore off, economics—and my predatory nature—won out. My wages as a busboy were pitifully low and did not even begin to meet my needs. I still owed Hank $1,000 for helping me get an early release. At $1.65 an hour—just over minimum wage at that time—there was no way I'd ever be able to take care of that obligation. Even my manager at work could sense the cloud of melancholy and defeat that hung over my head all the time.

"Hey, Floyd," she said one afternoon, pulling me aside, "I have a friend who manages a steel mill. It's hard work but it pays well. How would you like it if I give him a call for you?"

I took her up on her offer and was working at the mill within the week. From the very beginning it was terrifying—although *not* on account of the noise and scorching heat. The work itself was very physical, like lifting weights, something I found stimulating. My terror arose instead from having to see the apparent emptiness of those who worked alongside me. To me, they seemed like robots. I could see no struggle in their eyes; their dull, blank faces apparently had long ago ceased to reflect anything. Every day, I had to look upon their collective apathy and the underlying self-righteousness that had fed and allowed the "justice system" I so despised to flourish. Would I become just like them? Could I ever accept such mental mediocrity? To me, prison itself appeared to pale in comparison to the horror of such a monotonous existence among the sheep. There *had* to be a way of escaping this!

To that end, I called up an old friend from McNeil Island, Dick Hedges, who I knew to have money and operational contacts. I tried to interest him in doing a robbery in Los Angeles that J.P. had suggested would make for an easy and very lucrative target. I told him I needed his financial backing to get from Portland to Los Angeles, and I would repay him in full immediately after we finished the job. He refused to be included in any robbery in which the planner—in this case, J.P—wouldn't be actively participating, and there was just *no* changing his mind.

Not long after, I was about to take Kay to work early one morning when I received a call from Shakey, an old time "pete-man," a safe cracker who had been at McNeil for burglary. He'd just escaped from the city jail and he needed to get to Mexico. As I saw it, his call seemed heaven sent. My answer had come.

"Do you mind if we stop off in Los Angeles on the way?" I asked.

"What for?" he asked in turn.

"For an easy $20,000."

I heard a knowing chuckle. "Sure, why not? That will help make Mexico even better!"

When we got together later in the day to discuss our plans, I felt a certain stirring inside me that not even Kay's warm, giving body ever made me feel. Filled with a sense of euphoria, I started recalling all of the details that J.P. had given me about a prime robbery target: a nightclub restaurant in Los Angeles. After Shakey borrowed the money to get us to L.A., I got on the phone and made reservations for the 7:00AM flight to LAX. Then I went to the steel mill to announce in front of one and all that I was quitting my miserable job.

"If you quit without giving proper notice," my supervisor told me, "you'll *never* be allowed to work here again."

"I'll *survive!*" I cracked in response to his words, feeling nothing but contempt for him and all the other working stiffs who were standing nearby. I was ready to launch my reign of super-criminality upon the sheep and the goats. As I glared at this collection of pathetic farm animals who were now my *former* coworkers, I realized I hadn't felt this exquisite since that first night Kay had shown me the sweet pleasures of her bedroom.

This job in Los Angeles was to be my first armed robbery. During the flight to L.A., I spent my time mentally preparing myself for the reality of confronting another human being face to face with a loaded gun in my hand. All that was necessary, I told myself over and over, was that I not lose control. Loss of control would result in violence, and no professional ever wanted that to happen. As Blackie had once told me, "violence reveals a lack of preparation. If you are not totally prepared, you shouldn't be doing the job." Admittedly, I was still nervous, so I was glad I'd be walking into the lion's den with an old pro like Shakey at my side.

Blackie had also taught me about Element X—the unknown quotient—and the need to predict and plan for the unexpected. In this particular stickup, the "unexpected" turned out to be the amount of cash being held in the safe. When we grabbed the nightclub manager at gunpoint and demanded to know how much money he had in the safe, we were shocked when he stammered that he had just $5,000 locked away inside.

"We *know* you take in $20,000 a week and you don't bank until Monday" I growled, driving my gun into his back. "So, you'd better do better than $5,000 or you're dead!"

"You guys… you guys have old information!" he whimpered; eyes wide with fear. "We switched banking days six months ago. They pick it up on Fridays now. All I have in the safe right now is the weekend receipts."

It dawned on me that over a year had passed since J.P. had told me about this place. We *should* have cased the club *ourselves.* Certainly, a real pro would have done exactly that before coming in here with guns in hand.

The manager shut off the alarm and opened a back door, revealing a middle-aged Mexican janitor who was mopping the floor. Above his head a wall clock showed that it was precisely 4:10AM.

"*Dios mio*!" he exclaimed when he saw our guns. "My God!"

"*No se mueve, viejo*," I shouted out in Spanish. "Don't move, old man!"

Shakey covered the Mexican while I took the manager over to the safe. As he worked the combination, he announced that, along with the money, we would also find a loaded gun inside. Inwardly relieved that he had mentioned the gun, I ordered him to step away after the combination was entered. I opened the safe myself, cleaned out the money, and escorted our two goats into a back room.

I ordered the manager to remove the padlock from the cooler. Then I told them each to grab a coat from the rack of work clothes that stood nearby. The Mexican complied without saying a word. The manager, on the other hand, said he didn't need one.

"Grab one!" I snarled, knowing that they likely would not be found or freed until 6:00AM or later.

I smiled inwardly at my own thoughtfulness, amused by the idea that I was a "compassionate warrior." I recalled a distant memory that really irritated the hell out of me. Years before, while in the Hole in reform school, I'd been locked in a cell that had had most of its small windows broken out, allowing the falling snow to blow in on me. I'd almost frozen to death. After two days of begging and pointing to the snow in my cell, I had finally been given a blanket. Oh, how I *hated* the world and every living thing on its surface when I was finally let out of that cell! And now that I had the opportunity to exact a bit of cold air revenge on the manager and his janitor, it really annoyed me that I was consciously choosing *not* to pay the goats back for what had been done to me. What good was a war without casualties?

As we sped away south toward Mexico, I turned on the car radio and tuned in to an all-news station. Just 90 minutes after our getaway, the details of our robbery were being broadcast over the air. Our goats must have been discovered and rescued within minutes of our departure. The news station reported a loss of over $8,000. We had taken only $5,000. Knowing that the nightclub's insurance company would be nailed for the higher amount, I had to laugh at the realization that there was a little larceny in *all* our souls!

When we crossed over the border into Mexico, I felt like I had crossed some kind of finish line and I was filled with a joyous sense of accomplishment. Another penal fantasy made real. Granted, I had not gotten away with enough to retire, but I knew in my heart that I was well on my way to riches and the high life. The next day we laundered the loot in Mexico. Shakey was still hot because of his recent jail break, so he decided to lay low there for a while.

ᔕ

I returned to Portland right away so I could meet with Dick about a $100,000 bank robbery he wanted to set up.

"It looks good to me, Dick," I told him later as we sat parked across the street from the bank he had chosen as our target. "But I really think we should go find ourselves a bank in another state. We *live* in Portland and a pro never robs in the town where he resides."

"What you say is true," he replied, clearly familiar with that very same adage. "But since neither of us has ever robbed a bank that line doesn't apply to us. We don't have records for bank robbery, so neither the police nor the FBI is ever going to suspect you or me."

He had a point, and it was good enough to justify our doing what we really wanted to do anyway. We stole a car and stashed it away for several weeks, intending to use it as our getaway car when we pulled off the heist. We burglarized a gun store for pistols and shotguns. Then, under assumed names, we bought an assault rifle and several magazines, thus providing ourselves with enough fire power to shoot our way out of a tight situation if anything went wrong.

We spent a full month setting up the job, mentally strategizing against any potential pitfalls. The remaining problem was the matter of who we would enlist to drive the switch car after we abandoned our getaway car. Neither of us wanted to bring in a third partner, but we *had* to have someone sitting ready behind the wheel of our second vehicle. In the end, Dick suggested his girlfriend, Edie.

I could hardly believe my ears. "You want to use a *square*?"

"She's not a square anymore," he replied. "I've been teaching her the ropes." He continued expounding the reasons why she should be our driver, emphasizing that she would not get a share of the loot, meaning that I would not be losing anything in the bargain. Finally, against my better judgment, I agreed to use Edie, and we proceeded with our plans.

The job was set for Tuesday at 2:20 in the afternoon. At that particular day and time, the local police would be at their farthest distance from the bank, and just a single highway patrol car would be assigned to our target area. We took care of *that* by calling in a terrible, non-existent head on collision, a call that sent the highway patrol car racing miles from the bank minutes before we made our move.

Dick drove the first car, the one we'd stolen and kept hidden until now. I was crouched in the back with my assault rifle at the ready. We both wore Army fatigues and ski masks. As he pulled up to the front door, I leapt into action without a moment of hesitation, heading straight into the bank.

"All right!" I yelled, my voice forceful yet controlled. "Nobody move!"

Our plan called for us to spend no more than three minutes inside with the first order of business being to grab the manager, Mary Boston, the one employee who had the combination for the main inner vault. We looked and looked for her, but she was nowhere to be found. Glancing at our watches, we realized our time was being used up fast. Giving up the search for Mary Boston, we looted three teller cages and dashed out of the bank.

Our getaway route had us running the car up a steep trail that led straight into the woods, a trail that dead ended at a gravel road. If we were unfortunate enough to be detected and pursued by the police upon fleeing the bank, this route would lead the cops to believe they had us cornered and trapped. Just 50 yards beyond the end of this road, across a narrow heavily wooded trail impassable to any wheeled vehicle, there was another road where our second car, with Edie at the wheel, stood waiting to make good our escape.

Still heavily armed and no longer wearing our ski masks, we leapt from the first car and were confronted by another Element X: a whole herd of small kids carrying inner tubes to the local swimming hole. They stood paralyzed, staring at us with their eyes wide open, as if we were creatures right off the TV screen. With a .38 caliber pistol on my left hip, an automatic handgun on my right, an assault rifle in my hands, and an array of extra banana clips attached to my chest, I must have been a very frightening sight to this crowd of youngsters.

"Run!" I hollered at them, trying to sound as menacing as I could. "Get out of here!"

I had meant for them to run *down* the hill, *away* from our intended destination. They all turned and ran *up* the hill, in the very direction we now had to navigate to reach the second car. Some of the kids crashed off the trail to get out of our way. Most continued up the trail in a panic, with us following right on their heels. One boy could not keep up with the others. Looking over his shoulder in horror as we gained on him, he tripped and fell, then started shrieking hysterically as if some monster was about to devour him. We hopped over him and continued making our way up the hill, finally reaching the second road, where our getaway car was clearly visible to all the kids who had gotten there ahead of us.

"Don't look at us or I'll shoot!" I yelled, waving my assault rifle before their eyes like some madman. One girl was not to be intimidated. Even as we climbed into the backseat of our getaway car, she was sizing us up, after which she took a good long look at our license plate. Element X was rearing its ugly head yet again!

Later, as we counted out our money—a total of $19,980—

Dick started laughing as he recalled the terror we had inspired in those kids.

"Yeah!" I replied, equally amused. "And did you see that one little chick staring at our license plate?"

"Oh yeah, I saw that little rat. No doubt she's been watching too many police shows on TV. She probably went straight home to call in our license plate number to the cops."

"Yeah… but just think of it," I said, an obvious sense of relief in my voice. "If we had not thought to put those stolen license plates on our second car, we'd be in a world of hurt by now. The FBI would be crawling all over us!"

"True enough," Dick replied, a big, confident smile on his face. "But that's why we're pros, right?"

ꕤ

After laundering the money in San Francisco, Dick and Edie went to Las Vegas, and I went on to Mexico, just as I'd done after pulling off my robbery with Shakey. I now had enough money that I could send Hank what I owed him for my early release. My relationship with Kay had undergone something of a negative transformation after I had returned from Mexico that first time around. I'd begun to discuss with her some of my problems, telling her about the five years I'd recently spent in prison and about the several years I'd spent in reform school before that. I told her all that in an effort to explain why I felt so incapable of truly loving another person. Kay seemed to understand my sense of isolation, but she simply would not accept my inability to love. She fully expected that she could teach me to become as *emotionally* intimate with her as I was *physically.*

Finally having some money on hand, I'd not had to work after my first return trip from Mexico. Instead, I set up a phony job with a construction company to keep my parole officer satisfied. I used my free time to meditate and sort things out—and to mastermind all the robberies I hoped to pull off.

Strangely enough, I also spent some of that time thinking about God again. I wondered why so much of man's existence seemed to be spent in search of Him, either to establish or to deny His reality once and for all. I could not believe in God. For the same reason, I could never ultimately find a way to believe in love. Was there some character defect within me? Did I believe that love, like God, was just an illusion? What after all was love? To classify love, it seemed, was as futile as trying to find and classify God.

In any case, after my first return from Mexico, Kay had correctly deduced that I was back into crime since I was no longer working but still had money. Even before I'd left for Los Angeles, my announcement that I would "be gone for a few days" had given form to her suspicions and had led to our first real fight. As we went back and forth at each other, she'd cried that "Frosty" was bent on destroying Floyd.

I'd found her tears to be utterly disgusting. Now that I was away from Kay, savoring the success of my second armed robbery in the comfort of a nice hotel in Mexico, I knew that I no longer wanted to remain with her when I returned to Portland.

When I got back to Oregon, I immediately bought a used sports car and leased my own apartment so I could move out on Kay. She still wanted me to love her. As I'd already told her, I felt completely incapable of that. I honestly did not know what real love would even feel like, and I had no desire to find out.

Chapter Nine

"HI! I'M YOUR NEW NEIGHBOR"

In the novel I'd written about the professional bank robber, my hero never let anyone know where he lived. Following my own blueprint, I told only my sister where I could be found, just in case she needed me in an emergency. Living alone depressed me to the point I spent much of my first day of solitude thinking of death—suicide in particular. I was not suicidal, per se. I *had* reached the conclusion that perhaps the one way I'd ever really break out from this omnipresent soul killing silence that seemed to press in all around me was through death. I had internalized my own violence. I was the victim of my own war and had been led, at last, to thoughts of my own extinction. I was therefore quite surprised and gripped with fear when, on the second evening in my new apartment, there was a knock at my front door.

I had been contemplating action, yes, but not of the sort that I feared was awaiting me behind that door. It *had* to be the FBI coming to tell me that it was time to cash in my chips. There was no way I would ever let them drag me off to prison again.

My fear mounted at the sound of a second knock. Death seemed embraceable now. The problem was *how*. My guns were buried in the woods. My stove was electric, so there was no way to gas myself. There were no beams from which to hang myself. I had no narcotics. No poison.

With my mind racing, I debated whether I should flee to my bathroom and slash my wrists with my razor as I had done before. I'd heard that, in a tub of hot water, the blood flows more quickly and the pain is minimal. Grimly, I chuckled over the thought that I was now so concerned with the avoidance of pain when life itself had become the biggest pain of all.

Another knock. This time, I forced myself to look through the fish lens peephole on my front door. All I could see was a blur of blonde hair. I opened the door.

"Hi! I'm your new neighbor."

I tried to reply, but I was quite literally stunned into speechlessness by the sight of the goddess who stood there before me. She was, without a doubt, the embodiment of every fleshly fantasy I had ever entertained while locked away in prison. Just 48 hours before, I had left Kay for good, convinced in my soul that I was pathologically incapable of love. Now, as I gazed upon the yellow haired Venus standing in my doorway, a thousand emotions coursed through my body, causing me to feel that perhaps true love had finally come beckoning me into its embrace.

I noticed she was dressed in Army greens, the same kind we had worn while robbing the Portland Bank 12 days earlier. An FBI trick perhaps? Why dress her like this, thereby giving away their diabolical plan to entrap me, as Sampson had been entrapped by Delilah?

My wordless staring began to make her feel nervous. "Well," she said shyly, "I just wanted to let you know that if my stereo ever gets too loud just pound on the wall. I'm in the apartment right next to you."

Again, she waited for me to say something, but still I couldn't reply. Strangely, the thought went through my mind that here stood a woman for whom I would not hesitate to betray my best friend. As my heart pounded away inside my chest, I *knew* I *had* to have her!

"Well, I just wanted to tell you about my noisy stereo," she said, turning to leave.

I still hadn't uttered a word. Every fiber of my being screamed out that *this* was my soul mate. Never in my entire existence had I felt more certain about another human being, no matter that she was a complete stranger. She could not understand my lack of a response and started to walk away. Frantic, air seemed to whoosh from every part of my body and revive my frozen vocal cords.

"I have a new stereo," I blurted, finally finding my voice. "Would you like to see it?"

Hank had taught me to be smooth and sophisticated with a woman, which is precisely how I had acted while seducing Kay. Now such pretentious games of seduction seemed vile and almost sacrilegious in the face of the pure and unadulterated passion that this woman had so instantly kindled within me.

She was tall, perhaps five-eight, a classic Greco-Roman beauty. Her blue eyes mirrored my soul's long-suffering sadness.

As she sat on my couch and started remarking on my apartment, my insides were pandemonium. I had to make her love me, I had to have her joined with me, to become entirely one with me.

"Would you like to read my poetry?" I asked, embarrassed by my own question yet compelled to lay myself open to her.

In response to her nod, I selected a notebook of my best poetry, baring my pain and sorrow. As she turned the pages, I wondered whether she had as yet comprehended we had once been one soul. With every passing moment in her presence, I became more and more convinced that this *had* to be so.

She read for more than an hour without lifting her eyes, without saying a single word. I felt my pain becoming hers and hers becoming mine. I struggled to hold back my tears, not knowing how or why I loved her so much. I knew that I had to release my hold on everything else and cling to her.

She put down the book and a strange look came across her face. She didn't seem to know what to say. She had caught a glimpse of the horror of my nature. She must have felt that I could see her troubled soul as well.

"My name is Nancy." We both laughed at the same time, realizing that we had not yet introduced ourselves. "And *your* name?"

I almost couldn't answer. "Floyd."

She was 21 years old, had just graduated from college, and was about to embark on her chosen career as a teacher. Looking into her face as she spoke, I was so mesmerized that I could hardly register anything she said after that. When she announced that she had to leave to meet up with some friends, I longed to go with her. I could hardly fathom the sense of desolation I felt as she got up to leave. I felt myself being overcome by weakness; my body seemingly being sapped of strength. I had to pull myself together and sort it all out.

"Stop by when you return. I'll leave the door unlocked. Just come in and wake me up."

She seemed to realize that my words were not an invitation to seduction. "Okay," she replied. She stood up, smiled gently, and left.

Before she had come knocking on my door some 60 minutes earlier, I'd been trying to find a way out of my world of ugly loneliness. Now I was drowning in the ocean of love that my soul had inexplicably summoned forth from out of nowhere for this woman... this girl who called herself Nancy.

Nancy... Nancy... Nancy! Softly, I called out her name, repeating it over and over. The mere sound of it had a quality of mercy that seemed to pardon and cleanse me of my sins, as if imbued with the power to exorcize even Frosty. I could almost hear him gasping, as if dying, as my love for this Aphrodite of Redemption began to push out and drain away the blackness and evil that had long seemed so at home inside of me.

A dream slowly began to form in my mind. At first, I didn't realize it because my dreams were almost always violent and this one seemed so calm, so peaceful. I was sitting beneath a tree at the edge of a forest. Leaning against me was a woman whose face I couldn't see. I sensed that I somehow knew her, and she was someone for whom I didn't much care. At the bottom of the hill, a young girl was walking along a stream. I called out to her. When she looked up, I saw it was Nancy.

"I love you," she seemed to say, although her lips did not move.

"I know," I replied, my voice trembling with emotion. "I know."

Nancy slowly made her way up the hill to where I was sitting. As soon as she arrived, the woman who had been leaning against me suddenly jumped up, and I finally recognized her face. It was *my* face! She reached for Nancy and the two of them began pulling at each other's hair, screaming and hissing. The one who looked like me let out a deep, maniacal howl of rage as Nancy sank her teeth into the other girl's neck. Blood started flowing everywhere. This trashing girl fight seemed so ridiculous to me. I started to laugh. My laughter seemed to tranquilize them. Their struggling stopped. They looked at me for several seconds and then looked at each other. They kissed as if to seal a truce and then turned toward me as one, their eyes glinting with a sense of mutual purpose. Together, they leapt on me and started tearing at my body with their claw-like fingernails and fang-like teeth. Chunks of me splintered off and flew in every direction. Finally, with parts of me scattered all over the ground, the two of them joined hands, turned, and started toward the stream at the bottom of the hill.

When I woke up, I was gripped by nausea. The dream was still fresh in my mind when, to my surprise, Nancy came gliding into my bedroom. The mere sight of her seemed to chase away my self-loathing. She sat next to me and started talking about a neat guy she had just danced with. For just a fraction of a second, it disturbed me to hear about this "other" guy. But I could see that she seemed happy, and that made me feel happy.

"We have many things to talk about," I said to her.

"I know," she replied, sounding as if she really did know.

"Let's go to the beach tomorrow, just as soon as it's light."

"Okay," she said cheerfully. "Knock on my door when you're ready."

A little while later, she got up and left. Allowing a smile to spread across my face, I laid back, closed my eyes, and slept.

ശ

When I showed up at Nancy's doorstep the next morning, she was not at all surprised by the early hour of my arrival. She packed a small bag and we drove off in my car. We sat silently for the first half hour on the road, listening to music but sensing that something beyond the ordinary was happening that would forever alter the design of our lives.

I gave her the novel I'd written in prison. She spent the rest of the trip reading my words, breaking the silence when she had a question to ask about the story. She quickly realized I was "Mike," the Super-Criminal, which would make her "Rodine."

"How long have you been out?" she asked without looking up.

"Just over three months," I said.

Matter of factly, she asked whether I'd really had sex with that many men. I replied in the affirmative, having already decided to be as straightforward and honest with her as was practically possible. Then she resumed her reading, finishing the short novel by the time we reached Seaside, OR.

Not surprisingly, the small resort town was crowded for the Fourth of July weekend. As soon as we got there we jumped into the spirit and fun. She had a sweet vulnerability about her that tugged at my heart, like that of a child who needed my love, my protection, my care. This made me feel, for the first time in my life, as if I had a genuine purpose. I could actually be complete. I could somehow reach a *compromise* with Frosty, if not totally destroy him.

There was much I couldn't tell her. So much of my past was a laundry list of crimes. Moreover, I knew of too many men who were doing hard time because they had confided in a woman who, either willingly or by compulsion, was later instrumental in sending them to prison. I wasn't foolish enough to risk that. We did share the truth about our inner pain and feelings of worthlessness, of botched suicide attempts, of living on the edge of destruction and despair. To cover for the many years I'd been in prison, I fed her the fiction that I'd spent seven years living in Mexico before I went to prison. My fluency in Spanish added credibility to the lie.

Such was the connection we formed in those handful of hours together that, as soon as we returned from the beach, Nancy moved most of her personal belongings into my apartment. We would be lovers *forever*. I was sure of it. Yet, try as I might, I could not make love to her when she offered herself to me. Love, as opposed to sexual conquest, I soon discovered was a *surrender*, a yielding of myself that seemed to have an emasculating effect on me. The thought of approaching her as an equal created such a tumultuous uncertainty within me that I felt I would die from the sense of inadequacy that overtook me. The fact that she knew from my novel that I possessed a poignant bewilderment about the opposite sex also filled me with anxiety.

That I could not make love to Nancy when, for the very first time in my life, this *really* meant "making love," made me realize I would have to surrender to and continue the War. Frosty was still in control. I still needed him. Frosty had always been there, absorbing all the blows of penal absurdity. Now the only way I would ever be able to measure up to Nancy sexually was to let *Frosty* handle her. Frosty could never love her; of that he was totally incapable. At least Floyd could love her, even as Frosty was called upon to conquer her.

Never before had I been able to harness those two forces together. In the past, they had always been at odds with each other, acting to pull me apart. The thought that I could harmonize these conflicting entities because of my need to feel like and be a man to Nancy made me love her even more. We spent the entire ensuing day in bed, alternately clinging to each other in our passion and breaking to read this or that. Even as we read, we kept our feet tangled together in an embrace, so as not to break the flow of love between us.

Seeing so much of myself in the criminal psychology book I was reading, I put it down and cried. She did not intrude to ask why I was hurting. She seemed to sense I was possessed of some demonic pressure I could not explain with words.

"Don't look back, Darling," she said. "They haven't beaten you. You have beaten them."

My tears continued falling like the spring rains, some of them spilling onto her warm soft shoulder as she embraced me. She didn't understand that I couldn't be entirely myself—that I couldn't be totally *me*—even with her. She could never possibly understand why I still needed the War, why I would probably live a Jekyll and Hyde existence the rest of my life. To her, she was my salvation and my war was now over. Having decided to represent myself to her as a man making his living as a professional gambler, our entire beautiful relationship was *already* based on a lie.

ᔕ

A call from Dick shattered our idyll. It had been two weeks since I'd last seen him in San Francisco. As soon as I heard his voice on the line, I knew in my gut that it was time for our next business venture. When we met, he immediately sensed something different about me and asked if I was well. I told him I was fine. He shrugged and proceeded to unveil our next job—a bank burglary.

"A *burglary*?" That meant hitting a bank when it was closed, unoccupied, and securely buttoned up. "Those vaults are pretty tough, aren't they?"

"Well, the steel doors are," he admitted. "Most of the older banks have regular concrete floors, and I've invented a tool that can punch right through two feet of concrete."

I was feeling very uncomfortable about making any changes to what I considered our successful armed robbery routine. An acquaintance of ours had pulled off a similar bank vault burglary over the Fourth of July weekend, and Dick was eager to try out the device he had invented for the job.

"What I want you to do now is drive around and find us a bank that has an empty building for rent right next to it. Be sure it's an older one. They are less likely to have an alarm system installed under the floor."

Within a week I was able to locate just such a bank in Kalama, 60 miles from Portland. Once found, we enlisted a contact from Arizona to rent the adjacent building for us, with that person agreeing to accept $5,000 or five percent of the take, whichever turned out to be the higher share. We figured the bank would be good for at least $100,000.

We would need a lot of tools for this one, everything from cutting torches to high speed drills with diamond tipped drill bits. It took me a full week to locate and purchase everything we needed from various nearby hardware stores. I was down to the last few items on our list when I noticed the manager of one of the stores behaving strangely. He offered to help me load the sledgehammer and some other tools into my car. I saw him take a subtle sideward glance at my license plate. Later, I mentioned the incident to Dick.

"I think we should dump everything we bought from that store," I said to him, explaining the manager's suspicious behavior. "He got my license number."

"Why dump the tools?" Dick asked. "You don't really think we intend to leave anything behind, do you? And, besides, why in the world would he have any reason to be suspicious of you?"

"I don't know. He *did* take my license number, I'm sure of it. All that stuff from his store, if found later, can be traced to *me*—"

"Wait a minute," he said, interrupting me. "That was $200 worth of tools. What did you pay him with?"

"A couple of C-notes," I replied.

"Don't you see? He thought those hundred-dollar bills were phony. Once he checked them out after you left and realized they were good, he no doubt forgot all about you and your license plate. Now what else is left on the list?"

"Just the truck and the camper," I replied. "I still don't see why we need the camper."

"You've been wondering how we'll know if we hit an alarm. Here's the plan. Edie will be hidden in the camper, peeking through its curtains, about a block away from the bank. She'll have a walkie-talkie, and we'll be carrying another one with us inside the building. If we trip an alarm, she'll advise us of cops in the area. They'll go to the bank, not our building. We'll lay low and they will think it was just a false alarm, after which we cut our losses and go home. Simple."

"But what about the jeweler?" I asked. Our rented building was sandwiched between the targeted bank and a jewelry store whose owner lived in a small one room apartment attached to the back of his shop. Unless he was either neutralized or incapacitated, *he* would no doubt sound an alarm upon hearing the noise of our tools."

"We take him hostage and keep him with us," he said. "If

necessary, we'll stick a 'CLOSED' sign on his door on Saturday. He's already closed on Sunday anyway. I'm sure we can do all we need to in one night."

Darwin once wrote that all feelings are a part of the survival instinct, both for the individual and the species. Sure enough, all that I felt about this burglary at that moment was one of the most important dynamics of the survival instinct: *apprehension.* Blackie's words kept coming back to me, warning me anew that really intelligent criminals knew intuitively when something was wrong, that they could feel the coming fall before it happened.

"Why would someone keep going at that point?" I remember asking Blackie at the time.

"Well," he said, "Freud called it self-destruction, whereas Menninger described it as a 'lingering suicide.' But that's what you're up against, kid, every bit as much as you're up against the FBI. You see, there's something wrong with your thinking—"

"What do you mean by that?" I'd said, interrupting him.

He had in fact taught me well up to that point. He'd given me 21 rules by which to increase my chances of success, and I knew all of them by heart. Never be impatient. If you need to eat between robberies, humble yourself and get a job. Never share your robbery plan with *anyone* who was not going to be an active participant in the heist. Never this. Never that. Most importantly, never, never, never go through with a job if you felt even the slightest bit of doubt or apprehension. I'd memorized it all like a monk studying scripture. Yet now he was saying there was something wrong with my thinking?

"You seem to think that someone disciplined and intelligent enough to make it as a thief can't also live their life successfully as a law abiding square. Most squares live better than thieves, Frosty. They usually live longer, too."

I'd chalked that last bit of advice up to his having wasted so many of his years behind bars. He'd *failed* at being a professional. I *wouldn't.* Yet *now,* as we drove up in front of the bank in Kalama, I mentally counted six of Blackie's rules that we'd already broken in planning this job. Seven if I counted my having allowed myself to fall in love.

We parked the camper a short distance down the street, with Edie in the back, giving her a clear view of the bank and all its surroundings. It was 9:00PM. By 9:30, we'd unloaded the tools. At 9:45, we put on our ski masks and went for the jeweler. We brought him back to the adjacent empty store we had rented and tied him up. We taped his mouth and stuffed cotton in his ears as a precaution against his crying out or accidently hearing our real names. As in all my robberies, I went by the name of Mike —Mike Weaver, the master criminal I had created in my novel.

It was 10:15 by the time we were ready to begin working. We quickly started cutting a hole in the floor to create a tunnel underneath our building and below the bank, where we would then set up Dick's invention. When the circular cut was completed, the round manhole sized piece of flooring fell inward. The impact, when it came, seemed far away

"I don't believe what I just heard," I said, instantly filled with a very sinking feeling.

"That makes two of us," he chimed in glumly.

As we aimed our flashlights into the hole, we discerned the problem at once. The entire town was built over a flood-control drainage system for the Columbia River! It was, at minimum, a drop of 15 feet to the bottom. Dick's invention would be useless. If we wanted to get into the bank, we'd have to drill directly through the wall.

Spurred on by disappointment and anger, we started drilling, making a lot of noise as the bit bore into the solid concrete wall. It was physically very hard work, and soon we were both sweating profusely. We stayed at it and had made substantial progress when Edie's voice crackled over the walkie-talkie.

"SP coming through," she announced, instantly getting our attention with her signal that the Sheriff Patrol was passing through the area.

We glanced at our watches. Eleven o'clock. The sheriff's

patrol was routine and right on time. We stopped drilling, waiting for Edie's follow-up call, which came maybe 30 seconds later.

"All clear."

We went back to work. No more than a minute or two after resuming our drilling, Edie's voice sounded over the radio again.

"SP coming through."

"So soon? They weren't due to be back for *hours*."

"Who knows?" Dick replied. "Maybe they're responding to an unrelated call and this is the fastest way for them to get to where they need to go. Don't get nervous on me *now*, kid."

"SP gone," said Edie, much to our relief, and we again resumed drilling.

Soon, my arms started getting tired, so I handed the drill to Dick. Right then, Edie's voice and message put us both on edge.

"Two SPs coming through!"

"*Two*?" I blubbered in panic, instantly alert. "We've never seen two of them together at once, have we?"

"Nope!" Dick reached for the assault rifle and cradled it in his arms.

I checked my automatic and tried to control my breathing. A full minute passed before we heard Edie's voice once again.

"Two SPs gone."

"What do you think?" Dick asked.

"I don't like it," I said, unable to hide my nervousness. "It breaks the pattern of their routine. Let's pack up this stuff and get the hell out of here."

"We'll be at the vault by two o'clock," he replied, clearly not wanting to quit just yet. "And we should be able to get inside real fast with the torch. We could have everything cleaned out in a few more hours."

"Well, let's at least play dead and do nothing for 15 minutes," I suggested. "There might be someone hearing us that we don't know about."

Dick agreed. We waited, saying and doing nothing as we

peered at our watches. The minutes seemed endless. I allowed myself to think of Nancy, her precious body curled up asleep on our bed. I should have been with *her* this moment, instead of here.

"Let's get back to work," Dick finally said, trading the assault rifle for the drill. He was just about to switch it on when, over the radio, Edie's voice crackled.

"Two SPs and one HP coming through!"

"This is it, Dick," I said, my voice sounding desperate as I grabbed up the assault rifle and slipped a shell into the chamber.

"Be cool! Be cool!" he replied, his own voice edged with a touch of desperation. He checked his magnum then took on a stance of defiance. "Maybe something else is happening outside tonight. If not, let *them* start the fireworks."

Just then, Edie's voice crackled over the voice again, clearly very panicked now. "They're on foot! Out on the street!"

My heart seemed to stop. For so many years I had fantasized about catching a handful of cops in a vengeful and deadly hail of bullets. Now, on the cusp of just such an opportunity, I thought of Nancy, and a foreign longing encompassed me. I fervently hoped that the cops would just melt away and leave, that they would not compel the Frosty within me to open fire and kill them all.

We could see them walking outside, their eyes glancing left and right. They barely looked at the bank, which was lit up like a Christmas tree, one of the cops pausing just long enough to shake and check its double doors. Then they moved on to the front doors of the surrounding buildings, checking each one. Finally, they got into their cars and left.

"Let's pack it up," I said, knowing that Dick would offer no argument this time around.

We gathered up everything, waited 30 minutes to make sure that the coast was clear, then radioed Edie that we were coming out. After loading our tools in the truck, I slipped behind the wheel, with Dick and Edie sitting beside me. Almost as soon as I pulled away from the curb, a pair of lights appeared at the other end of the street. Dick saw them at the same time.

"Cops!" he yelled. "Step on it!"

I wheeled around and turned in the opposite direction. More lights appeared. It was a trap! I shifted into second gear and turned onto a side street that ran up the hills surrounding the town. The old pickup didn't have much power. We had just reached the top of a three-block hill when two of the cop cars started up after us. We were only doing 40 miles per hour even with the pedal floored to the metal. Knowing that the upcoming road to the right was a dead-end street, I turned left, and wondered whether the police knew the layout as well as I did. I didn't have to wait long to find out. They did. A third patrol car reached the upper road from the other end of town, heading straight toward us. They had us trapped between them.

Knowing I'd soon have to pull over so we could make a run for it, Dick hollered to Edie to get ready to jump. A fraction of a second later, I hit the foot and emergency brakes, bringing us to a screeching halt.

"Hit the woods!" Dick yelled, leaping out the passenger side door.

I fell out into a ditch, then scrambled up and over its edge, darting into the woods. I looked back. The truck was now surrounded by cops, but there was no sign of Dick or Edie. They must have made it into the woods on the other side of the road.

The sky was overcast with almost no moon to speak of, and the trees blocked out whatever dim star light was able to peek its way through the breaks in the clouds. Barely able to see anything in front of me, I inched my way through the woods, using my hands to protect my eyes, as I'd been taught to do in boot camp. I was trying to make my way to the safe car. We had agreed beforehand that in case of trouble the first one to reach it should use it. I had just one weapon with me, my .38 special, with six rounds. It was slightly better than nothing at all.

In the dark, rough terrain, it was hard to tell how far I'd traveled. After maybe a mile, the earth disappeared from under my feet and I fell, my arms flailing wildly through the air in an effort to break my fall. It seemed as if I was suspended in space and time. Though my fall could not have lasted more than a second, it felt like I was plummeting for hours. Had I been dying, I supposed I would have seen my life passing before my eyes. As it was, I saw Nancy. She was in a birdcage hanging in a dark tunnel. I was reaching for her, but couldn't seem to extend my arms far enough. In the next instant everything went totally black.

It was very quiet when I regained consciousness. Every bone shouted out its location in my body, but none felt broken. Apparently, I had fallen into the brush by an abandoned logging road. It was still dark and I was missing my .38 but at least I was still in one piece.

"This *has* to be my last job," I muttered to myself. Now that I believed myself genuinely in love for the first time in my life, I had wondered what I would feel while committing a crime with my beloved sitting at home—and I didn't like it. I now had something to lose. More than ever before, I did *not* want to return to jail.

I began walking along the logging road, which eventually led me out of the woods to a nearby freeway, next to which I spotted a 24-hour truck stop. I immediately headed for the restroom, where I cleaned myself as best as I could and called a cab. Two cheeseburgers and four glasses of milk later, the taxi arrived. The fare to Portland was $50, which I was required to pay up front. "Always carry several hundred dollars on any job," Blackie had counseled. At least I'd followed *that* rule. I had the driver drop me off at the after-hours club, where I quickly found a pay phone and called Dick. He and Edie had been home for several hours, the two of them having reached the safe car ahead of the police. I was relieved for them. Even so, things were not altogether good.

"Everything is gone," Dick moaned. "We lost everything."

"Well, *I* ended up losing the .38 when I fell down a cliff," I added miserably.

"The assault rifle, the .357, the automatic, and your .38?" he said, tallying our material losses. "I guess we really blew it!"

"Yeah, but at least we got away," I said, trying to find a silver lining, "and that's all that really counts."

"Maybe so, but we've got problems buddy. Those drills you bought and the pickup can be traced back to *you*, Frosty. We'd better not have any contact with each other for at least a few weeks."

I suddenly realized *I* was the one who had bought everything. *Mine* was the vulnerability—and mine *alone*. Not Dick's. Not Edie's.

"But don't worry about it," he continued soothingly, clearly not worried in the least for *himself*. "If they pick you up, I'll scrape up the money for a lawyer to fix it."

"What about the old man?" I asked, referring to the jeweler we'd left behind, still bound and gagged, in our hasty departure from the bank.

"The jeweler?" he repeated. "What about him?"

"It could be days before they find him," I replied. "Just because they discover a bunch of burglary tools in the truck doesn't necessarily mean the cops will ever look in the back of the store where we left him."

"Do you really think that square would give a damn to help you or any other ex-convict for that matter? He deserves what he's getting! My, oh my, it almost seems as if you're turning soft. What in the world has gotten into you, Frosty?"

I really couldn't answer that, my being every bit as perplexed as Dick was over my uncharacteristic concern for our victim. Embarrassed at feeling so *human*, I mumbled something about how he was right after all, that the goats truly deserved their doom, and hung up.

I couldn't stop thinking about the old man. While still on the road, I was reminded of a time in reform school when, while in the Hole, I'd been so cruelly handcuffed to the bars I could hardly move. The old jeweler, as I knew all too well, could not move at all. I wondered whether he'd be able to resist urinating for as long as *I'd* had to hold in my own piss before finally letting go in my pants. The fact that the old man might end up having to wet himself, as I'd had to do all those years ago, just didn't seem an appropriate revenge.

ᔓ

When I got home, Nancy was surprised and delighted to see me. I had told her I would be gone for a week, the time span I'd allotted for Dick and me to launder our stolen money in Mexico. Her delight turned to shock when, as I changed my clothes, she saw I was covered with bruises.

"My God!" she gasped. "What happened to you?"

I lied and told her I'd been in a car wreck.

"Was anyone hurt?" she asked.

Her question made me think about the old man lying bound and gagged in the back of the empty store. Her concern, so automatic and natural for a normal human being to feel for the physical wellbeing of a complete stranger, made me realize I couldn't leave him there for days without food or water. That *I* had once been forced to live on bread and lettuce for weeks at a time, with one warm meal every 14 days, somehow did not justify what was happening to him. Besides, after hearing the deep concern in Nancy's voice, I knew I could never look her in the face again if the old man ended up dead because I chose to do nothing. I answered her question by posing a question of my own.

"If someone was in an auto accident and was lying hurt somewhere, and I could make a simple phone call to alert the authorities so they could come to help that person, what would you want me to do?"

Before responding to my question, Nancy looked at me strangely, as if I were from another planet. "How could you not know the answer to that?"

Her words and expression haunted me. I had at least a half a dozen answers to her question, most of them entirely self-serving, and this made me wonder whether I would *ever* be able to think or feel like a "normal" human being. For the first time in many years, perhaps since early childhood, I felt rising up inside of me a long-forgotten emotion: shame. I did not like it one bit. "Get dressed," I finally said. "We need to go to a pay phone."

We crossed the Columbia River into Washington and found a phone booth in Vancouver so that my call would not originate in Oregon. I dialed the bank manager's home. When he finally answered, I feigned what I hoped would sound like a passable Italian accent:

"Now you gonna listen to me real-a good, 'cause I ain'ta gonna tella you but-a once," I began, pausing several seconds to give his groggy brain enough time to wake up and focus. It was 6AM on a Saturday morning and he had taken a very long time to answer. Clearly, he'd been sound asleep when I called. "De bank-a yousa manager of wass-a robbed, and-a the old-a jewelry man issa all up inna da empty ztore right-a next door-a to you building. Pleass-a givva him zome help-a zo's he no die. You got alla dat?"

"Yes, I understand," he replied with feeling. "God bless you."

I hung up the phone, my composure rattled by the banker's closing words asking God to bless me. Why this should shake me up, when I didn't even believe in God in the first place, I didn't know. I decided I just needed some rest. It had been a very rough night. One of the roughest.

Nancy had noticed I cradled the phone in my handkerchief, but said nothing until we got home. "Would you care to tell me what all *that* was all about, Floyd?"

She put a motherly emphasis on my name, making me feel like a juvenile delinquent. I *really* wanted to be open with her about this last festering part of my soul. She could cure me. She could make me well. But she was, first and foremost, an innocent bystander in the criminal drama that was my life. She *wasn't* involved, and I couldn't risk any disclosure that would legally render her an accomplice by simply knowing and not reporting my activities.

"*No*, I would *not*," I replied, surprising even myself with the tone of my voice. I was still operating by Frosty's Laws. I hadn't meant to speak to her so harshly. I was *still* not used to the rules of a genuine personal relationship, its need for authentic tenderness, its dependence on thoughtful give and take. Everything I knew about relationships I'd learned in prison. In prison you just *took*.

Saying nothing more, yet still feeling guilty over the pain I'd just caused Nancy, I went to bed and fell asleep. Soon, I was dreaming. In my dream, I was asleep in prison, dreaming within my actual dream I had been freed from prison, had found Nancy, and I was asleep right next to her in our bed. In that same dream I suddenly found myself back in prison, then together again with Nancy, then back yet again in prison.

Like a man desperately trying to wake up from a dream where he was drowning, I tried to wake myself. I woke up one more time in prison. Somehow, I could not reach any level of consciousness that I absolutely knew to be real. Finally, a gentle voice reached through this seeming madness and said: "Let all your dreams be gathered together into one place. Let all your fears become as one."

The voice belonged to Nancy. As soon as she finished speaking those words, continents of reality rose up and took form within me, originating from the spiraling nebula that swirled around me. The sea of my intellect was filled with fish, each one a memory. One fish was my birth, one my childhood. Another one, a ghoulishly ugly serpent fish, was my father's untimely death. All of these gave a sense of order to my previously formless state. I began to see the pattern—or, more accurately, the plan—and found at long last my place in the endless span of time from which I had somehow slipped. I knew now with complete confidence I was still really and truly asleep next to Nancy, that I was still dreaming, and that it was now okay to wake myself up whenever I chose to do so.

As it turned out, I was alone when I opened my eyes. I was confused to find Nancy's side of the bed empty. I heard a noise in the kitchen, got out of bed, and went to her. When I saw her, I drew her into my arms and kissed her, knowing in my heart that she was all I really needed. At that moment, I didn't care if I had to work again among the goats and the sheep. I would quit the War. I would make peace with the world. I would live my life with my beloved Nancy. The next few days we spent together were a perfect expression of that idealized vision: Our hearts sang and rejoiced, so happy we were to be alive for each other, to be in love with each other.

∽

A few days later, I stopped by Matt Dillon's place. He still hadn't lost any of his "con-wisdom," and thus smiled knowingly when he saw my brand-new car.

"The cards must be turning up pretty good for you, Frosty," he said. "How long have you been out now?"

"About four months."

"So tell me, is the hate and resentment gone?"

"It's starting to go," I replied.

"Frosty, why don't you just cut loose whatever it is you've got going and make up your mind to go straight? I promise you, once the bitterness is gone, you *can* make it. The *only* way to overcome the bitterness is to steer clear of the bad choices long enough to start feeling like a part of the free world. Do you hear what I'm saying, my friend?"

"I'm just about there, Matt. Really. I'm almost there."

It felt good to see someone who had "made it," and who seemed so at peace with himself and with the world at the same time. It had been Matt who'd gotten me the busboy job when I was fresh out of McNeil, at a time when I was still struggling mightily to fit in again in the outside world: buying clothes that fit correctly and were not coarse, reacquainting myself with everything around me, getting used to the faster pace of life and doing without the daily nap I'd always taken between "afternoon yard" and "evening chow," listening to far away little voices that called me "Uncle Floyd" and climbed on me with a gleeful joy, contrasting the charred ruins of my soul.

Now that my heart and mind had so much invested in Nancy, I was better able to see what he'd meant back then. I thought not at all about the years of abuse behind bars, and had felt almost completely devoid of hate, especially over the past few days. Perhaps Matt was right. Once you got over the hate, there was nothing to do but to get on with your life.

Chapter Ten

THE "BIG SHOW"

Dick and I had decided to wait at least two weeks before making contact again. I thought seriously about calling him before that to tell him that I was *through* with crime. Just a week after our failed bank burglary, Dick ended up calling me ahead of schedule.

"A little premature, aren't you?" I asked when I recognized his voice on the other end of the line.

"Hey!" he replied, sounding much more chipper than when we'd last spoken. "If they had anything on us, they'd have grabbed you up by now. Come on over. I need to see you."

An hour later, I was sitting at his kitchen table, listening to him outline a new robbery he'd been planning. When he was done, I took a deep breath and told him of my decision.

"I'm quitting the gang, Dick."

He looked at me for several seconds, as if waiting for a punchline. When none was forthcoming, he started laughing. "Quitting? *You*? Man, this is not the time for any stand-up jokes. I'm broke and I've got bills to pay. House payment. Electricity. Gas. My car payment is due next—"

"I'm quitting," I repeated, interrupting him mid-sentence. "And I'm *not* joking."

"Well, I never thought I'd see them break *your* spirit," he said, not specifying just who he meant by "them." "You're the heaviest dude I know, Frosty. Why in the world would you let them do this to you?"

"They didn't," I replied wearily. "I'm just tired of it all."

"I guess that fall in the woods must have really rattled your brains. Tell me, just how do you intend to earn a living? Washing dishes? Mowing lawns? A paper route maybe?"

"I don't know," I said, ignoring his belittling sarcasm. "I'll be a laborer. I'll find a job doing something."

He continued talking for more than an hour, all the while trying to shame and persuade me into changing my mind, reopening old wounds of revenge that were still tender beneath their crusting scabs. I'm still not sure why I gave in to him, agreeing to just one more robbery. He didn't force me to say yes, but he knew what buttons to push, digging deeper than all of my good intentions. Just a quick teller robbery. Grab the money and run. My responsibility would be the switch car. Dick would find us another assault rifle.

I told Nancy I'd be gone a week again. Leaving her tore me apart. This job really had to be the last for me. I left home at noon. A few minutes later, I realized I'd forgotten my gloves. I couldn't bear the thought of saying goodbye to her again, so I stopped and bought a brand-new pair at a local hardware store. My uncharacteristic forgetfulness rattled my confidence, and a sense of doom seemed to take hold, tightening its grip on me with each passing minute. I was losing control.

Like a recording stuck on "replay," Blackie's lessons started playing over and over in my mind. If you don't feel right, don't do it. If you start losing confidence, quit. If the ice feels thin, get off the lake. Loud though this mental recording was as it played inside my head, I forced myself to turn it off as I pulled in front of Dick's place. From the curb, I could see into his garage. He was taping a set of cool plates over the hot ones on our stolen getaway car.

The switch car was already in place, parked near the library that was to be my drop point. Everything was ready. Edie left at 2:00PM. Dick and I left about 15 minutes later. As we neared the location we had chosen to switch license plates, a green car hung on our tail so closely that we couldn't stop and make the change. We doubled around the block and pulled over, but then noticed a man in a grey car parked nearby, our own car directly in his line of sight.

Unable to switch the plates, and with the man in the grey car watching us, we climbed back into our vehicle and drove off to find another spot. Everywhere we looked, there seemed to be spectators, potential witnesses who prevented us from stopping.

"This is absurd!" I swore, growing more and more frustrated by the moment. "A whole stretch of road and we can't find a single damn spot to change the plates?"

"I don't understand it," Dick growled, as frustrated as I was. "There's usually not this much traffic in this area."

"What's Edie going to think?" I asked, knowing that we were now a full 30 minutes off schedule.

"Don't worry about her," he replied. "She'll sit there all day like a good little soldier if necessary."

Moments later, Dick settled on a good spot to switch the plates, and he quickly pulled off the road. When we got out of the car, we scanned our surroundings, making sure no one was around to see us make the change. As I was pulling off the rear plate, a green car came rolling slowly around the corner, the driver glancing left and right as if looking for something then sped up on the straightaway.

"Hey! Did you see that car?"

"Yeah, so what? He didn't see anything."

"That driver seemed to come around the corner way too slow," I pointed out, "as if he was looking for something—or *someone*—and then he sped up as soon as he saw *us*."

"You're letting your imagination get the best of you, Frosty. *Everyone* slows down around corners. They don't all practice high speed power slides like you do! Shake off the nerves and let's get this over with."

The bank stood at the edge of a small shopping plaza at the bottom of a hill. Dick pulled into a shaded area near the crest of this same hill, and it was here that we readied ourselves for action. I took my assault rifle out of the laundry bag I carried it in. Then I handed Dick his pistol and ski mask. Just then, a green car came around the corner, and the old man behind the wheel really looked us over.

"Did you see that?" I screamed. "That's the same old man who saw us changing the plates!"

"Impossible!" Dick replied, an irritated look on his face. "Snap out of it, Frosty. You're acting like this is your very first job. *Relax*, will you?"

My head was spinning as Dick released the brake and we blasted down the hill toward our target. I pulled on my ski mask just as he pulled up to the back door, then we jumped out and ran into the bank.

"Everyone down on the floor!" I yelled. All the bank's customers wilted like flowers and fell to the floor. Several tellers remained standing behind the counter, evidently believing they would be needed to empty the cash drawers.

"You too!" I screamed, waving my assault rifle at them. Dick was now behind the counter looting the cages. We were out of the bank in minutes. Dick drove off as I sat in the backseat, where I immediately stripped off the jumpsuit I'd been wearing over a pair of corduroy slacks and a Portland State sweatshirt.

"I think that Volkswagen is following us," Dick reported, glancing into the rearview mirror. I turned and looked.

"Are you sure?" I asked.

"It's made the last three turns with us. If it turns with us one more… time, *blast* it."

We turned down another side street and the Volkswagen did the same, sealing its fate. I grabbed the assault rifle and leaned out the window. For years I'd dreamed of blasting to pieces any goat who might dare to foil my escape after a robbery, as *this* one evidently was trying to do. Now that just such a moment had arrived, with the barrel of my assault rifle aimed directly between the eyes of my pursuer, I couldn't bring myself to play God. I raised my gun sights about a foot above the goat's head. For a second, I was distracted by the look of absolute disbelief I saw on the face of a man we passed as he was mowing his lawn. I calmly refocused my attention on the Volkswagen behind us and squeezed the trigger.

The first shot missed the VW completely and the assault rifle immediately jammed. I quickly ejected a couple of shells and aimed at the VW. I fired. To my immense relief, the driver stopped in the middle of the street. I lowered my weapon, withdrew inside the car, and removed the magazine holding the shells. Minutes later, as we approached my drop point, I stuffed the assault rifle and magazine inside the laundry bag along with the money.

Sirens filled the air, sounding like so many angry bees, as I hopped into my own switch car. It was very hot inside, so I pulled into a Dairy Queen to take in the action while I cooled off with a milkshake. I noticed a bunch of men laying asphalt across the street. They were covered with dirt and tar and were repeatedly raising their arms to their faces to wipe the sweat from their eyes. Could I really do manual labor? Was this *really* to be my very last bank robbery? Now that it was over, I felt better for having agreed to do it. I felt a renewed sense of pride over a job well done. With that, I knew in my gut that this very probably was *not* the last time I would ever race into a bank and take its money at gunpoint.

I finished my milkshake and returned to my car. As I pulled onto the roadway and started to drive off, I thought I noticed the same old man in the green car sitting in the parking lot across the street from the Dairy Queen. I wondered if I was losing my mind. Just in case, I watched especially carefully as I drove to Dick's house to be certain that I was not being followed.

Dick was having a beer when I arrived.

"You did okay on that VW, Frosty. I wasn't sure you'd hold it together today, with your getting so spooked about seeing that old man."

"Would you believe it?" I said. "I think I saw him *again* at the Dairy Queen just before I came here."

"Man, you'd better start drinking something other than just milkshakes," he laughed. "You want a beer?"

"You *know* I don't drink."

"Well, you *do* like money," he said, holding up our bag of loot. "Let's count it up."

It didn't take long. We flipped to see who would have the hassle of tallying up the coin. Dick lost. Soon enough, we had our total: $10,049. We smiled and laughed it up. Then, in an instant, our easy atmosphere was shattered by Edie bursting wild eyed into the bedroom.

"My god, Dick!" she shrieked. "There's cops all over the place outside!"

I jumped up and looked out the window. Two city cops with shotguns were running across the backyard. A sheriff and a highway patrolman were darting along the hedge that bordered the neighbor's yard.

"Forsberg and Hedges!" boomed a voice over a bullhorn. "This is the FBI! Come out with your hands above your heads!"

"They even know our names!" Dick screamed. "How could they know our names?"

I dashed to the living room and peeked out through the curtains. I couldn't believe my eyes. There were so many cops I couldn't even begin to count them. Every police agency seemed to have four or five cars parked on the street, with at least four uniformed officers behind each unit, pointing their weapons at the house. An ambulance was visible halfway down the block. Off to my left, a TV van from a local station was filming the whole scene. I hurried back to the bedroom. Dick was still looking out the window.

"How many out front?" he asked.

"Too many to count."

"There's at least six in the back," he said matter of factly.

"Well, let's gear up," I said excitedly, reaching for the assault rifle and slapping in a fully loaded magazine.

"Are you crazy, Frosty? We can't shoot our way out of this! There's too many of them!"

"I know," I replied. "But we can at least take a few of them with us before they take us down."

"That's insane! I'm giving up, Frosty. Rocky Butte Jail is escapable. *This* situation is *not*!"

With that, Dick walked out and gave himself up. Edie was nowhere to be found when I glanced into the living room, so I figured she must have gone out with him. I turned around, went back to the bed where all of our loot was still neatly stacked, and sat on the edge of the mattress. The FBI continued calling out my name over the bullhorn, but my mind was so full of clamoring thoughts that their words seemed unintelligible to me. My moment of truth had arrived.

Now that Dick had given up, I had no desire to shoot it out with them. Instead, I felt an intense longing to kill myself. As I picked up the automatic it occurred to me that all my years of struggle had seemed to revolve around exactly this: getting this insanity called life *over with*. Yet my very next thought reminded me that my life hadn't been quite so insane since Nancy.

Nancy. How would she react to my death, were I to end it now? Would she return to the emptiness of her past?

I could hear the tear gas being fired through the windows. For just a short while time seemed to stand still. If I died now in a shootout with the Feds, Blackie and all of my other prison associates would *know* that I had lived and died a true warrior. On the other hand, if I postponed the decision to go down fighting, even for a week, perhaps I might see Nancy one more time—and learn whether she could ever love or want the real me. Before opening death's veil and stepping inside its perpetual blackness I *needed* to know which way her heart would go—*for* me or *against* me!

I picked up the phone and knew instantly I would not be able to handle a call to Nancy. I dialed my sister instead, and Sharon answered on the second ring.

"You won't believe this, baby," I said evenly, "but I'm trapped in a house surrounded by a hundred cops. They're shooting tear gas through the windows and there's no way I'll ever be able to shoot my way out of here."

Surprisingly, now that my mind was made up, I was quite calm. Sharon was crying and asking me to give myself up. Thinking logically now, I made her hush up and told her to go to my apartment and remove all the valuables before the police arrived and treated everything as spoils.

"And please be sure to tell Nancy what happened," I said. Then I hung up the phone, walked to the front door, and hollered that I was coming out.

As ordered, I walked out backwards, with my hands held behind my head. Someone knocked me to the ground. I felt the cold steel of a shotgun barrel pressed against my temple while my hands were cuffed behind my back. When I was jerked to my feet, I stood face to face with the old man I had seen all over town. A minute or two later, the TV crew approached and started filming me inside the cop car, where I sat with an FBI agent on each side of me and two others in the front.

Someone *must* have followed us from the bank, I thought to myself, trying to figure out what had gone wrong. How could they have gotten so many police agencies involved and in place around Dick's house *so quickly* after we committed the robbery? And what about the ambulance and the media? I simply could not figure out how they could have gotten there so quickly on such impossibly short notice.

At the Federal Courthouse, my attorney enlightened me. It

turned out that I had been under around the clock surveillance since the aborted bank burglary in Kalama. Since our first meeting a week after Kalama, Dick had also been under constant FBI surveillance. The Feds had watched all of our preparations and had documented *everything*. I was sick with humiliation.

My attorney could scarcely control his mirth. "I've never had a case where the FBI watched the planning of a robbery, the switching of the license plates, the placing of the ski masks, and then simply tailed and followed the oblivious robbers straight to the targeted bank. Just imagine what kind of a case they've got. *All* of their witnesses are Federal agents!"

As I absorbed my attorney's words, I realized that Federal agents had been all over my life, unseen but ever present, since the day I'd thought I'd gotten away scot free after the failed burglary. They'd had enough evidence to arrest me within 48 hours. After I'd been traced through the sledgehammer and identified as the buyer of the abandoned truck and camper, the Kalama police had developed leads indicating that there were at least three of us working together. The FBI quickly figured I probably would not implicate anyone else if they picked me up immediately. The decision was made to set up the surveillance, confidently believing I would lead them to their John and Jane Doe.

"But how did they know one of us was a woman?" I asked.

"You *really* don't know how they figured out that something was going on that night?"

I didn't know. I asked my attorney to fill me in.

"Well, when the first sheriff came through, he heard a woman's voice on his radio say, 'SP coming through.' A person doesn't have to be a rocket scientist to figure out what 'SP' meant. You and your partners should have taken some cryptography lessons, as well as some lessons on how to spot a tail!"

One of the agents following me had spotted me stealing keys for the new getaway car, and they quickly determined we were planning another robbery. At this point, they secured authorization from J. Edgar Hoover to let us proceed with our bank robbery, which they would film and televise in its entirety to generate publicity for the Bureau!

Their single miscalculation was that they'd believed we were going to rob the Hillsdale Bank, two blocks from where I'd parked the switch car. It was there they'd set up all the cameras to catch us in the act on film. At the last minute they realized that the First National/Burlingame branch bank was our actual target.

Agents had watched Dick leave the stolen getaway car several minutes after he'd dropped me off at my switch car. They saw him struggling with the heavy cash filled laundry bag and could have easily arrested him right then and there, but the Feds wanted to surround his house for a 1930s style capture on camera, a la Elliott Ness and the Bad Guys. So, they'd let him go, just long enough for the cameras to be set up outside his front yard. The absurdity of it all made me smile. We had robbed a bank for the glory of the FBI.

All over town cops were no doubt laughing and the other inmates would tease us unmercifully. Still, I was glad I hadn't killed myself. For one, Dick was already working on an escape plan. More importantly, I'd heard from Nancy. She'd left a note at the jail the first night after my capture.

Darling,

None of this matters as long as you meant what you said about loving me.

I'll be up Sunday, unless you tell me that you don't want me.

I love you.

Nancy

Chapter Eleven

"JAILBREAK!"

My transition back into the regimentation of incarceration was not an easy one this time. A part of me was still very much on the outside. This, combined with raucous laughter-filled reports of guards clustered around police radios on the afternoon of my arrest, made the readjustment all the more painful.

Dick, Edie, and I were charged with the August 16th robbery, as well as with the first robbery we had committed together, the June 21st heist where we had run into a bunch of kids during our getaway. The M.O. was the same for both robberies, except that we hadn't used Army fatigues for the second job. The first robbery was eventually dismissed for lack of evidence. Dick pled guilty on the remaining charge, whereas Edie and I entered pleas of not guilty. As for the attempted burglary in Kalama, only I was formally charged with this crime.

Curiously, Nancy thought my arrest to be our biggest and best opportunity to destroy Frosty. She made me promise to seek psychiatric help. I absolutely dreaded the idea of allowing anyone, except for her, to actually see all that lived inside of me. Initially, at least, I resolved to abide by Nancy's wishes. After all, with three robbery charges on my plate, things couldn't possibly get any worse, no matter what anyone might see during a psychiatric evaluation. In the end, Frosty's pride found this prospect altogether intolerable, and he wrote to Judge Solomon telling him that Floyd was not crazy and would not submit to the probings of a head-shrinker. Floyd simply could not survive prison without Frosty and, while I seriously doubted any psychiatrist could ever destroy that darker persona inside of me, I couldn't take that chance.

I soon received several letters from old friends. Royale persuaded a guard to smuggle out some words of encouragement for me, adding that my old job in the kitchen pot room would be available for me whenever I got to the Big House. Although meant as a kindness, the message drove home the fact that I was really on my way back there. Back to Royale, J.P., Blackie, and all the rest. Equally deflating was a letter I received from Delores, one of Nancy's friends, asking if there was anything I could suggest to help Nancy, who was not handling the stress of my arrest well.

I could no longer afford my regular lawyer and had no respect for court appointed counsel so I decided, at least at first, to act as my own attorney. As a result of this decision, I was provided access to all the judicial documents and evidentiary items that had been amassed against us.

I noted with interest the indictment's claim that we had taken, "by threat and intimidation," the amount of $11,049—a figure that was $1,000 higher than the actual amount Dick had counted out in my presence. I assumed that the bank had simply lied to the insurer, as most normal business persons would typically do under similar circumstances. However, when I examined the inventory list of all the evidence removed from Dick's residence, I saw $1,000 in twenty-dollar bills had been found and removed from a book stashed in one of the bedrooms.

My first impulse was to accuse him. I quickly decided that, in the larger scheme of things, it didn't really matter. In my eyes, as a robber he was a solid pro, and he had shown some class by how he'd handled himself after our arrest. He'd even told the FBI that I had not wanted to be involved in the score in the first place, and that *he'd* been the one who had fired at the Volkswagen during our getaway. Since I'd been to prison just once as an adult, he figured that I'd have a much better chance of getting a lighter sentence if I feigned cooperation. He encouraged me to pretend to work with the Bureau, to tell them anything I wanted —except about Edie's role in the heist. The sooner we could get *her* out of jail, the sooner we could take a shot at the jailbreak we had planned.

Dick realized I knew about the $1,000 he'd skimmed from our take. He offered the explanation that Edie, unbeknownst to him, had been secretly saving some money on her own. I pretended to believe him. Before the robbery, he and Edie had been so broke they couldn't even afford to buy groceries. I couldn't believe Edie wouldn't have dipped into her "secret stash" of cash for *food*, at the very least, if she'd really had any money set aside and at her disposal.

I spent one entire afternoon being questioned by two FBI agents: Mr. Barton, the old man whose aged face had become so familiar to me, and his partner. Both men impressed me with their intelligence. Neither man believed, as we were claiming, that Edie had "unknowingly and unwittingly" driven the switch car. Nor did they believe that Dick had fired the assault rifle at the Volkswagen. They knew he had remained behind the wheel of our getaway car the entire time. We all seemed to realize quickly enough that we were just wasting each other's time. They were polite and professional throughout the interview, more so, I should add, than any regular cops who had ever questioned me before.

When I was finally brought before a judge, he immediately tried to persuade me to accept a court appointed defense attorney. By then, I had already seen *all* my files and had my strategy all mapped out. The burglary case was airtight; I'd *have* to plead guilty to that. I'd also have to change my plea to guilty on the robbery charge and then pretend to cooperate with the Bureau against my partners. With any luck, I might not have to escape. With that in mind, I opted to accept the judge's offer of court appointed counsel.

Dick was sentenced to 18 years. I was hoping for 10. Realistically, I could be paroled in half that time, which would still leave me under 30 years of age upon release—and I figured that Nancy might be willing to wait that long for me. Any longer than that, I didn't know whether she could or would stick with me.

Edie was scheduled to go to trial in December. I was amazed they would actually proceed against her on the basis of what was nothing more than pure speculation on the part of the FBI. My attorney spelled out their rationale for me.

They were counting on *my* testimony to convict Edie.

"They figure they can always get one member of any gang to testify against the others," he explained. "In this case, they're convinced that *you* will accept a deal at the last minute."

"Well, they're wrong! There's no time cut they could ever offer, or one I would accept, to make me a rat!"

Later, when they came for me without notice, I figured I was being taken to Edie's trial, which I knew had already gotten underway. Instead, I was taken to my sentencing hearing. Apparently, the Feds wanted to get my sentencing out of the way first, before taking me to Edie's trial, so my expected testimony against her could not later be challenged as "purchased." Not surprisingly, the U.S. Attorney claimed to have "misplaced" half my paperwork, so I was sentenced on the robbery charge alone. I would be sentenced later on the burglary charge, he said, "when we locate the rest of the paperwork." I received 18 years for the robbery, but the judge stated he would probably run my pending burglary sentence *concurrently* with the 18 he'd just given me.

From there, I was taken directly to Edie's trial. After taking the stand, I testified that, on the day I first met Edie, her husband Dick told me she was an "honest square" and that we were never to discuss any of our business dealings or criminal activities in her presence. By the time I was done speaking, she could have been canonized as a local saint by the jury. Not surprisingly her acquittal came just moments later.

My attorney advised me to prepare for the worst when I was finally sentenced for the Kalama burglary. "The FBI and U.S. Attorney's Office are *not* accustomed to losing," he said, his voice every bit as grim as the expression he had on his face as he spoke.

With an 18-year sentence and more sure to come, I could not imagine Nancy could ever endure or hang around for that long a period of "rehabilitation." The only rehabilitation, I thought to myself, was *escape*.

We got the hacksaw blades in through the Marshal's office. Edie's attorney, formerly an assistant with the U.S. Attorney's Office, still had a lot of influence with the U.S. Marshals. On the premise of needing to meet together to discuss Edie's burglary charge—the FBI had immediately re-charged her on the Kalama case after failing to convict on her robbery charge—we used her attorney to arrange a special visit in their offices where all three of us could be in the same room at the same time. I kept the attorney distracted with a list of legal inquiries while Edie passed six blades to Dick. The breakout was set for Sunday night, when the jail operated by a skeleton crew.

I planned to wait until the very last minute to tell Nancy of my intentions. I'd hoped the sudden and unexpected prospect of a life together would be enough to persuade her to come with me. When she came to see me on the day we'd slated for our escape, she could tell something was up. Sharon had told her I'd given Edie a substantial sum of money for some dubious undisclosed purpose.

"Who am I visiting today?" she cried after I disclosed our escape plans.

Frosty immediately came to the fore, resorting to self-serving reasoning. "Baby, you don't understand. This is the *only* way we'll ever be together. If I stay behind bars, everything we have will be destroyed. The system will drive us apart. I've seen it happen too many times to others."

"*Forget* the system!" Many heads turned in our direction. I couldn't help notice the guard at the visiting desk looking up at us as well. "You want me to help *myself*, Floyd, yet you allow Frosty to keep digging his and *your* grave ever deeper and deeper. Don't you realize you're destroying *yourself*?"

"But Baby, I've got an 18-year sentence and things are going to get worse—"

"Floyd!" she cried, cutting me off. "You've got to draw the line! If you escape, don't expect me to go, and don't ever try to contact me again. If our love isn't worth waiting for, then we may as well call it quits *right now*. I love *you*, Floyd. *Not* Frosty."

We made a deal: If I put away all thought of escape and stayed put, she would wait for me.

A few days later, I pulled Dick aside and told him I'd be staying behind.

"You're getting to be a real clown," he said in response. "If we don't make it, a lot of people are going to die. We're not playing games. This is for real."

"I'm not going," I repeated firmly. "But good luck to you, Dick."

The escape began well. Dick and his friends made it through two sets of doors, took one guard hostage from the maximum-security unit, then set about cutting through the iron frame window that stood between them and freedom. At this point, a voice squawked over the intercom, asking the officer to send an inmate to the dining room where the medical doctor was conducting his biweekly meetings with prisoners who had asked to see him.

"Maximum, send down Coleman," said the voice. "The doctor is here."

Coleman was not a heavy. He belonged in another, lower

custody part of the jail, and had been placed in maximum custody simply because he had refused to eat all of his breakfast swill one morning. He had only a month left to serve before his release, so he wanted nothing to do with the escape. The call for Coleman to be sent to the dining hall provided the six fleeing inmates with the opportunity to capture the entire facility.

Irish, a convict who had a previous escape from another state after receiving a death sentence, grabbed Coleman and told him to walk to the door as expected. "If you say one word to the guard before he opens the door," Irish warned, "I *will* kill you."

The six plotters crouched out of sight by the ramp as Coleman approached the door. The guard on duty was an ex-Marine. When he heard Coleman coming, he unlocked the lower door and then walked away, taking for granted that everything was secure. He was ten feet away when, too late, he heard the pounding of many footfalls coming down the ramp and through the door before he had any chance to react and slam it shut.

Irish, who definitely *was* a heavy, demanded the keys. Instantly possessed by mad courage, the young guard backed into a corner, assuming a fighting stance.

"I'm not giving you *anything*," said the former Marine, his voice even and calm. "Now get back upstairs!"

Irish and a man with a knife jumped the guard and managed to overpower him, took his keys, and left him crumpled on the floor. The six then slipped into the kitchen, where the doctor and the jail nurse were conducting examinations. Just then, the one guard assigned to the other side of the jail happened to wander into the kitchen for a cup of coffee. He, too, was quickly subdued. At this point, every guard was a prisoner, except for the one in the Control Room. If the Control Room could be taken, this would mean machine guns, thousands of dollars in inmate funds—and freedom.

The Control Room guard would have to open the kitchen door from the outside to let the doctor out. The six convicts knew that as soon as this guard came out with the keys, he, too, could be seized. Since the doctor had just arrived, they decided to wait 30 minutes before ordering the doctor—at knifepoint—to call for the guard.

In the meantime, Coleman returned to the unit and told us that the jail was under inmate control. Other inmates began to wander out of their cells. I began to wonder whether I'd done the right thing by staying behind. But then, as if rising from the dead, the old jailer who had been taken hostage in our block lurched out of the cell where he had been left tied up with strips of torn bed sheets. Having managed to free himself, he looked at all the inmates milling around the unit and quickly deduced that we had chosen to take no part in the escape. Reassured that none of us meant him any harm, he left the unit and locked the door. We were again prisoners. He then locked the door to the maximum-security section and began yelling for help. Irish and the others had already cut the telephone lines and destroyed the intercom system, but the old guard had a powerful set of lungs. His loud cries could soon be heard in the courtyard, on the street, and in the kitchen where the six were holding their hostages.

"Jailbreak!" he screamed. "Jailbreak! Jailbreak! Jailbreak!"

Dick and Reese, who numbered among the six, rushed back toward the unit to silence him and discovered that a locked door now prevented them from reaching him. The old guard continued shouting until his voice finally gave out. Soon enough, sheriff cars started arriving on the scene, tires screeching, surrounding the jail, dancing their spotlights across the windows.

The opportunity to capture the whole jail had been lost. Irish began demanding a car in exchange for the lives of the hostages, but by this time Sheriff Clark himself had arrived, machine gun in hand, to take charge of the situation. No prisoners would be released, he announced, no matter how many hostages might be killed. He gave the gang of six just ten minutes to give themselves up before ordering an armed assault he personally would lead to take back the jail.

The six prisoners quickly recognized the hopelessness of their situation. Irish decided to kill one of the captives anyway—one of his personal tormentors.

"I'm taking this one down to the Hole with me," he said, grabbing both a guard and the doctor's medical bag. "I'll kill him myself. Anyone else want to come?"

The situation had spiraled completely out of control. If they murdered the guard, it would all be over. Reese understood intuitively that Irish fully intended to kill himself with drugs from the doctor's bag and decided to join him. He couldn't take it anymore and decided that he, too, wanted out. He followed Irish and the drugs down into the basement area where the Hole was located.

Irish and Reese stuffed pills in their mouths all the way to the Hole and then freely handed out what was left over to the others who were locked up in the Segregation Unit. Predictably, their hostage begged and pleaded for his life, which Irish and Reese found very amusing as they stood menacingly over the guard. Both men laughed and giggled at their captive's terror—until Irish, and then Reese, lapsed into unconsciousness from all the pills they had ingested. By the time Sheriff Clark and his minions stormed into the Segregation Unit, Irish was dead. Reese would be saved by the timely use of a stomach pump. The hostage managed to walk away unharmed, his life spared by the powerful narcotics that so quickly caused his captors to pass out at his feet.

The siege was over. The end result: one inmate dead; one guard in critical condition; and, best of all, one Nancy in control of Frosty. Dick, on the other hand, was in far deeper trouble than ever before, and I could very easily have been faring the same dire consequences that he was to face after this escape attempt. For the first time in my life, I had made a decision to do the right thing. Nancy was proud of me. I was proud of me.

Chapter Twelve

SELLING MY SOUL FOR NANCY

December 25, 1966. Another Christmas in jail, my eleventh behind bars. I was 25 years old.

I remember thinking to myself it was time to get serious about changing and bringing the madness to an end. With Nancy vowing to help me every step of the way, I really believed I could do it.

To lessen the tension after the failed escape attempt, the courts worked hard to purge the jail. As soon as each man received his sentence from a judge, he was shipped directly to prison, rather than returning to county lockup. It wasn't long before I found myself shackled inside a boat taking me to the Island once again. Admittedly, were it not for Nancy and the love that connected our hearts, I would have felt right at home as the boat pulled into the dock of this island prison.

The rules of submission kicked in automatically and almost naturally as I shuffled my way silently through the admissions process. I spent the remainder of that first day shaking hands and being welcomed back by friends and acquaintances. Very few of my buddies had left. As for the guards, the more humane officers whispered hushed refrains of "Sorry to see you back" or "I'm sorry you didn't make it out there, Frosty," apologetic bursts of warmth and decency that made both them and me a bit uncomfortable. Mr. Monroe, an older guard who had often treated me like a son, actually had tears in his eyes. At the same time, the more sadistic guards seemed to lurk in the background with glee in their eyes, *waiting* for the opportunity to say something nasty, mean-spirited, and hateful. It never ceased to amaze me how such presumably well-adjusted law-abiding men could derive such joy from the misfortune of another human being.

I was back in a world of no purpose, where time was measured in years, not hours. Once again, I was just a number, a file, a mere piece of paper tucked away inside of some prison counselor's Filing Cabinet of Absurdity. I was "doing time," my mind trying to keep scattered images of normalcy somehow glued together within my intellect, while at the same time trying to bring order to the varied personal identities that hid beneath my facade of adjustment. All this I tried to do while pretending not to be a vegetable.

There *had* been some changes for the better during the ten months I'd been away. Men were now allowed to wear their wedding bands, so I was able to keep on my finger the ring I'd worn since the day Nancy and I spent at the beach. That day I proposed to my soul mate, she accepted, and we exchanged rings. Now I would be able to wear the symbol of my purpose and newfound freedom. Also, letters were no longer restricted to just one single page, although we could still only place eight friends or family members on our approved mailing list.

To ensure Nancy would be approved for visiting without delay, I listed her as my wife when I submitted her application form. Within four days, she was placed on my list, and I was allowed a three-hour visit that was so intensely emotional it left me utterly drained by the time it ended.

Royale still had plenty of pull and promptly had me placed back at my old job in the pot room. I recounted to her all of my forays into self-destructive behavior over the past ten months, and then I shared with her my completely unexpected discovery that I was actually capable of loving. Royale was genuinely saddened by my return to prison but was genuinely happy to see me touched by love.

Toward the end of my first week back, I spent an entire afternoon with J.P. He was very disappointed that the big breakout we had intended for him was spoiled by my capture. He was still very interested in escaping, and I normally would have felt a certain rush or thrill at the mere mention of planning an escape. Ordinarily, I would have been instantly committed to any plan J.P. had in mind, but not this time. He was still ensnared in his own inadequate realities, haunted by the ghosts of his long past, long dead ideals. Although we would always be friends, I could no longer be part of his unrelentingly negative world.

Sometime that first month, I was chained up and transported back to Portland for sentencing on the Kalama burglary. As I stepped off the elevator on the sixth floor of the courthouse with a U.S. Marshal on either side of me, Nancy was there with Delores. I could see that Nancy had been crying.

"What's the matter, Darling?"

"Oh, Floyd," she said, choking back a sob, "They're going to give you more time!"

My escorts pulled at my arms and hustled me away before we could exchange another word with each other. Minutes later, my court appointed attorney, Mr. Hurley, arrived at my holding cell to explain what the judge had in store for me.

"I'm afraid I have some bad news for you, Mr. Forsberg."

"How bad?" I asked, suddenly feeling sick.

"The FBI persuaded Judge Solomon to give you a consecutive sentence in order to force your cooperation."

"But Solomon already said in open court that he wouldn't give me a consecutive sentence!"

My attorney simply shook his head and shrugged. The judge's previous pronouncement didn't mean a damn thing now. Sure enough, when I was brought before Judge Solomon, he added a seven-year consecutive sentence to the 18 he'd already given me. I immediately protested, reminding His Honor that I *had* cooperated with the FBI as promised, and thus did not deserve this additional time. Judge Solomon would hear nothing of my complaint.

"'Cooperation' does *not* mean giving the FBI a few morsels of information that they already knew," he snapped. He ordered the bailiff to get me out of his courtroom.

For the next hour or so, Frosty raged inside of me as I sat in my holding cell, infuriated over what had just transpired in Solomon's courtroom. Then Nancy appeared outside my cell. At the sound of her voice, her words cut right through Frosty's anger, reaching and touching Floyd's heart.

"Hi, Darling," she said softly. "Are you all right?"

"How did you get in here?" I asked. "Who set this up for you?"

"Mr. Barton and the FBI arranged this for us."

"How nice of them! First, they get the judge to give me more time. Then they arrange this special little visit for us, the purpose of which I can easily guess." I felt a rise of bitterness inside of me, *not* toward Nancy, but at the FBI for so cynically using her innocence and naiveté to try to get at me.

"Don't you see, Floyd? This is our chance to kill Frosty. The FBI really wants to help us. They want to put Dick away for good and give *you* another chance to—"

I interrupted her breathtakingly naïve spiel. "Nancy, don't you realize what you're asking me to do?"

"I'm only asking you to do one thing," she replied, speaking firmly as she looked directly into my eyes. "I'm asking you to do whatever it takes to come home to me and make our babies and have a life together. If that means you having to rat every day of the week, then that's what you'll do. You *have* to put an end to Frosty! If you don't, we'll never make it."

"Baby, baby, you don't understand," I could feel Frosty insinuating himself into my speech. "A rat is a lowlife! He is absolute scum! Not just to everyone else, but to *himself* as well—"

"Stop it!" she said, cutting off my Frosty persona, her facial expression making it very clear that she'd hear no more of his crap. Clearly, the FBI had been reading our mail and knew they could easily manipulate and use her to elicit the cooperation they desired. As for Nancy, our love was the ultimate reality, the ultimate everything. In her mind she believed the only way we could ever get recognition for our love was to play the game their way. It was that cut and dried to her. She refused to listen to my objections and left with my promise I would play the FBI's game.

Barely two minutes later, Mr. Barton and two other agents arrived to question me. I confirmed their suspicion that Dick and I had planned all three robberies as a team, and that Edie had been in it to the hilt from the start. I also told them that had it been left to me alone, I would have preferred to keep quiet and do my time. I was no longer speaking for me alone. I was selling my soul for Nancy.

The three agents assured me I would never be housed in the same prison with Dick, adding I would be a free man many years before him, time enough to disappear and start a new life with Nancy. Then they left, satisfied with the information I'd been compelled to give them.

ღ

Not long after I was returned to McNeil Island, I confided to Royale that I'd been given the opportunity to get a sentence reduction by agreeing to help the FBI convict Dick and Edie on the Kalama burglary charge.

"Poor Frosty," she said with a mixture of sadness and

profound sympathy as if I'd just announced I'd been diagnosed with leprosy. "Don't you know you'd be much better off keeping your mouth shut and doing your time? The system doesn't care whether you straighten up or not. Prisoners are political tools. It's just a big game. One of the rules of the game is *don't* be an informer. That's not just *our* rule, either; it's *their* rule, too. Sure enough, cops *do* use informants. They just don't respect them."

"Don't you think that the Parole Board will consider my cooperation a genuine attempt to break free from my criminal identity?"

"Do you really believe *any* man ever gets paroled because he's 'ready'?" she asked in turn. "Look around you, Frosty. When was the last time you ever saw *that* happen?"

Royale's words were depressing. Judge Solomon had 120 days to change my sentence. I knew that Dick would make every effort to stall his trial as long as possible. I finally decided I'd have to play it close until my sentence reduction came through, then I would recant everything and serve out my original shorter sentence.

Nancy, fearing the U.S. Attorney's Office might be harboring some animosity toward me for helping Edie beat her robbery conviction, asked me to write to them and in some way convey to them I was on their side now. She also wanted me to write to Judge Solomon and try to convince him I was now truly worthy of a substantial sentence reduction. She naively believed that he'd understand that my war against the world was over.

What could I possibly write to Judge Solomon that would in any way seem credible to his discerning eyes? How could I ever convey to him I really wanted to change, that I'd already begun to change, or that I was even capable—all of a sudden!—of genuine change? How could I ever explain to him what I had been before—or why I had been that way—or what was so different about me today?

I wished that I could scream that *society* had done me wrong, but deep inside I knew that *I* was the cause of my own present circumstances. I had wasted my intelligence, rejected common sense, repeatedly chosen wrong over right, and had squandered my life. This ever-increasing realization that I had condemned *myself* to spend my life in prison was not an easy thing for me to stomach. When I was released from McNeil Island some ten months earlier, I had no real sense I'd be doing anything truly "wrong" by picking up where I'd left off in my chosen life of crime. Anger and bitterness were simply the norm for me, as was the guiding philosophy with which I'd been indoctrinated in prison and reform school: that "only squares carry a lunch-pail" and "people are honest because they lack the courage to steal."

In the past, I hadn't ever valued my freedom because I hadn't ever valued myself. If I put down these thoughts on paper, would Judge Solomon ever understand any of that? Or would he simply consider it a whole lot of self-serving psychobabble? I didn't know. The one thing I knew for sure is that, after stumbling through life searching for some kind of truth and finally finding it, I now wished I could forget it. The truth was simply too painful to bear. All my life, there had been an energy burning inside of me that, if channeled constructively, would almost certainly have made me a genuine success story. The realization, when coupled with the knowledge I'd now have to pay grievously for that which I'd allowed to happen in my life before making this newfound discovery, would be the greatest punishment I'd ever have to bear.

For whatever it was worth, I took Nancy's advice and wrote to Judge Solomon and to the U.S. Attorney, asking them to give me back something I'd never truly felt was entirely my own: my life. Not long afterwards, I received a short reply from the U.S. Attorney, a two-sentence letter that filled me with hope:

Dear Floyd,

Rest assured that neither I nor anyone else in the U.S. Attorney's

Office wishes you anything but the best of luck in your desire to change your life.

It must be hard to have to return to prison after finding someone who means so much to you, but you now have something constructive to work for.

Sincerely yours,

Charles Habernigg
Asst. U.S. Attorney

Judge Solomon's 120-day window for my sentence reduction came and passed without incident. Clearly, he was not going to bring me back into his courtroom until after Dick and Edie had come to trial, thus ensuring I would *have* to testify against them before he would grant me any sentence relief. Dick's trial was scheduled for October, 1967. In late September, Nancy and Delores came to see me, both of them making it very clear they *expected* me to go through with testifying against him.

As I reflected upon my past relationship with Dick and Edie, I recalled Edie's refusal to bring us a pair of guns during another visit in the Marshal's office, guns which Dick and I had intended to use to make our escape. Both Dick and I felt betrayed by her refusal although, admittedly, she'd probably saved our lives by saying no to the guns. Then I thought about the $1,000 Dick had skimmed off the top from our last robbery. For a fleeting moment, I felt a rise of anger. Then I remembered Dick's effort to help me by encouraging me to pretend to work with the FBI. My inclination was to keep my mouth shut and swallow my 25-year sentence, as Royale had advised. Even the U.S. Attorney's Office seemed to think my love for Nancy was something they could leverage to compel me to control Frosty. The mere thought of them *working* me, as if I were some kind of puppet, caused the bile to rise up in my throat. I decided it was time to break free.

Dick's lawyer came to see me a week before the trial.

"My client has total faith in you, Forsberg. I've told him of your cooperation with the authorities and have even shown him your statements, but he refuses to believe you'll testify against him."

"Why are you here?" I asked. "You'll both know in a week."

"True enough," he said. "But the government is offering Dick a deal. Five years if he'll cop a plea. I'd like to see him take it. It's better than the 20 he'll get if he goes to trial and is convicted by a jury."

"Tell him to take the deal," I said. Such a plea bargain would spare me the stigma of actually taking the stand against him. Moreover, if Dick took a deal, neither the FBI nor the government could credibly accuse me of failing to cooperate with them. Dick, at the very least, had to believe he had no shot at an acquittal and thus no choice but to accept the government's deal. "I *am* going to testify."

"If you really intend to testify against him, Dick has asked that you verify this by telling me something that only he and you would know about."

I sat in silence for about a minute, thinking about what to say. Finally, I spoke. "Tell him the FBI knows nothing about where we got the walkie-talkies because I didn't want to involve his sister."

The lawyer, who seemed to sense intuitively I was walking a tightrope and acting under duress, thanked me sincerely and left. Shortly thereafter Dick and Edie both pled guilty and each was given a five-year sentence. For his part, Agent Barton ended up keeping his word. He went to Judge Solomon on my behalf. The judge then bumped down my recent seven- year sentence to run concurrently with my original 18-year number, then he reduced that 18-year sentence to 15 years maximum.

Despite this sentence reduction, I still felt betrayed. I had been promised a new life. The way I looked at it, Judge Solomon almost certainly would have given me concurrent sentences at my *initial* sentencing hearing if the U.S. Attorney hadn't conveniently "misplaced" my case file on the Kalama job. The government had effectively shaved off just three years from the sentence that I *should* have received. Three years off for selling out Frosty was a far cry from what I considered a "new life."

I returned to McNeil Island and was assigned a one-man cell. Sooner or later, it would become known that I had given statements against Dick, and my life would be endangered.

Chapter Thirteen

"DICK SENDS HIS REGARDS"

In July of 1968, I heard Smitty talking to someone on the tier above my own. Smitty, a bank robber from Seattle, was an extremely creative modernistic painter whose abstractions were the talk of the institution. He always signed his work with a thumbprint. Normally, I would have tuned out such conversation. This time, his tone and manner made it clear his visitor was neither a convict nor a guard. My ears perked up and I lifted myself off my bunk, pressing my face against the bars of my cell to try to catch what was being said.

He was explaining to his guest what his painting ability meant to him, and how it had changed his whole outlook on life. The visitor, who asked many pertinent questions, not only seemed sincerely interested in what Smitty had to say, he also seemed highly knowledgeable about why men committed crimes and ended up in prison in the first place. Clearly, this person understood all the frustrations of prison life, so I was convinced that he had to be an ex-convict, though a highly-educated one. *Whoever* it was, the man was undeniably full of compassion. When their conversation ended, I watched the stairs to see who left Smitty's tier. Down the steps came a heavyset, pipe smoking man in a brown suit. When he was gone, I went up to see Smitty.

"Who was *that*?" I asked, full of curiosity.

"That's our caseworker, Mr. Hubbard," he replied. Both Smitty and I had a prison number that ended with a "2." Since caseworkers were assigned on the basis of one's final digit of their prison number, that meant Smitty and I shared the same caseworker.

"A caseworker?" I asked, incredulous. "I've been in these cesspools all my life and I've *never* seen a caseworker visit someone in his cell or care one iota about what any of us felt in here!"

"Well, Mr. Hubbard is for real," Smitty said. "He won't lie to you or give you any of the usual bureaucratic B.S."

I wondered whether I could share with Mr. Hubbard how much Nancy meant to me, about how desperately I wanted to change. I went back to my cell and pulled out some writings I wanted to show him—a short story, several poems, and a copy of the letter I'd written to Judge Solomon. Such writings were considered contraband, but I felt I could take this man into my confidence after seeing that he cared enough to visit a prisoner in his cell.

According to Smitty, Mr. Hubbard had an open-door policy for all the men on his caseload, which was something totally unprecedented in my prison experience. During lunch hour, I went to his office and knocked on his door, which was already open a few inches, enabling him to see my face.

"Come in, Forsberg!" he said cheerfully.

This surprised me. "How did you know my name?"

"Well, I've already gone through your file a number of times, and you're one of the few on my caseload I've yet to meet face to face." He paused to look me over, then resumed speaking. "What can I do for you?"

"Wow, this is unreal!" I said, shaking my head in disbelief. "What are you doing in this place?" He seemed to know exactly what I meant and smiled graciously at my unintended flattery.

"I'm doing some advanced work on my degree," he replied, his manner both forthright and direct.

"You know, I've *never* seen a caseworker visit an inmate in his cell or show the least interest in any inmate's feelings or concerns." He had no idea I was referring to his visit earlier that day with Smitty. I realized this had not been his first such visit to the cell of a prison inmate.

As if Mr. Hubbard were my confessor, I opened up to him, telling him about Nancy, about the emptiness and uncaring coldness I'd felt before she came into my life, of how much I wanted to change and become a better, more worthy human being. At great length, I explained how hard it was to focus on that end, with there being so much negativity and so much hatred generated inside prison walls.

Mr. Hubbard listened intently to my every word. He understood all I had to say. He was responsive and supportive. By the time I left his office I felt infused by hope, believing that someone who had power actually understood me and was on my side, willing and ready to help me move forward.

That summer also brought another change for the better. A new captain was brought in. Captain Mobley believed that prisoners would benefit from taking pride in their dress, and he started allowing us to dress as individuals. Although we still wore our prison uniforms, we were allowed to roll up our sleeves and untuck our shirts, among other small liberties. In addition, he permitted everyone to paint their cells in whatever color they wanted. I painted mine blue, to match Nancy's eyes.

Two months later, however, a black cloud moved in and settled over my existence. One of Dick's friends from Leavenworth arrived at McNeil Island. The inevitable hit man, it seemed, had materialized. His message, when delivered to me, was both simple and cryptically menacing: "Dick sends his regards."

Nothing more. No overt threat. No promise of deadly violence. Just four little words that prompted me to get my hands on a shiv and start watching my back.

It felt odd to be packing a knife as Floyd. *Frosty* was the one who always liked the feel of cold steel, the power and sheer menace that surged through his soul when cradling such a weapon. As for me, I could think only of survival as I debated whether to take out Dick's Leavenworth friend first or wait for him to make his move. Frosty would not have hesitated; he would have nailed him at the earliest opportunity. Floyd had so much more to lose and could not risk blowing everything by acting rashly and out of pure self-interest. I decided to keep my powder dry and just watch... and wait.

ꕤ

November 25, 1968 was my 27th birthday. Nancy came to see me. She was, as she'd always been, simple and complex, a wondrous mixture of mystery and magic that I ached to understand. I thought I would be able to remove her mask, but I soon learned she wore a thousand veils. Every time I lifted one, another would appear in its place. None of her disguises was completely her, and yet each one was part of a slice of her dynamic, multifaceted whole.

On that day, she was self-aware enough to recognize and admit to me that she was still as sick as ever on the inside, despite her seeming frivolity on the outside. I already knew that, as I knew the same old emptiness, fear, and confusion still reigned just beneath my *own* veneer of postured self-composure and calm.

Despite her openness, however, I sensed we'd begun to put up barriers against self-disclosure. Our conversation gradually devolved into idle chatter about our separate worlds, and we were soon listening for the significance and meaning of those things left *unsaid.* I sensed pain, unexpressed but undeniably real. If we could just fly away, lie in each other's arms, and allow the nakedness of our bodies and souls to heal our throbbing wounds! But it was not meant to be.

Here, away from Nancy, I had become a homosexual. It was the only available release. I once believed prison homosexuality was "900 of *us* using 200 of *them.*" I had since learned that almost every man in the prison was a homosexual in one sense or another. These were not the stereotypical "queers" or "punks" or "weak" individuals. These were men who were simply starved for love and who longed for affection and tenderness in their world of penal brutality.

At first, this discovery sickened me, filling me a sense of self-loathing. I discussed this inner revulsion and confusion with Mr. Hubbard, with whom I felt secure enough to be completely open with. He told me of several studies which indicated that, among men confined in prison for a period of more than three years, about 85% of them engaged in homosexual behavior, with the figure jumping up to 98% among women prisoners who were surveyed. This wasn't true homosexuality, he said, adding that most behaviorists referred to this phenomenon as "situational homosexuality." Apparently noticing my discomfort, he told me not to feel guilty about being among the 85%.

"There is serious damage done to one's self-respect by participating in situational homosexuality," he said earnestly, "but I don't think it's all that scarring. The mind is usually very good at justifying whatever the body needs. As I see it, the worst aspect among men who engage in this behavior is that, in many cases, their marriages begin to fall by the wayside, leaving them with even less motivation to reform."

Mr. Hubbard paused for a minute, allowing me to absorb his words. Then, as if thinking aloud, he added, almost rhetorically, "And isn't it one of the most embittering factors about this place that you are being filled with hate and rage under the guise of being helped?"

He understood so well!

"Seriously," he continued, looking me straight in the eye, "wouldn't you feel less enraged if there were no pretext or pretense of rehabilitation here? Not one single program to make you believe that there might be genuine hope?"

"How can you…" I said haltingly, trying to organize my thoughts. "How is it that you can so clearly see all the hypocrisy that chips away and destroys the souls of men here and yet be a part of it? How can you bring yourself to work here?"

He smiled. "Where would you have me work? Should I give up and not try because I'm chained to a wretched prison system, hundreds of years in the making, that does not and will never work? No! I will keep right on doing what I can, and accepting what I cannot change. That's what mature people do, Floyd. It is this very same level of emotional maturity that you still have to learn."

In December of that year, 1968, the prison increased the number of allowed visits to three per month. The third visit had to be taken on a weekday, and Nancy's job precluded her from coming during the week. This did allow Delores to come see me more regularly. Previously, she'd been able to see me on a hit or miss basis, depending on whatever lie we could concoct to justify an extra visit.

Dolores wanted to see Nancy and me make it as a couple. Twenty years older than us, she was from a generation of women whose marriages were that of subservience and submission. She had never been treated as a complete person in her own right by the man she married. He knew nothing about her inner feelings, her private thoughts, her needs or wants or fears, and he couldn't have cared less about any of that. Looking back on the emptiness and quiet desperation of her married years, Dolores could see what Nancy and I had together and was cheering for us to make it through.

I would survive those years with the help of those three visits per month, the many letters I received each week, and the interaction I enjoyed with Mr. Hubbard, who continued to be my ally and friend. Where most caseworkers did not even like to talk with the men on their caseload, Mr. Hubbard and I shared many long and deeply personal conversations. At times, he would simply speak off the top of his head, expressing his opinion and inviting and showing interest in my feedback.

"The judicial process recognizes the difference between premeditated murder and the less serious crime of manslaughter," I remember him saying one December day. "And yet it refuses to recognize the difference between a desperate unarmed man driven by lack of alternatives to rob a teller and the heavily armed, greed driven predator who robs as a way of life."

"But there *is* a difference between the sentences for armed and unarmed robbery."

"Oh, yes," he laughed, realizing he had not as yet sufficiently fleshed out his argument. "I know, I know. That five-year reduction in sentencing is really just a prosecutor's tool to get guilty pleas. Do you honestly believe an unarmed robber is only five years less dangerous than the armed robber?"

His question made me feel a bit confused and uncomfortable. Perhaps he was a wolf in sheep's clothing, more hardline than I could have ever guessed.

"Are you saying armed robbers should be receiving a longer, heavier sentence than they are getting under current laws?" I asked.

"No, Floyd. Not more time. Twenty-five years is quite a heavy enough penalty, especially if meted out uniformly. What I'm saying is I think the penalty for *unarmed* robbery should be *less*. This country is obsessed with passing out long sentences, completely ignoring the inevitable consequence that this makes men even *more* desperate to avoid capture.

"I am sickened, Floyd, when I see so many young people

come in here for non-violent crimes. Have you ever wondered how different *your* life might have been had you not been incarcerated all those years for cashing some stolen money orders? If instead you had been sent to a community-based treatment center and not isolated from the things that make a person feel human and worthwhile? I really believe you could have been helped."

"Wait! Are you saying I'm beyond help?" I tried to sound lighthearted, but was actually feeling a bit uneasy about the implication.

"No, not at all," he replied. "I consider you a borderline case with the advantage of having more things going *for* you than *against* you. If *I* had any real say in the matter, I would get you out of this place as soon as possible so you and Nancy could start building a new, purposeful, and truly meaningful life together.

"Floyd, I don't mean to depress you with the realities of this system, but the Parole Board usually doesn't care one iota about what a man has 'going for him' on the outside. In your case, they will probably hold you until you've served the entirety of your sentence, until you and Nancy have drifted apart from the simple frustrations imposed by such prolonged confinement, until you are embittered to the point where the Board can smugly proclaim 'Aha! You see? We *knew* he was beyond rehabilitation!'

"Of course, by then, we would *have* to release you, because you would have completed your sentence. Honestly, I *wouldn't want* to release you at that point. I don't think you'd make it after all those wasted and embittering years behind bars. My biggest worry would be the very real possibility of you killing someone the next time around. We would have *no choice* but to free you if the Board compelled you to serve all 15 years of your sentence. If that happened, *everyone* would lose. That's why I'm going to recommend you for early parole when you see the Board in April."

When my mind finally grasped the significance of that last

sentence, I grinned from ear to ear. He beamed a huge smile in return.

"Someday, Floyd," he continued. "Maybe not in our lifetime, but someday, when enough honest thinking people get tired of mass-producing criminals in places like this, perhaps there will finally be a complete and much needed overhaul of the justice and penal system."

"What is the alternative?" I asked.

"It's really not that hard, Floyd. In fact, I'd bet that you could draft a whole new approach for identifying and rehabilitating those who are most amenable to such a positive change. A whole new concept that would not only help redeemable young men like yourself, but that would also protect society and perhaps do away with these medieval bastilles. Why don't you try it?"

I laughed. "Right. Who would listen?"

"Probably no one," he chuckled. "But I can't help observing that you do have a very keen insight into the whole process. I've read some of the things you've written about the factors underlying the dismal failure of prisons. Diagnosing the problem is precisely just that: a *diagnosis*. I'd be interested to see what you think would be a workable solution."

His sincerity and belief in my intelligence embarrassed me at first, then profoundly touched and encouraged me. Among the most frustrating aspects of prison is that so many inmates are treated like morons, incapable of logical thought. True, many inmates have the I.Q. level of a pet rock, but the same is true of many guards! For the first time in *my* life experience as a prison inmate someone was acknowledging I had a brain capable of more than finding my way to the chow hall for a tray of breakfast mush. I appreciated that far more than Mr. Hubbard could have ever guessed.

With my hearing and Mr. Hubbard's parole recommendation just four months away, we started lining up a parole plan with the help of friends and family on the outside. My sister found a job for me with a wholesale meat cutting outfit in Portland. Bill McConnell, my instructor from the local union, arranged for me to get in as a second-year apprentice. Mr. Hubbard, who helped tremendously with calls to outside contacts, felt it was one of the best parole plans he'd ever seen.

Finally, April and the day of my hearing arrived. Walter Dunbar, the Chairman of the Parole Board was there to conduct my hearing. We talked for about half an hour. He listened attentively as I explained how wrong I'd been to hate the system all these years; how, for the first time ever, I *wanted* to change for the better; and how, at long last, I felt ready to live out my life responsibly as a man of honesty and genuine integrity. Things were changing. There was hope. Life—a *real* life—was just around the corner.

Mr. Dunbar recommended parole. Upon hearing the news, Nancy cried like a baby. Even Captain Mobley was happy for me and congratulated me by giving me a new job. Believing that I would be leaving soon, he decided I should be given a little more freedom, so he assigned me to a position outside the fence in the machine shop. How wonderful it was, during my breaks, to sit on the beach and look *back* at the prison!

Then, from almost 3000 miles due east, in Washington, D.C., there came a political decision that instantly and profoundly impacted the lives of thousands of federal prisoners all across the country. Richard Nixon established a tough new parole policy. Mr. Dunbar was replaced. I asked Mr. Hubbard if he believed Mr. Dunbar's parole recommendation might be reversed. A wave of relief passed through my body when he replied that, in his opinion, all was well and I *would* be paroled as recommended. I'd been counting my lucky stars every day since my hearing before Mr. Dunbar because I knew how fortunate I was that I would be getting out after serving just three years on a 15-year sentence. I finally understood how my friend Matt, the vacuum cleaner man, felt after getting a genuine, near miraculous break from a long prison sentence. Like him, I was going to get out early and be so far ahead of the game I would be a fool to return to a life of crime.

In May, Mr. Hubbard handed me my official parole board notice—and my heart sank. I had been set off for two years. Shock and devastation nearly caused my knees to buckle at the realization I wasn't going anywhere. I thought of Nancy and tears ran down my cheeks. Mr. Hubbard felt as helpless as I did. He tried to ease the anguish by telling me about all the many other denials that had been handed out under the Board's new "get tough" policy. All of his well-meaning words were blocked out by thoughts of Nancy—and the blow this news was sure to inflict on her. After such great anticipation and excitement, I didn't think she could muster up the will to endure two more years of just one letter a day and two visits per month. Out of desperation, I asked Mr. Hubbard to request a review.

The following month found me staring across the table at a Mr. Reed, who had been assigned to the Board to replace Mr. Dunbar.

"I understand you don't agree you that should have received a two-year set off in April," he said.

I glanced at Mr. Hubbard, who was seated at the far end of the table. He nodded for me to speak. Once again, I recounted at length my newfound desire for change and about how ready I felt to lead a constructive, productive life. I reminded Mr. Reed I had been sentenced with an "A" number, which meant I could be released whenever the Board deemed me ready.

"Judge Solomon told me that if I really tried to straighten out my life, I could make parole in a reasonably short time," I said, winding down my presentation. "And I *have* tried hard. The question now is: Does the Board feel, as I do, that I am ready?"

Mr. Hubbard smiled, clearly convinced I had spoken well for myself. Mr. Reed, on the other hand, simply stared at me for what seemed like an hour before unleashing his response.

"An 'A' number?" he hissed sarcastically. "When you are

'ready'? Do you think I care one iota whether you might be 'ready' for release? The President of the United States has appointed me to *stop* the revolving door of recidivism, and *that* is what I intend to do!

"You think your two-year continuance is 'unfair'? Well, I've got news for you, buddy. When you get done with *that* two years, you're going to get set off another two years, and then another. We aren't going to release *anyone* unless and until we are 99.9% sure of them, and we're not going to parole *anyone*, period, with violence on their record!

"You can just forget about parole. You're not going anywhere for a very long time. As far as I'm concerned, you've *already* gotten all the consideration you ever deserved for your role as an *in-form-er*, when the judge cut those ten years off your sentence!"

From the disdainful manner in which he stretched out the word "informer," I knew that Royale had been right. To the powers that be, I was less than nothing. I was garbage. I was disposable. Mr. Hubbard saw the frustration building up in me and signaled me to restrain myself. It was too late.

"Well, I'm sure glad you told me all that!" I snarled. "I just wish I'd known your position beforehand. I didn't become an '*in-form-er*,' as you put it, just to get myself a sentence reduction. I did it because someone I love *asked* me to do it, being convinced that 'doing the right thing' would be a bridge to a new life. Apparently, as *you* see it, there are no such bridges. There's no way out—"

"Mr. Forsberg!" He cut me off. "I've heard enough from you! What you *are* speaks for itself. This interview is terminated."

His words rang inside my skull. At that moment I wanted nothing more than to leap across the table and wrap my fingers around his throat, to strangle him on the spot and savor the feel of his life oozing out between my fingers as I looked into his dying face. Although I controlled myself just enough to not act out this vengeful fantasy, I left the room with Frosty screaming maniacally in my mind, crying out for blood.

Later, Mr. Hubbard told me not to become too discouraged. By the next time around, he said, I'd have a third of my sentence completed, and he felt certain I would be granted parole. I asked him for permission to marry Nancy, adding that she was already thinking of writing the Bureau of Prisons to get the okay.

"Oh God, don't do *that*!"

"Why not? The worst they can say is 'no.'"

"You forget that she has been visiting you as your *wife*," he said, reminding me I had also spoken of her as my spouse when laying out my parole plan before the Board. "If they find out that the two of you are not really married, they just might remove her from your list. I've seen it happen before."

ꕤ

Two months later, Nancy broached the subject of marriage yet again. This time, it was to tell me she wanted to fly to Peru to marry "Jorge," who was living in the United States on visa. She wanted a relationship that was more stable than our few monthly visits. Since we couldn't and wouldn't be together for at least another two years, I reluctantly agreed, on the condition that she made it clear to him that she would remain with him for only two years, and she would immediately file for a divorce as soon as I was released from prison. Even if he agreed to such a temporary arrangement, I was still deeply worried he would object to letting Nancy return to me.

"But he has never raised any objections about you, Darling," she said when I expressed my concerns out loud. "He knows of you and, from what I've shared about you, he likes you." She laughed. "He's just a temporary measure until you can come home and we can make our babies."

I wanted desperately to say "no" to this marriage of convenience, but I also wanted her to be happy, if not with me, then at least *temporarily* with him. Our twice monthly visits were barely enough to sustain a friendship. I'd long ago come to realize I had ceased to be a flesh and blood man to her. She had stood by me for three years on a foundation of just 46 days. I could ask no more of her.

Dolores could hardly believe I could love Nancy enough to permit her, under any circumstances, to marry another man. I confided my fears that this arrangement was a mistake, that I would probably end up losing the only woman I had ever truly loved.

"I'll do everything I can to make sure she doesn't lose sight of what she has in you."

"And what makes you think you really know what Nancy 'has' in me?" I teased.

"A woman *knows*, deep in her heart," she said, her voice serious. "She *knows* when she is in the presence of a real, all loving man. The reason we settle for less is because there are so few of these men around, so few who can love us as individuals, who can love us unconditionally. Believe me, if you were mine, I'd wait for you the whole 15 years."

Dolores's husband began to resent my continued presence in her life. He threatened to inform the prison administration that Nancy, who was still visiting me faithfully, was actually married to someone else. Clearly, he believed that if he could remove Nancy from my life it would also squash Dolores's interest in our growing friendship.

His threat, if carried out, certainly *would* bring an end to all my visits. Neither Nancy nor Dolores would be allowed to see me, and I would have *no* physical contact from the outside world. I also knew that Dolores's husband was right about one thing: Nancy would never be able to experience any semblance of genuine happiness with Jorge as long as she continued visiting me in prison. There was no denying she was being emotionally torn in half by her spiritual connection to me and her strictly physical connection to Jorge, who quickly grew to resent her habit of writing to me on a nightly basis. He demanded she cut back our visits to one per month. When this happened, I asked Nancy, in the name of our love for one another, to divorce him. She refused. It was *then* I realized the end was near.

I knew what I had to do. If I really loved Nancy, I would have to cut her free and *insist* she devote herself entirely to Jorge. He was among the living. He could give her, at least for the time being, more than I could. I decided that during our next visit I would *have* to do the right thing and tell her goodbye.

When that next visit arrived, the mere sight of her entering the visiting room flooded me with emotion. No creature quite as beautiful or as loving had ever before been a part of my miserable existence. She had given me purpose and hope. Now, with *me* being the reason for her inability to give her husband the things he demanded, I would release her, albeit with the promise that, when the marriage failed, as I was certain it would, she would return to me.

Her cheerful greeting just deepened my gloom, while our single permitted kiss seemed to extinguish whatever tiny flame of hope still flickered deep inside my crying heart. Memories of our 46 days in each other's arms insinuated themselves, bittersweet now, into my thoughts as I prepared myself for what I had to do. Where would I ever find the courage to tell her goodbye?

I had intended to cut right to the chase so she could leave immediately and catch the 1:30PM boat to the mainland. Before I knew it, it was 3:20PM, leaving me with just ten minutes to gaze at the only human being who had ever held any meaning for me. The moment I had avoided finally arrived. My voice cracked and my words were an agonized whimper.

"This is it, Darling," I said, tears welling up in my eyes.

She knew. The tortured expression on my face left no doubt as to my meaning. "Oh god, no, Floyd! Don't let it destroy us!"

"*'It'* destroys everything. Why should lovers of just 46 days survive?"

"I'll divorce him! Honest I will!" Even as the tears ran down her cheeks, she understood intuitively that we had already been crushed underfoot by the grinding weight of our circumstances and our disparate realities.

"I cannot watch you walk away," she finally said, accepting our fate. "I'm going to the bathroom until you are gone."

I leaned across the table that separated us and kissed her on the forehead. Then, turning her face away from mine, she rose up out of her chair.

"Take care of yourself, Darling," I whispered, barely holding myself together.

She walked away, and I died. Blinded by my own hot tears, I felt my way along the familiar corridor to my unit. Blurred images of fellow prisoners registered faintly as I made my way to my cell.

I had often heard men cry when their wives and families slipped beyond their grasp. Now *my* turn had come. Why this had to be a part of my punishment, I did not understand, nor did I care to know. Exhausted by my inner anguish, I collapsed onto my bunk and drifted off into sleep's protective embrace, my last conscious thought was of all I had lost when Nancy walked away.

Chapter Fourteen

"FROSTY HAS RETURNED"

In the fourth year, Nancy stopped coming to see me. I had pushed her away. Even though I couldn't bear to live without her, I was unwilling to endure any more pain.

After five days of brutal heartbreak, I realized I could not survive without her. I wrote to her, begging her to return. Her eyes never saw my pleading words; she burned the letter without opening it. I wrote another, and then another. All of them went unopened.

On the 21st day, I wrote my fourth and final letter, threatening suicide if she didn't come back to me. I asked Dolores to personally deliver it into Nancy's hand, and she agreed to do so. It did no good. It was over.

I ate little and lost 20 pounds in the month after Nancy left me—or, more accurately, the month I left her, the distinction no longer quite so clear in my mind. My body lost so much of its insulating fat stores that I felt very, very cold in my cell. One night, after donning a sweatshirt and covering up with three blankets, I fell into a deep, fevered, and troubled sleep. Subconscious thought swallowed reality as curtains of prior knowledge burst into flames.

My dream was a maze of corridors, passageways, and doors.

Stumbling, I came to a wide door marked: "WARNING: FOOLS ONLY." I entered, but this just led me to more doors. One was marked: "PRECONCEIVED SOUP." Another bore the label: "PRETENDED PURPOSE SOUP." Behind the first, men in religious garb were talking and laughing as they placed their own brand name on ideological cans. Behind the second door there was a nonterrestrial world of events—not *things*, but rather gestures, rhetoric, and movement that floated endlessly across the panorama stretched before me. The same show played over and over again. I watched as long as I could bear it, and then withdrew, seeking another door.

I left the main passageway and walked toward a row of doors that all bore the same sign: "FOR THOSE WHO DON'T LIKE SOUP." When I got there all the doors were sealed. I was about to return to the main corridor when I noticed a small hatchway in the ceiling. Climbing up a dangling rope ladder, I squeezed myself through the narrow opening and entered a room of music and light that beguiled me. There, I found my Nancy again. She was but a vapor. Ethereal though she was, she smiled at me, and I became a vapor too.

In that moment, I understood nothing had really changed. As long as she was alive, I could survive. My life returned to me, and I knew I could open my eyes. When I did, I found myself in a darkened room that was not my cell. I staggered to the toilet, my heart empty and confused. Wet pajamas clung to my body. An inmate nurse from down the hall came rushing in at the sound of the flushing.

"Well," he said brightly, "it seems Frosty has returned to the land of the living!"

My eyes hurt as I tried to focus them in the direction of that familiar voice and I started to lose my balance. Before I fell on my face, a pair of arms caught me and guided me back to bed.

"You'd better take it easy, man. You were one sick boy!"

The voice tucked me in and explained I'd been out of my head with a fever for three days. It spoke of other things, as well, but my mind quickly drifted back into the realm of dreams and vapor and mystical oneness with Nancy.

I was released from the hospital after a week of observation. Although I was still wobbly on my feet when I left, I at least felt a renewed sense of purpose and desire to live on. I would continue to gain control over Frosty. I would keep Nancy alive in my heart through my connection with Dolores. I would endure until I made parole. Then, one fine day, I would knock on Nancy's door and say, "Hi, I'm your new husband!" If Jorge was still around, he'd simply have to leave or face the consequences.

Knowing that the minimum custody camp had a higher percentage of paroles granted than the main prison, I asked Mr. Hubbard to take me before the Classification Committee to be considered for a custody reduction and a minimum custody transfer. Actually, I tried twice. The knifing at Lompoc left me classified as a "Violent Offender," and I still had too much time left on my sentence. I was turned down by Mr. Tennison, the Chief of Classification and Parole. Eventually I decided I'd have to forget about minimum custody. I'd been living in Cascade Hall since I'd been released from the hospital and soon realized I enjoyed its much freer atmosphere. There were no bars on the windows in this unit, and no guards to hassle us during the day. Moreover, I was keeping myself busy, continuing my project for Mr. Hubbard devising a new concept for prisons and the justice system.

As for Dolores, her husband continued to give her a bad time about her coming to see me after Nancy stopped visiting. Dolores and I both laughed at the ludicrousness of his blaming *me* for the failure of a marriage that had been cold, stagnant, and devoid of any real closeness since before I had even entered the first grade. Nevertheless, the menace that could result if he carried out his threat was very real, so we did not laugh overly long or hard. If I lost Dolores, I would lose my most dear and supportive friend, as well as the only link I still had to Nancy. Dolores seemed to understand all of this

"I really want you two to make it, but that won't happen if you fail to stay on the right path. I don't think you can do that if I quit visiting you and you end up hearing nothing more about Nancy or the outside world. Besides all that, breaking away from my marriage is something I need to do for myself."

"But what happens to *you*, Dolores, when I get out and marry Nancy?"

"Well," she replied, "sometimes filing for a divorce helps the two involved parties reflect upon and reestablish their sense of values. It might do Bob and me some good to be apart for a while. *As* things stand right now, there's nothing there to hold us together. Nancy is becoming more unhappy with Jorge each passing day, so she should be back in your life soon enough. When *that* happens, Bob will lighten up and relax about my interactions with you."

Delores made the decision to divorce. It was good for her. She started to come out from behind the wall of protection she had built around herself and Bob started treating her better. They even went on several dates and actually spoke far more than they had ever done the previous 15 years.

ഗ

Dolores's divorce proceedings went forward, and the dissolution of her marriage became final in July, 1970, almost exactly four years to the day since Nancy walked into my life. Dolores wanted to visit me on July 2nd, the anniversary of the date Nancy first showed up outside my apartment door to introduce herself to me. Just in case Nancy planned a surprise visit on what had previously been our special day, I told Dolores no. Hoping against hope, I woke up early on "The Day," got all dressed up and eagerly awaited the calling out of the day's visiting list. To my considerable disappointment, my name was not on the list.

That summer, I incurred other painful losses besides Nancy. Chief among these was the loss of Royale, who was shipped off to Leavenworth for helping one of the "legal beagles" win the freedom of over a hundred men. Royale and the inmate legal aide had established an office and purchased $7,000 worth of law books, all of which they put to good use by learning to file expert legal briefs. After they were shipped out, nothing of their office remained.

Old Troy was killed that summer, too. Troy was an old African-American who had sold me the .22 Magnum I used in my first armed robbery. An addict for most of his 62 years, he always managed to support his drug habit by running his own gas station. When he was 61, he was caught up in Tricky Dick Nixon's campaign to put "users" in prisons along with "pushers" and he was subsequently shipped off to McNeil Island. Troy was killed by a young black thug for refusing to steal sugar from the Camp kitchen supply room to make a batch of home brew.

I also lost Mr. Hubbard. Someone dreamed up a new program to reclassify everyone according to their potential for rehabilitation, and Mr. Hubbard was assigned those inmates deemed most likely to change. *I* was placed in the category least likely to respond to rehabilitative treatment. No more Mr. Hubbard.

Not long after this, I saw a memorandum stating that Mr. Tennison would soon be absent for three weeks, and that Mr. Hubbard would be acting in his place. This was my one opportunity to be transferred to Camp, and I approached Mr. Hubbard on the very first day of Tennison's absence. Perceiving my plan at once, he smiled as I entered his office.

"Well," he said, after hearing my reason for coming to see him. "Go to your caseworker and get him to present your case to me right away."

My new caseworker was one of those empty husks of humanity who merely acted out his function in the bureaucratic maze. To my relief, he agreed to present my case the following Tuesday.

This time, it worked. I was assigned to Camp! It was such a big step I felt like I'd been granted parole. At Camp, there were no gun towers, no bars, and the guards treated inmates like human beings. It was all set. I would work in the slaughterhouse so I could learn that end of the meat cutting business. Most encouragingly, Mr. Hubbard told me several times that I almost certainly would be paroled the next time around.

When Mr. Tennison returned, he was outraged. He immediately typed a report to the warden informing him that he had previously denied me a transfer to the Camp on two separate occasions, and that I'd been told to wait a whole year before requesting further consideration. As the fourth man in the prison hierarchy, ranking higher than even Captain Mobley, Mr. Tennison assumed his request to reverse my transfer would be routinely approved by the warden. It was not.

The warden, Mr. Parker, had known me since the very first time I'd arrived at McNeil, over seven years before. He had seen the change in me since I'd been back, and he believed I could handle the responsibility of the lesser security Camp.

I heard through the grapevine that Mr. Tennison was fit to be tied. I had no idea why he hated me so much. Then again, I didn't care. The only thing that mattered to me is that I'd gotten away from him.

At least I *thought* I'd gotten away from him. Just eight days later, I received a note from one of the "girls" inside the main prison that completely turned my world upside down:

Baby Doll:

I don't know what you did, and I don't care, but Mr. Tennison has got you in his crosshairs big time now. In the morn-

ing, they are coming after you and they plan to cuff you up and take you straight to the Hole. Mr. Tennison has recommended your immediate transfer to Leavenworth. He has removed Nancy and Dolores from your mailing and visiting lists. The only thing I know for sure is that you'll never be allowed to see them again. I know what you'll probably do about this. Although I think such a reaction on your part would be foolish, I know how much they mean to you. I'm sorry that we didn't get to know each other any better.

Good luck!

Love, Bobbie

Frosty and I decided to make a run for it that very night, just as soon as the 7:30 evening count was completed. What a friend he had been to forgive me after all I'd done to suppress him. Frosty recognized even before Floyd did that Dolores's husband somehow *had* to be behind this sudden reversal of fortunes. I didn't need Frosty to persuade me that I had but one purpose now. Somehow or another, I *had* to get off the Island, make my way to Portland, and *kill* Dolores's husband for whatever he had done to so royally screw up my world.

I could not guess at exactly what he had said to give Mr. Tennison the wherewithal to destroy me. It could be he told the Administration I wasn't married to Nancy or perhaps he called and blamed me for his divorce. To be dragged off to the Hole from Camp and then summarily shipped off to Leavenworth seemed an overly severe punishment for falsifying a visitor's relationship status.

All of these thoughts ran through my head as I made my way toward the Sound, having impulsively decided to swim my way to the mainland. Stopping to vomit before reaching the water, I suddenly felt a pang of sorrow for Captain Mobley. He would be blamed for this, and Mr. Hubbard would catch hell too.

I reached the water's edge and sat down to cool off and catch my breath before beginning the swim to the mainland. I glanced at my watch—the one that Nancy had given me—and her face filled every square inch of my mind. The realization slammed into me like a fist. If I escaped, Nancy and I would never be together again. She would blame herself—and would be the one most hurt by my fleeing in this way.

Frosty played tug-o-war with Floyd until the cold crept into my bones, coaxing me to be reasonable, forcing a change of mind. I began running back. Frosty started laughing at me, mocking me, but I pushed him away as I returned to Camp. When I got there, I was too wet from the woods to chance using the front door, so I used the fire escape to sneak back into my dorm. If a guard saw me, he would realize instantly I'd been out in the woods, which was considered out of bounds for all inmates.

In the morning, I caught a bus to the main institution right after the 8:00AM work call. I couldn't just sit around and wait for them to come for me, chain me up, and throw me in the Hole where I could do nothing to help myself. I left Camp while I could still do so on my own.

As soon as I got to the main prison, I went straight to the Captain's office, but he was not in. I had to do something, so I went to see Mr. Hubbard, who wasn't at all surprised to hear I had learned of Mr. Tennison's plans to destroy me. As Mr. Hubbard knew me better than any other staff member, the only thing I needed to explain was what kind of person Dolores's husband was and my belief that *he* was the one behind my present misfortune. After hearing me out, Mr. Hubbard suggested I go and explain everything to Mr. Tennison.

"Mr. Tennison?" I blurted. "Are you crazy? He hates my guts!"

"He's not quite the ogre you make him out to be, Floyd.

You're personalizing your feelings to such a degree you're not recognizing his side of things."

"But you *know* how he tried to keep me from Camp," I said. "And you *saw* how mad he got that we pulled a fast one on him while he was gone. You *must* understand he's really got it in for me now!"

"That may be so, Floyd, but you cannot ignore or deny him his individuality. You'd be mad, too, if you were in his position and came back to work to find out you'd been manipulated. You pulled a fast one and got away with it."

"But why is he so against my being at the Camp?" I persisted. "Why is he so against my helping myself?"

"I don't think he's against your trying to help yourself." He smiled, trying to break through my hatred of the man, "He just doesn't think you're Camp material. He is entitled to his opinion, isn't he? When he learns you didn't escape, I think he might just change his mind on that too. Just tell him the truth."

I went to see Mr. Tennison. Not surprisingly, our conversation lasted a mere ten minutes before he threw me out. The only reason it lasted *that* long is because he repeatedly demanded to know how I learned of his plans to ship me to Leavenworth. After the fourth or fifth time I refused to give up the name of my source, he ordered me to get the hell out of his office.

When I left Tennison's office, I learned Captain Mobley had arrived, so I made a beeline for his office. He listened to my story and thanked me for not escaping. Then he listed the charges lodged against me. Dolores's husband *had*, in fact, called the institution. As luck would have it, he had been connected to Mr. Tennison, who he spoke with at length. His charges, although loosely based on facts, contained just enough lies to seal my fate.

His list of accusations was long and creative, and contained just enough truth to be dangerous. I'd stolen $10,000 of his money (I hadn't). I was trying to break up his marriage (he was doing that just fine on his own). Nancy was *not* my wife (that much was true). I was destroying Nancy's marriage to her husband Jorge and, as a result, they were living in fear of my release because I had "threatened" to kill them (I would never have done that!). There was one final malicious mention of Dolores being "afflicted" by menopause, and this "female condition" was the reason she was so easily manipulated into "making a fool of herself."

I sat there stunned as I listen to the charges. I was going to be disciplined for making false statements on my visiting form about my relationship with Nancy. In my own defense, I explained to Captain Mobley I had misrepresented Nancy as my wife to avoid the typical three-month delay that came with seeking approval for a girlfriend. I reminded him that I *had* been able to help myself by helping Nancy, and that I was still planning to go back to her as soon as I was released. I knew nothing about the $10,000 that Bob claimed I'd stolen. I explained Dolores *was* intending to place $7,000 on my inmate account so that the Parole Board could see I would not have any need to steal anything once my $30 gate money was gone. I emphasized it was her money, *not* his money, that was going to be deposited in my account. I reminded him that Dolores's husband was now an *ex*-husband, and thus had no legal right to object to her visiting me.

"Are they *really* divorced?" asked the Captain.

"Call the County Courthouse and check it out for yourself," I replied, looking him square in the eye.

"If they aren't divorced, I'll be very inclined to believe all the rest of the allegations that have been leveled against you," he warned.

"If they aren't divorced, you can send me to Alcatraz, and you'll never hear another word of complaint out of me," I said, making it very clear I was speaking the truth. "But please call Nancy. She'll tell you how much we still love each other and what kind of person Dolores's husband really is. He is a vicious and vindictive egomaniac who feels the need to manipulate and control everyone around him."

I gave him Nancy's phone number. He spent the rest of the day on the phone calling the courthouse, Nancy, and then Dolores. Before day's end, he had me called to his office, where he told me he had pretty much confirmed my story to be true.

"I'll consider putting Dolores back on your visiting list," he said, "but only if you promise not to let her put $7,000 in your inmate account."

"But it's *her* money!"

"Yes, it is," he replied. "But, if you're just swindling her—as her ex-husband seems to think is the case—then it makes *us* look bad, too."

"What about Nancy? Do I get to place her back on my list?"

"She's *married*," he said, shaking his head from side to side as he spoke. "Why don't you just forget about her? You already know married women aren't allowed to visit men who are not their husband."

"She's only married to *him* because *we* can't get married while I'm still locked up in here. Didn't you call her? Didn't she tell you how much she loves me? Didn't she tell you she'll get a divorce and marry *me* the very minute I walk out of here?"

The Captain got up, walked over, and slowly sat down beside me on the couch. "Listen, Floyd," he said, speaking to me in an almost fatherly tone. "I don't think you're being realistic about Nancy. She has a new life and she's very happy. You should be happy for her."

"But she *can't* be happy with him? She is *not* happy!" I broke down crying, feeling as if the last vestiges of my world with Nancy were now completely crushed underfoot. Somehow, weeping in front of Captain Mobley didn't embarrass me in the least, so overwhelming was my heartbreak and grief.

"Well… happy or not, she's married," he said softly. "You will not be allowed to see her as long as you are here."

"What if she gets a divorce?" I asked hopefully.

"Not even then."

"But *why*?" I asked, my voice a mixture of anguish and defiance.

"It's not your place to question our decisions," he replied, speaking sternly now. "If you continue your good behavior, we may allow Dolores to visit. That will be entirely up to you."

"What do you mean?" I asked as he got up and went back to his desk. I sensed immediately he was expecting more of me than simply continued good behavior.

"You and I are going to see the warden tomorrow afternoon. We'll be very interested to hear how you found out we were coming out to the Camp to lock you up. There's a security leak, and we intend to get to the bottom of it."

He looked at me, waiting to see whether I intended to spill my guts right then and there. Captain Mobley was one of the most fair-minded staff members in the whole prison. At times, though, even he could not help playing the game. Expectant as he was of a response, I said nothing.

"Well," he continued, "Dolores said for you to be strong, and that she would be certain to visit just as soon as she is permitted to do so." He understood perfectly well the intended effect of his measured words.

"When will that be?" I asked, realizing just how much I needed Dolores to establish and maintain a sense of order within me.

"Well, I see no reason why she can't be put back on your list as soon as we plug that leak..."

I refused to reveal the identity of the person who had warned me. As it turned out, it took Dolores nearly two months and cost her $2,000 in attorney fees to get back on my list. I was deeply touched that she went to such lengths to win back the opportunity to visit me.

Chapter Fifteen

I RESOLVED TO GET OFF THE ISLAND

In January of 1971, just two months after Bob's malicious and near disastrous phone call to Mr. Tennison, Nancy divorced Jorge. I fully expected she would try to get back on my visiting list right away. I soon learned she had taken an 18-year-old lover and apparently now had no intention of coming back to see me. Even so, I still held on to the hope of making parole and showing up at her door to take her back into my arms.

Demoralized, I could feel my sense of purpose slipping away. Although I'd never believed in risking my money on bets or games of chance, I started gambling, a practice that quickly morphed into a habit. To my surprise, I found that I was quite good at it. More often than not, I ended up winning, and the thrill of that helped to ease the emptiness I felt from trying, seemingly in vain, to become a better person for Nancy through my reading, studying, and exercise routines.

As for Dolores, she and I eventually had a very heated argument over her ex-husband. I wanted her to quit spending time with him since he had attempted to destroy me. She refused, making it very clear I had no right to be making that kind of demand of her. She was deeply hurt that Bob had dragged out their marital problems in public and was very upset and sorry his actions led to Nancy's removal from my visiting list. However, she could not and would not answer evil with evil by breaking off all contact with him.

Around this same time, more and more college students started arriving at McNeil for refusing the draft in protest against the unwinnable Vietnam War. As their numbers grew, they began to organize the criminal inmates for the purpose of striking for better treatment. Predictably, the FBI came to me, asking me to infiltrate one of the student political organizations taking shape.

"Why ask *me*? I'm no political radical." I made no effort to conceal my contempt for the immaculately dressed G-man. He seemed embarrassed but continued presenting his offer.

"You've cooperated with us before, and we thought you would want to help yourself out. As you know, you'll be coming up for parole soon." He smirked self-righteously, clearly believing he held the winning hand. This time, I wasn't playing.

"Listen up, pig!" I snarled, pointing my finger in his face. "Floyd became your little rat *only* because he wanted to show his woman how much he loved her. Well, she's *gone* now! And gone with her is all the hope he ever had as well as any power or leverage you ever had over him." With that, I stood up and stormed out before I gave in to the violence I so wanted to inflict on his smug face.

I genuinely believed in the cause of the strikers and openly rooted for them. I was simply too close to the date of my parole hearing to risk losing my good time or jeopardizing the possibility of early release by joining their ranks. I was one of only five men who worked throughout the shutdown. By the tenth day, there were maybe 20 of us who worked in the kitchen, while several others were driven out of their cells by sheer boredom to work in the laundry.

Before long, word came from Washington, DC to end the strike at any cost. For Richard Nixon, all this organizing by smart imprisoned college kids had become a political embarrassment. One by one, the guards brought each inmate out of his cell and gave him the choice of returning to work or losing all of his good time and winning a ticket straight to the Hole. A few diehards still held out. Most chose to work. For all practical purposes, the strike was crushed.

That same year, Captain Mobley was transferred and replaced by a new Captain, one from the "Old School." Every privilege that Captain Mobley had given to us was immediately stripped by the new guy and, predictably, tensions increased exponentially. I had not yet formally lost my minimum custody status, so I decided to ask the new Captain if I could be sent back to the Camp. I doubted very seriously he would let me go. To my great surprise, he allowed it. Mr. Tennison didn't give me his vote of approval, but at least he did not raise any objection. The rest of the committee, including the new Captain, passed me.

My renewed sense of freedom at Camp almost instantly cleared my head of the hate that had been starting to well up inside of me. I was again in the slaughterhouse, doing the very same work I had enjoyed previously. I also adopted Blacky, a big, black, lazy old feline that slept at the foot of my bed every night. Although I still had 14 months to go before my next appearance in front of the Board, I sensed that, somehow, I was really going to make parole this next time around.

Curtis Ray Michelson arrived at the Camp the following month. Having already served almost seven years on a 22-year sentence, he also had an "A" number, meaning he stood a good chance of making parole with a third of his sentence completed.

Curtis had also gone the reform-school-and-then-straight-to-prison routine, having served time at San Quentin before coming to McNeil. He had been arrested for bank robbery in California and was bailed out, and he had continued robbing banks without let-up while awaiting trial. At that time, he made his periodic court appearances, but the Los Angeles federal judges were too backlogged to try his case and kept pushing back his trial date. One day, Judge Solomon came from Portland and, brooking no further delays, fast tracked Curtis's trial and ended up putting him away for 22 years. Curtis's wife committed suicide when he was sent to prison. This tragedy spawned a deep and intense hatred in him for the federal judge who, in Curtis's opinion, bore the responsibility for his wife's death.

When I first met Curtis, his sole preoccupation was escape, escape, escape—and studying how to become a better bank robber. Now he decided he was going to go straight. On a purely logical level, he had done the math and figured out he could make just as much money in the long run by working at a real job as by stealing. Once he'd arrived at that conclusion, it was enough to put robbery out of his mind. The change I saw in him seemed real, and almost as dramatic as my own.

By the time we got to working and living together at Camp, we were of the mindset that crime was a loser's game. We believed that, after serving their sentences, many ex-cons are simply pressured back into crime by parole officers, cops, and the collective hatred that eats away at them after years of having their identities and their self-respect ground underfoot in prison.

The irony of it all struck me when, in November, a month after his arrival, I tried to persuade him to escape with me. He made it clear that he thought my reason for fleeing was utterly ridiculous.

"*No* woman is *that* important!" he growled. "Turn them upside down and they're all the same."

Still, I resolved to get off the island.

ᔓᔕ

The next time Dolores came to see me she could tell I was upset. I usually greeted her with a hug and a kiss, but this time offered her neither when she entered the visiting room. She seemed to feel my pain before we exchanged a single word.

"Floyd, what's the matter?" she asked. "You haven't written in the last week and a half."

"I'm going to escape," I said matter-of-factly.

"Why?" she asked softly, taking my hand and holding it in hers.

I had learned to trust Dolores with my most secret innermost thoughts and feelings. I knew it was safe to tell her.

"Nancy is the reason I've been denied parole the last two times!" I said, my voice a mixture of grief and rage. "I found out she backed up Bob's story to the Administration. She told Tennison that she lives in constant fear of the day I get out. She also told him she believes I'll probably kill her as soon—"

"On, no!" she gasped. "How can you be so sure of that?"

I explained to Dolores about a conversation I'd had very recently with my caseworker after Dolores's youngest daughter, Sylvia, had been summarily removed from my approved correspondence list. When Dolores and I started growing closer, she had suggested I get to know Sylvia a little better. To this end, I had her added to my mailing list and had just started writing to her when, out of the blue, Dolores's now ex-husband made the phone call that stirred up so much trouble and got *everyone* removed from my visiting and mailing lists. When things got cleared up to the extent that I could again correspond with Dolores, I requested that Sylvia also be placed back onto my list of correspondents.

My caseworker at the Camp routinely approved her. By chance, Mr. Tennison soon learned of this and immediately had Sylvia removed from my list a second time, telling my caseworker that Bob's entire family was desperately and deathly afraid of me. My caseworker, who was still young and idealistic, had been as mystified as I was as to why I'd been denied parole two times already, even with strong recommendations from the institution and Mr. Hubbard. After all he heard from Mr. Tennison, my caseworker understood all too well why I was getting shafted, and he didn't hesitate to tell me of it.

"Now you know the *real* reason," he said, after calling me into his office for an honest sit down. "You'll *never* receive parole until and unless you disabuse Mr. Tennison of his belief that Nancy—*by her own admission*—lives in constant fear of your release."

ᔕ

After recounting all of this to Dolores, she looked at me incredulously, as if unwilling or unable to wrap her mind around the possibility that Nancy might really have turned against me.

"I don't believe it," she said. "*Bob* could be that vicious toward you, but *not* Nancy."

"I don't care," I replied angrily, not appreciating her questioning what I now damn well *knew* to be true. "I'm getting out of this place, and I need your help."

"What do you want me to do?"

"I want you to be waiting for me on the other side with dry clothes and money. I have a friend from Mexico who will come with me. We can be at the airport and on a plane before they miss us."

Dolores mulled over my words in silence for a minute or two. Finally, she looked at me and said, "There *must* be another way to work this out."

"'Work this out'?" I hissed. "Nancy *betrayed* me! She and Bob painted me as some kind of homicidal maniac in Mr. Tennison's eyes. So just how do you think any of *that* can be 'worked out'? Do you really think it's that simple?" I sneered. "Just get her to send in a letter?"

"Well," she replied, trying to sound encouraging, "for one thing, a letter from her would make it possible for you to make parole the next time around. Your next hearing is just 11 months away."

"*Can't you understand?*" bellowed Frosty from deep inside of me. "Even if I got paroled tomorrow morning, I could *never* forgive her for telling such a lie! As far as I'm concerned, she's a *snitch!* What difference does it made when or how I get out? I probably *will* kill her now!"

"But what about *us*?" she asked softly, almost timidly, as if afraid to know the answer.

"Us?" I asked in turn. "What *about* us?"

"Well, you may have lost Nancy but you still have *me*."

"Now you're talking like the frustrated, middle age housewife that Tennison and everyone else thinks you are!" I said, ignoring the hurt and embarrassment my words were causing. "Do you really think you could last even a week out there on the street with me? Why, you're so damn square you wouldn't even be able to—"

"Floyd," she said, interrupting me, "You don't have to talk to me like that." Then, like a crushed flower, she lowered her face, staring silently into her lap.

"Look," I said, suddenly ashamed of myself for hurting her. "I'm just trying to tell you like it is. You were just something to fill in for Nancy until I got out. Now there's no Nancy and no need for you to keep coming here. I want only one more thing from you, and that's a ride to the airport for Benny and me." Benito was the friend and citizen of Mexico who would help me establish a new life.

"Floyd," she replied, taking my hand yet again. Then, very solemnly, she uttered the words, "I love you."

I started to interrupt her, but with fire in her eyes and a sternness of voice that altogether surprised me, she said, "Shut up and listen to me! I've been writing to you and visiting you for over five years now. I would have given anything to see you and Nancy get back together. I've never seen anyone love another human being as much as you love her. I've seen the depth of pain and anguish you've felt—and how it almost destroyed you when she decided not to come back to you.

"All this time, I've loved you both, and I will *always* love the two of you. For years now, I've felt that I could be more than your friend. I *know* I can never replace Nancy or ever be as loved by you as she was, but I would rather have half of you than all of any other man.

"I know I'm a 'square.' And you're 29 and I'm 50 years old. And, compared to Nancy, I am sexually naïve. I'm not even half the woman you need, but if you'll give me a chance, I'll be anything you want. Just never ask me to hurt anyone. Please don't ever again talk of killing Nancy. I could never forgive you for that."

I sat there speechless, numbed by her words. I wanted to laugh at first, all of it sounding so ridiculous. I had never thought of Dolores as a "woman" before—at least not as my woman. She had to know I was incapable of loving, just as I'd been before Nancy had so unexpectedly come into my life. I had clung to Dolores to keep Nancy alive. Now I resented Dolores for the very same reason: She kept Nancy alive when I wanted no further remembrance of her! I wanted to *forget* I ever loved her. I wanted to be Frosty again. *That* being the case, it was Frosty who came to the fore to address the present situation.

"Okay," I said, sitting higher in my seat. "You can be my woman. You must fulfill my every need. You must become *totally mine* in *all* ways."

Dolores's eyes began to sparkle. I could almost see inside her soul and read her mind. What were her thoughts saying? That she, with *me*, would regain her misspent years. That she, through me, would become young again. I leaned over and kissed her.

"Okay, Floyd," she said, "you have a deal."

Pain shot through me, but it was a good pain. Somehow, I knew that with Dolores I could burn up all the love Nancy had inspired and reduce it into semi-endurable embers of suppressed hatred.

"From now on, there is to be no more Nancy," I said. "I never want to hear you mention her name ever again or anything about her. If she dies, *then* you can speak of her. Otherwise, not a single word. Understood?"

Dolores nodded in agreement.

"And one more thing," I continued. "I am going to kill Bob when I get out. It was his fault I lost Nancy. There's no way she would have ever called the prison on her own. I have taken an oath to kill him. If you can't accept that, you can't be my woman and should forget even thinking about it."

She made no reply and voiced no objection, so I spent the rest of the afternoon explaining what was expected of her. The Frosty inside of me smiled the entire time, clearly intending to turn Dolores into the freakiest old lady in the whole damn world. I was Pygmalion and I would create my own Galatea and bring her to life.

Chapter Sixteen

"SOME POOR BANK IS IN FOR IT NOW!"

Not long after this momentous visit, Curtis Michelson rejoined the War. As it happened, he was taken inside the main prison and thrown into the Hole on a phony escape charge after he unwittingly ran afoul of one of the most hated guards on the Island, Mr. Troy.

Along with two other inmates, Curtis had been working at Mr. Troy's on-island residence, installing 220-volt electrical service in the guard's home. As was the custom with many of the guard's wives, Mrs. Troy offered them cookies and milk after they finished the job. When her husband arrived home and found the unsupervised prisoners sitting around his kitchen table, he flew into a rage, ordering them to leave at once or face the Hole. Mrs. Troy, who had returned to ironing clothes in the living room as the inmates munched on their cookies, heard the ruckus in her kitchen and came rushing in like a mother cat defending her kittens.

"Just wait one minute!" she said to her husband. "You may be the Big Man inside, but this is *my* kitchen! You're not going to tell me who can and can't be here. These boys worked hard all morning long, so *I* invited them to sit down and enjoy a little snack!"

Turning toward the three inmates, she told them to go right ahead and finish eating their cookies. Mr. Troy crept away with his tail tucked between his legs. Later that day, when Curtis recounted all of this to me, we both got a big laugh out of Mr. Troy's humiliation. Curtis should have known that Mr. Troy would *not* forget the incident.

The written rules of the prison clearly prohibited inmates from wandering around in the woods at night. In practice, few staff cared about the rule as it applied to the inmates at Camp as long as everyone was present where he was supposed to be during the prison head counts. Unfortunately for Curtis, Mr. Troy knew that he was one of the prisoners who typically wandered off into the woods just as soon as the 7:30PM count was over. This afforded the cantankerous bastard the opportunity to screw Curtis over for having the nerve to enjoy some cookies at his kitchen table.

Two days after being skewered by his own wife, Mr. Troy watched as a number of inmates, including Curtis, wandered off into the woods after the 7:30 evening count was cleared. Waiting until they were all too far away to hear the count bell, he rang it briefly, ordering a special unscheduled 8:00PM head count. At the first roll call, 12 inmates were missing. Mr. Troy rang the bell again. Moments later, seven hippies who had been smoking pot up in the barn all heard the bell and hurriedly returned. Now only five were missing. Again, the count bell rang. Two more inmates wandered in. Finally, Mr. Troy locked all the doors and called in a "possible escape attempt" on the three remaining missing men.

Oblivious to the ruckus, Curtis and the other two "missing" inmates sauntered back to Camp at 9:00PM. They were immediately confronted by Mr. Troy. Curtis's two companions were placed on restriction. Then Mr. Troy gruffly ordered a pair of guards to haul Curtis off to the Hole. The guards objected, pointing out that this obviously was *not* an escape attempt, but simply the missing of a head count—a surprise, unscheduled head count at that! Mr. Troy growled that *he* was the shift supervisor and advised them they would be wise to keep their mouths shut.

By the time Curtis got out of the Hole, he had been stripped of everything he had worked so hard to earn. He was again in Close Custody, back in the cell house where he had begun more than seven years before. Bitter as he was over Mr. Troy's treachery, he was still determined to go straight. It was December, 1971, and he was just six months away from seeing the Parole Board. He was still confident he had a chance. However, Mr. Troy's devious frame job and the bogus report he submitted to the Board about this so-called "escape attempt," led to Curtis getting a 24-month set off when he finally appeared before the Parole Board. He remained in a state of shock for over a week. Then, consumed by a silent but boiling rage, he reenlisted in the War. By November, he'd found a way off the Island.

ᔕ

"Five thousand dollars?!" I exclaimed when he told me of his scheme and offered to buy my assistance.

"That's right," he said. "You're the key. You help me off the Island and $5,000 from my first bank heist is *yours*."

I took a couple of days to think about it. I had been in prison off and on now for over fourteen years. From age 15 until now, my days as a free man numbered less than a year! On the other hand, if I helped Curtis and was later implicated in his escape, I would lose *everything*.

The money was a great temptation. Dolores and I already had $6,000 in a safe deposit box. I'd started running drugs and was doing some loan sharking to make enough money to go to Mexico as soon as I was done serving all my time. With an extra five days off per month for good behavior, I figured I could finish this 15-year sentence in eight years and eight months. An extra $5,000 would certainly help make life easier when I got out and moved to Mexico, where greenbacks were much more valuable than pesos. I could settle down and go to school. Of course, I *would* first have to settle a little personal business here in the States with Dolores's ex-husband. After dispatching him, I would *finally* be able to begin a new life.

The more I thought about Curtis, the more I realized he was no ordinary convict. I'd come to admire him as a professional. I respected the way he maintained his focus and self-discipline by refusing, unlike so many behind bars, to engage in all the drama of homosexual relationships. I'd also come to identify with him with great empathy for the whack job they'd done to his mind. In the end, I felt Curtis deserved my help and I decided to give it to him.

The way off the island started opening up just weeks after Curtis's trouble with Mr. Troy. Not long after Curtis was returned to the cellblock, a mentally unstable inmate accused Curtis of giving him "the evil eye." A fight ensued, landing both men in the hospital, after which they were sent to the Hole for fighting. The Captain had long been aware of the vicious assaults provoked by the problem inmate and was pleased Curtis had given the kook a taste of his own medicine. Accordingly, he released Curtis from the Hole the next day. Realizing he'd been pretty unfair with Curtis the last time he'd been brought before him, he returned him to medium custody, with a promise of granting him minimum custody in the near future. With medium custody, Curtis could again work outside the fence, albeit under the watchful eye of a supervising officer. Knowing he would want to run off immediately by ditching his overseer, I advised him to wait at least a few months before attempting an escape, explaining he'd get a much better head start if he waited until he earned his way back to full time Camp status.

"Man, I'm not waiting anymore!" he growled in response to

my advice. "I've had it with this place. There's so much tension around here, I could very easily end up getting killed the next time someone decides to butt heads with me. I just want out. I can't take it anymore!"

We started brainstorming, and it felt good to be plotting again, to be putting together and then picking apart a plan, studying its components and assembling them again in our minds to eliminate any and all weaknesses. When we were done, we felt certain the plan was sound, that nothing could possibly go wrong.

His friend Kurt in the upholstery shop made him a knapsack, and I stuffed it with a hundred bags of peanuts, five pounds of raisins, a jar of peanut butter, fish hooks, fishing line, and some extra clothes. Along with an air mattress some guard's kid left in a swimming pool the summer before that I had managed to get a hold of, I had one of my friends steal a truck inner tube out of the auto shop, both of which were to be used as floating devices. Blackie, who now worked on the tugboat, stole a tide table so we could determine exactly when the current would be most advantageous. Those of us who possessed contraband cash chipped in a total of $60 for pocket money, which would last him a week or two, to be used when Curtis finally hit the streets after two weeks of "laying low" in the woods.

Dark grey clouds filled the sky on the morning set for the escape, an unexpected bonus. Old "Driftwood Annie," an elderly crone and year-round resident of the island—who had been the downfall of many a fleeing prisoner who she spotted while on her morning forays to collect driftwood—would pose a smaller risk in the rain.

Curtis's work outside the fence was with the electrical crew, a group of men whose custom it was to sit around the first half hour of every morning drinking coffee and discussing the work duties they'd have to perform throughout the day. He went outside to check in with his supervisor, then walked around behind the fire department, where I was waiting in my pickup.

By this time, with Nancy out of my life, I felt no need to learn a trade, so I was no longer working in the slaughterhouse. I had been working in the fire department for over a year and had the run of the island.

Curtis slid inside the truck and crouched low beneath the dashboard. The guard at the checkpoint, with whom I'd just spent 20 minutes grousing over all the work I had ahead of me that day, waved me through without leaving the warmth of his guard shack—and without inspecting the cab of my truck. Once over the hill and out of sight, I floored the gas pedal. From this point on, every second counted.

Curtis began stripping himself and was completely naked by the time we reached the hay barn. I pulled the truck inside and tossed him a stolen can of grease to lather all over his body for insulation against the cold winter waters of the Sound.

I had made an outrigger out of the air mattress, lashing a piece of plywood at a right angle to support the weight of the pack.

"What's *that* for?" Curtis asked, pointing at the wood. I had not told him about the change I had independently made in the design of the outrigger, so I started to explain.

"I don't want the board," he said, interrupting me. "Take it off."

We were both tightly wound up by the stress of our unfolding drama. He'd soon be missed and *still* had at least a half hour swim ahead of him. I again tried to tell him why he'd be needing the board. "Listen, man, that pack weighs 60 pounds! You'll *need* the board to support the weight of the..."

"Take it off!" he insisted, cutting me off in mid-sentence. "Take it off NOW!"

Sheathed inside the pack was a knife we'd made for use in the woods. I pulled it out and began hacking at the rope that lashed the air mattress to the board.

"Hurry up! Hurry up!" he urged. Then, with his voice

suddenly taut with emotion, he blurted out. "What in the hell is that sound?"

Too stunned to answer, I tried desperately to plug the inch-long gash I'd punched through the skin of the air mattress with the knife. It was no use. Grimly, I stood up and looked at him.

"Dammit, Curtis, I cut a hole in it!"

He looked silly standing there all naked, his body completely covered with grease. His face, on the other hand, was a perfect picture of utter disbelief.

"What did you say?" he asked, his voice an anguished gasp.

I couldn't answer. He walked over to the air mattress, which was still hissing, although not quite so loudly now, as the last of its air made its escape.

"Where's the inner tube?" he asked, his voice hard and determined.

"Over in the corner, under that hay," I replied.

"Get it!" he said, taking command. "Get it now!"

"But I didn't fill it! I didn't think we'd need it—" My voice trailed off into silence. I felt sick. I had failed him. He was such a professional. Now the whole escape had been ruined—by *me!*

"Jee... sus Chr... ist!" he cried, leaning defeated against the truck while looking abjectly at the beckoning waters. I had let him down. My mind raced, searching for a solution—*any* kind of solution. I grabbed the tide book.

"Look," I said excitedly, "There's a low tide at 12:05. I'll get the tube blown up and have everything ready by lunch. In the meantime, take my t-shirt and wipe all that grease off your body while I hide all this stuff."

He was dressed by the time I finished. We jumped back in the truck and raced down the gravel road, sliding around corners, twice nearly losing control as I drove back to Camp at speeds approaching 80 mph. Driving by the shop area, I saw Curtis's boss looking for him. As I pulled behind the motor pool, Curtis jumped out, then hopped over the fence and quickly went to work. I went to the fire department to fill some empty fire extinguishers with air for the inner tube. By the time I returned to the shop for lunch, Curtis had cooled down. He even joked with me about how our blunders reminded him of the Keystone Cops.

As Curtis was still in medium custody, he was supposed to eat inside the main prison. He spoke to his boss and got the man's okay to let him remain at the Camp to eat with his coworkers. This would allow for a much greater head start, but I was still faced with the problem of how to get Curtis back inside my truck without being seen. I quickly came up with an idea and left to set it up.

Louie, a small fry Mafioso who had taught me the ropes of loan sharking, was the one inmate assigned to live at the fire department. I asked him if I could use his garage for a few hours and then got him to agree to stay out of sight. Ten minutes later, I met up with Curtis at the gym.

"Did you get the tube blown up?" he asked.

"Yeah. Let's go," I said. "The truck's in Louie's garage."

"Louie?" His face twisted into an outraged sneer. "Are you *crazy*? Louie is a *rat!*"

"He won't say anything," I assured him. "We're partners in the loan sharking business, and he won't want to blow that."

Curtis turned and started to walk away.

"Where are you going?" I asked, irritated.

"Man, I'm *not* going to let that snitch see me doing *anything*!" he answered in a loud, angry whisper. "I'll just wait for another day."

"We can't do that!" I retorted. "Everything is already set. Besides, we can't just leave all that stuff stashed in the barn where someone *will* eventually find it!"

He just stared at me. His face was full of resolve and I couldn't have admired him any more than I did at this moment. Another inmate would have continued with the escape. Only a professional could walk away when something didn't seem right to him. He was truly a master. I could see he was weighing *my* argument as well, knowing that this opportunity wasn't likely to come his way again any time soon. After a minute or two of heavy silence, I saw a flicker in his eyes that told me all I needed to know.

"All right," I said, "I'll get the truck out of the garage and pick you up behind the gym."

Curtis grinned and patted me on the shoulder. "Let's go!"

We executed the plan once again, this time without any mistakes. He greased up his body while I placed the tube and the pack in the truck and headed for the water.

"Don't get caught, Curtis!"

"Don't you worry about that, Frosty. I'm ready! Once I get my hands on a gun, they'll have to kill me. I won't forget you, buddy. I'll send your money as soon as I do my first job."

We shook hands on the path that led from the road to the water. With the dazzling prospect of escape shimmering from the Sound, Curtis started for the beach.

It was a full hour before he was missed. Even then, his boss assumed he was just off somewhere nearby smoking some grass. Curtis was one of his best men and he was very reluctant to assume the worst and mistakenly call for a search too soon. We had counted on this and, sure enough, it bought Curtis some extra time. At last, when he realized he'd been beaten, the supervisor made the call, and boats quickly roared to the back of the island. It was too late. With a full two-hour lead, Curtis had already reached the mainland and was holed up in the woods.

The prison was locked down and every available staff member was dispatched to conduct a thorough grid search. On the 10th day, the search was terminated. Cold and hunger usually drove a man out of the woods within a week. Those who made it any longer than that were presumed to have succeeded.

"Some poor bank is in for it now!" a guard was heard to say shortly after the suspension of the search. The War was again underway.

Chapter Seventeen

"OH, YES, YOU WILL BE BACK."

Despite the ebb tide, Curtis spent an hour and a half swimming in the freezing water before he reached the other side. Numbed and exhausted, his body shivering uncontrollably, it took all of his remaining strength to carry the inner tube and pack into the woods. As quickly as he could, he put on some dry clothes, dug a foxhole for himself, and fell soundly asleep.

Curtis was nearly discovered by ground search parties twice during that first week of living in the wet underbrush. Once, even after he had buried himself up to his neck to hide his scent, he was discovered by one of the search dogs. To his great surprise, the dog did not sound the alarm. Instead, it actually came nose to nose with him to sniff his face.

When the search was terminated, he abandoned the gloomy, forbidding safety of the woods. When the nights became too cold to continue sleeping out in the open, he broke into an empty summer residence to use as his base of operations. After three days of indoor comfort, Curtis was surprised by the unexpected arrival of the residence's caretaker, an elderly man who he immediately took hostage so he could use the old man's 1949

Ford to take him to Seattle. He left the car in a long-term parking lot at the airport and checked into a Skid Row hotel.

I learned all of these details from Dolores during our second visit after Curtis's escape. It was then that she told me that Curtis had phoned her from Seattle and had been living with her for three whole weeks.

"Wait a minute!" I said after doing the math in my head. "We've already had one other visit since he moved in with you. How come you didn't tell me any of this before today?"

Dolores lowered her eyes. "I'm sorry, Floyd, but he asked me not to tell you. He says you trust too many people."

That part was certainly true enough, I had to admit. Curtis's implication was that I might put him at risk if I casually mentioned to a mutual friend that he was hiding out under Dolores's roof. I also wondered why a professional would violate such a basic rule as running to and involving someone as close as a best friend's woman. If Curtis had asked me beforehand, I would have told him a woman and a traceable car were the two biggest risk factors in the ever-present threat of apprehension—and would have insisted he *not* approach Dolores or get her involved in any way.

With that in mind, I asked Dolores, "Has he even mentioned to you the fact that I am very probably considered a strong suspect in helping him escape and that someone just might think to check your house?"

"Yes, he did," Dolores replied. "But he's convinced that, due to the lack of communication between the bureaucracies, the prison personnel won't pass on such suspicions to the FBI. Besides, it won't matter if they search my place because we're leaving for California tomorrow."

"'We'?"

"I've taken two weeks off to take him to California so that he can get his gang started again."

Her words and tone were so matter of fact I could only sit there stunned, wondering what kind of monster I had created. A part of me, admittedly, was impressed. As for the rest of me, I wasn't so sure I liked what I was hearing.

"Dolores, do you realize what you are doing? Do you really understand what you're getting yourself into?"

"Yes, I do," she replied. "Curtis *wanted* to go straight. Just as with you, he has been destroyed by a system so blind that I can no longer identify with it or believe in it. Aside from that," she grinned, "I'd *like* to go!"

I inventoried my feelings about Dolores's involvement in Curtis's plans. I quickly realized that if I complained too loudly, he might not send me my $5,000. In the end, the money won out.

Dolores spent her vacation with Curtis in California while he re-formed his gang and cased several banks. Then she returned alone, carrying with her a promise from Curtis that I would have my money soon.

When Curtis struck, he took particular delight in hitting Portland, Judge Solomon's hometown. Robbing Portland banks was Curtis's way of saying "hello" to the man who had sentenced him to 22 years in prison—and his wife to death.

Curtis, along with J.B. and Ed Malone—the Old Professor, as Curtis called him—had just pulled off what the newspaper headlines were reporting as Oregon's largest bank robbery: a heist of $127,000, But what utterly surprised me was that Dolores told me she had sat watching it unfold from inside a small cafe across the street from the bank. Curtis, who had suggested that she would "get a huge kick" out of watching his robbery team in action, had encouraged her to be there so she could enjoy the show. When the team gathered at Dolores's place to split up the spoils, Curtis and the Professor each gave Dolores $1,000, but J.B. wouldn't go along. Moments later, when everyone threw their coveralls into the fireplace, two .38-caliber shells that J.B. had forgotten were in his pocket exploded! Curtis swore he would never again have anything to do with J.B.

ᔓ

In the meantime, I had other things to worry about, like staying alive. The undercurrent of violence, an ever-present reality in all prison settings, had magnified under the tighter control of the new administration. While it sometimes occurred that these frustrations were unleashed against the prison staff, such prisoner on guard violence was always extremely costly, and thus quite rare. More frequently, the victim of an inmate's attack was another inmate.

There had been at least seven or eight murders of informants since my return to McNeil Island. As it happened, I too became careless and ended up getting sliced up one side and down the other by someone wielding a leather cutting tool. It had been a simple argument about a radio. I had forgotten that some inmates don't have simple disagreements and always carry weapons. Fortunately, the attack took place on a very cold day, and the heavy coat I was wearing saved my life. Even so, it still took 50 stitches to close me up, and the doctor worried me that I'd likely never again regain the full use of my left hand. I had to give up lifting weights after this, and started running instead, eventually building up to five miles per day, five days per week.

The attempt on my life had been so bold, carried out in full view of so many witnesses, that there was never any doubt as to the identity of the man who assaulted me. Because I personally refused to name him, I was stripped of my lower custody status and returned to the main institution. After this outrageous unfairness, it was clear that Floyd could not survive the madness of incarceration much longer. I surrendered almost completely to Frosty.

When I protested that it seemed most unusual and unfair to punish the *victim* of a knifing and *not* the assailant, whose name they knew without my having to finger the guy, the assistant warden told me that I was being sanctioned for "other reasons."

"Like what?" I asked.

"Like gambling away hundreds of dollars every week," he replied. "Like betting $100 at a time on a single football game. I'm convinced the only way you could ever have that kind of money to throw around is by being a drug trafficker."

"Hey, I don't even drink coffee!" I said. "I'm a big health nut!"

"That's what really puzzles me," he replied. "I know all about your health routine. I know you despise those who need the artificial escape that drugs provide. I'm really curious about where your money is coming from. Would you care to offer an explanation?"

The trafficking accusation was true. I wondered whether he'd ever believe that *Frosty* was *my* euphoric fix, or that the only mind-altering substance my psyche needed was hate. Admittedly, a part of me still wanted to tell someone about Frosty. Now that I was nearing the end of my sentence, however, it was simply too late for honest self-exploration.

"Well, you've heard about the losses," I said, responding to his query. "So, you've certainly heard about my winnings too. Whatever money I have I've earned gambling, and I usually lose it all back."

He seemed to believe me, so I kept talking.

"But is my gambling habit any reason to take away everything I've achieved and earned over the past seven years? I mean, I was at Camp for 18 months and never once considered escaping. *That* should be the only criterion for removing me or allowing me to stay there."

"Maybe. I wonder just how much you had to do with Michelson's escape."

"Michelson?" I said, feigning surprise.

"You knew the man, didn't you?"

"Sure, I knew him. He worked for me in the butcher shop."

"And that's *all* you know about him?" he asked, his expression and voice incredulous.

"Well," I laughed, trying to appear at a loss, "I know he escaped. But *everyone* knows that, don't they?"

"Forsberg," he replied, his eyes boring straight through my soul, "I feel sorry for you."

My eyes narrowed. "Why?"

"Well," he sighed, "I know you were somehow involved in his escape, and I know you're behind a lot of the drug trafficking in here. I also know that during your first five years in here you were one of the most rehabilitated men in this place. Now you've reverted to being a criminal. Your words deny all of that, but your bearing belies all your outward expressions of real change. It's sad. You'll be back. Oh, yes, you *will* be back."

I remained silent. What could I say? We both knew that what he'd said was true.

Not long after this exchange with the assistant warden, I quit loaning money. I didn't fear getting caught; I'd taken several heavy losses recently. The largest and most painful was a $2,000 loan to one of my best friends, Big Frank, who had decided to blow off repayment of the debt. I could forgive others, but I'd always considered Frank a trusted partner. I'd have given him anything he asked for. Now, with his decision to keep my money, he was leaving me with no other choice but to kill him.

There were so many people on my death list I would have to kill after my release that it would probably take me several months to knock them all off. Aside from this resolve to exact vengeance, I had no other concrete plans. But I knew that if I didn't go after my perceived enemies, I would lose my sanity, there being so little meaning left to my life at this point.

I was so plugged up with hatred I decided to try smoking some of my own grass in an effort to relieve some of the tension that held me in its grip, which soared especially high after I learned Dick had been paroled before me. It didn't matter that he had received extra time for two escape attempts and one assault. It made no difference that he entered prison with a 27-year sentence, 12 years more than my 15-year sentence. I had sold out to the FBI for nothing. *For nothing*! They had played me like a fiddle, promising me a new life with Nancy and assuring me that Dick would serve a longer sentence than me, thus ensuring he would not be around to harass Nancy and me as we got on with our new life. Now both promises were but smoldering ashes.

Every day after that, I fantasized about taking one of the boning knives from work and running through the prison, stabbing to death as many prison guards as I could before they brought me down. I was certain I could kill at least ten before they could initiate a tactical response. More than once I came within seconds of pressing forward and carrying out this deadly fantasy. The only thing that stopped me was the knowledge that if I went through with it, I'd have no choice but to kill some guards who were not deserving of death. There was always at least one decent, considerate, humane guard working during every shift. I realized I could never kill Mr. Monroe or Mr. Ellege. Eventually, I quit the butcher shop altogether to get myself away from the knives.

After being transferred back to Cascade Hall, I asked to be assigned to one of the janitor positions. The Captain reminded me that the Parole Board seldom ever granted early release to men who settled for and worked at such menial jobs. I laughed contemptuously in his face.

"Do I have to remind you how many years I've already worked in the butcher shop?" I said, pointing to my work record in the file he was holding in his hands. "And how many times was I recommended for parole throughout all those years only to be denied each time by the Board?"

He glanced at my work card, embarrassed, and approved my request for a janitor job without further protest.

Chapter Eighteen

HE COULD SEE FROSTY TOO CLEARLY

January, 1974. I met with Mr. Tennison and had a conversation that completely changed my view on wanting to kill him. For a while it had seemed I might be robbed of the opportunity to take his life. He had had a serious accident, and was gone a long time recovering. When he returned to work, I was so relieved and excited by the renewed prospect of getting my hands on him that I made a point of avoiding him, lest my eyes betray the depth of my homicidal hatred for him.

One day, while walking through the hospital tunnel, I noticed him coming toward me from the opposite end. I thought of retreating, but decided to keep my course. Instinctively though, I lowered my head so that I would not have to look at him.

"Good morning, Forsberg!"

His bright and cheerful greeting startled me. I thought about it all day long. I'd heard, but had refused to believe, he had changed since returning from his accident. Now that I'd seen with my own eyes that some change might have in fact taken place, I decided to go see him, whatever happened. I no longer cared about being paroled.

I was waiting in front of his office with eight other men

when he returned from lunch and announced he would not be conducting any interviews. Disappointed, I heaved myself out of my chair and turned to leave when, noticing me, he called out my name.

"Forsberg?" he asked, his voice sounding altogether surprised. "Did *you* want to see me?"

I nodded. He waved at me to follow him, and I stepped inside his office.

"What can I do for you?" he said, sounding genuinely helpful. "I suppose you want to go back to the Farm again, right?"

"No," I replied, "I'm quite happy right where I am. What I'd really like to do is go home."

He looked at me without speaking, his expression conveying that I was free to continue.

"As you probably already know, I go to the Board in two weeks, and I have—that is, I *will* have—only a year to serve after they see me, no matter what they decide to do with—"

"Just a year?" he exclaimed.

"That's right, one year. I've actually been here longer than you," I laughed.

"So, you want me to recommend you for parole?"

"Not exactly," I replied. "I think it would be enough to ask if you just didn't sabotage me."

His eyes narrowed momentarily, but then he let out a long sigh, releasing the tension that had started to pinch his face.

"Do you think *I'm* the cause behind your having been made to serve almost all of your sentence?"

"I do," I replied. "What else could you do? With people telling you that they live in constant fear of my release, you *had* to keep me. You wouldn't have been doing your job if you hadn't."

He seemed, at least, to respect my straightforwardness.

"Hell, Forsberg! You've been around long enough to know how little weight any of us prison officials carry with the Federal

Parole Board. I *try* to get men out of here when I know they're ready, and I fail more often than I succeed."

"That may be true," I retorted, "but I bet they'd damn well listen to you if you told them that I *shouldn't* be paroled!"

"You surely do believe the worst of me," he said, sighing yet again.

"Why shouldn't I?" I snapped.

He looked at me a long time before he started to speak.

"Maybe I shouldn't tell you this, Forsberg, but I'm going to give you my straightforward opinion of you.

"First of all, I think you are an extremely dangerous man. You may not project it outwardly, but inside you are a seething man of hate. I feel the Board made a huge mistake when they didn't parole you in 1969. I think you might well have responded very positively to a little good fortune at that time.

"You are the type of individual—and there are many others in here about whom the same could be said—who could actually derive great benefit from a few years of incarceration. Say five years or less. After that, your type starts to build and embrace fantasies where *others* are always to blame for all your troubles.

"If I had any say about the system, I would rather parole your type before five years or never let them go at all. Now, I believe your chances of making it on the outside are quite slim. In fact, I'm inclined to believe you would probably kill someone if you ended up in a stressful situation that you couldn't handle. That's why I never wanted you placed out on the Farm. I wasn't concerned you'd try to escape. I was convinced someone would get his head bashed in while you were on the way out.

"Let's face it, Forsberg. You are the type of person who finds it necessary, at least every few years, to release his frustrations by way of an act of violence. You may not agree with me, but that's how I see it."

I was so stunned he could see so much of Frosty that I dared not speak, lest I reveal even more of my hidden persona to him. When Tennison saw I wasn't going to respond, he continued. "I guess you understand now why I won't be pushing for your release. I cannot in good conscience recommend you for parole. You know as well as I do that this is your final Board hearing and they *will* parole you. After you get out and fail, someone will scream long and loud about how you should never have been paroled. No one will ever bother to mention you would have been out within ten months anyway when you completed your entire sentence. No one will ever mention you were paroled five years too late for your good *or* the good of the public. That's just the way things are."

That he could even recognize and describe the chaotic mess of the parole system really shattered all my lesser opinions of him. Even Frosty seemed impressed. I could almost visualize him scratching Mr. Tennison off the hit list.

As I stood up to leave, he told me I was welcome to stop in and see him any time I wished. I knew I never would. He could see Frosty too clearly.

When I finally came before the Board, the parole judge seemed to be incredibly young for such a weighty position. Almost immediately, I noticed the hint of a smile on his face. When he spoke, I realized his voice was not yet jaded and hadn't lost its humanity.

"Do you have anything you'd like to open with before I ask some questions?" he asked, his voice courteous.

"What is there to say?" I answered straightforwardly. "It's all been said before."

"What are you back here for, Mr. Forsberg?"

"I'm back here for bank robbery."

That seemed to disturb him. "Do you mean that, after we paroled you, you went out and robbed another bank?"

Obviously, that was *not* the case. I asked him to explain what he meant.

"What I mean is that you were arrested for bank robbery in 1966, you were paroled in 1969, and then you came back again for robbery."

I shook my head. "I *didn't* get out in 1969. That 1969 parole you mentioned never happened. It was cancelled. Never in my life have I been granted parole."

He began flipping pages, stopping here and there as he examined my file, checking one sheet against another. Finally, he looked up.

"You have less than a year left to serve on a 15-year sentence, yet you were recommended for parole *three times* and were never released? I find this quite unusual."

"How long have you been a parole judge?" I asked.

"This is my first Board hearing," he answered. "Why do you ask?"

I laughed good humoredly. "You'll figure it out soon enough."

The hearing was brief. I didn't ask the young judge for any clue of what his decision might be. It didn't really matter; one way or another, they would have to let me out in less than a year. In February, 1974, I was notified I would be paroled directly to the street on March 28th. No halfway house, no work release, no weekend passes in the interim. I would have liked a little time to adjust, but that's just the way it was.

ꕥ

More than five years had passed since I'd last heard the name "Nancy." That March, I began to ask about her. I learned she'd had a steady lover for almost two years and that the two of them were thinking of marriage. Like ripping a scab off a festering wound, the thought of her building a life without me tore anew at the wreckage of my heart. I felt totally adrift, completely without purpose, except for my resolution to kill the nine people on my revenge list before heading off to Mexico where my friend

Benny, who had finally escaped, wanted me to join his drug operation.

The thing that really crushed me was the discovery that Dolores wasn't all that I had wanted and thought her to be. During our visit on the day before my release, she announced she would *not* help me kill her ex-husband when I got out. Then, adding insult to injury, she made it very clear she did not want *me* to go through with my plan to kill him

"What are you talking about, bitch?" I raged, using the expletive that escaped my lips only when I was extremely displeased with her. "We've been planning this out for *years*!"

"*You've* been talking about it," she retorted. "*I've* just let you rant and rave, providing you a listening ear, all the while thinking this was just another of your time passing fantasies."

"Do you really think I'm not going to pay him back for what he did to keep me in here all these years?" I hissed, my anger almost completely overtaking me. "You're supposed to be my woman, Dolores! From the very beginning I made it clear to you that if you couldn't accept my killing your ex-husband as a necessary payback for what he did to me then you would just be wasting your time and mine by staying in my life."

A look of anguish spread across her face as my words slammed into her like blows from a sledgehammer. At least she had the good sense to cry. It felt good to see her hurting after her betrayal of me. And I did feel betrayed.

"Listen," I said through gritted teeth, "Tomorrow, we go to the bank, get my money, and then you and I will call it quits. I don't want your 'square' ass anyway!"

I felt sick to my stomach. For such a long time she had seemed so docile and compliant, I'd convinced myself I might actually come to love her. Now I felt like the ultimate dupe.

"Floyd," she said, drying her eyes, "I am your woman. I'd do almost anything for you. But I *won't* help you kill Bob. If you *really* love me, you *won't* hurt him."

"You don't seem to know whose side you're on, do you,

Dolores?" I said, my voice full of contempt. Admittedly, I wanted to see her cry some more. She maintained her composure.

"Floyd," she said, refusing to call me *Frosty* as always. She looked me straight in the eye. "What Bob did to you was wrong. That he drove Nancy and you apart is something I'll never forgive him for. But he's the father of my daughters and, as such, I still have feelings for him. I probably always will. If you really love me, you'll accept that part of me, that part of my past life, just as I accept that part of you that will always love Nancy."

"But I *don't love* that bitch!" I screamed.

"Poor Floyd," she sighed, her voice almost maternal. "Do you think I believe you'll ever quit loving her? Do you really believe there's absolutely no love left inside your heart for her?"

She was right. There was a part of me that would never stop loving Nancy. Dolores's sympathetic tone caused me to soften a bit, persuading me to at least reconsider my resolve to kill Bob.

Chapter Nineteen

"THE BIGGEST BANK ROBBERY EVER"

The next day, March 28, 1974, I looked back at the Island and watched it fade in the rain and mist. The water, as always, was cold and rough. The wind seemed to blow an elegy of chilled enthusiasm for the man who was being released that day. The crime for which I had been sentenced to prison had so long ago escaped my consciousness. My soul had leaked out through all the wounds inflicted by society's retribution.

Life and death, I thought. The line between them seemed so frightfully thin. How harrowing it was. In my own soul at the present moment, both seemed to be one and the same.

I was in Nancy's world of life and freedom, a world in which she could be held and fondled and loved. But it was Dolores who stood waiting for me on the dock. It was Dolores who drove me to a nearby motel. The lovemaking was too heavily burdened by the memory of our last visit back at McNeil. As far as I was concerned, she *had* led me to believe that as *my* woman she would help me to destroy Bob. Now she was begging for his life as a repayment to *her* for services rendered. "For keeping you alive all those years," as she phrased it.

I now had $14,700, all from Delores. Almost comically, $700 had fallen from her boots when I undressed her earlier. She was still trying to "obligate" me to love her, to surrender my heart to her for having stood by me. I felt I owed her everything *but* that. What I could not verbalize to Dolores was that her warm, naked body simply evoked too many vague images of Nancy. It was a piercing reminder that whispered the betrayal of the one I thought would be my forever soul mate. Yet, if I just seized the moment and enslaved Dolores with my lovemaking, perhaps I could persuade her to not stand between me and Bob's annihilation.

After several hours in bed, we got up. I encircled her diminutive body in my arms in front of a full-length mirror.

"Look at that, Darling," she said out loud at the sight of our reflection. "The world's most ridiculous couple."

After a while, I started feeling encased and restless in our motel room so we gathered our things and left, the matter of her ex-husband still unresolved.

"You know, Dolores," I said as we drove south toward Portland, "I do understand how Bob will always be a part of you and why you don't want me to kill him. But he is a vicious human being. You yourself were victimized and hurt by that call he made to the prison. I've thought it through, and I think you'll be very happy with my compromise for settling the score with him."

I had learned from years of manipulating Dolores that she did not fool easily. She was silent now, a motionless little rabbit, her eyes and ears cautiously alert for whatever snare I had in store for her.

"My plan will in no way cause him any physical harm," I continued, "but it *will* afford you the opportunity to prove to me you *are* really my woman."

"What do you want me to do?"

"Call him, let him know I'm out. Tell him you *never* want to see him again. In no uncertain terms, tell him he never satisfied you even once throughout your entire married life. Tell him that now that I'm out and you had the chance to be alone with me, you finally know what a real man is."

"I suppose you'll be listening on the extension?"

"Of course!" I replied. "Where else would I be? The point, after all, is for *me* to savor this bloodless revenge. Isn't that what you wanted, no blood?"

Dolores refused me even this. Once again, I felt she was betraying me. It became clear there was almost no chance of happiness between us.

∽

I drove by the hardware store of my future victims. The sign indicated they were still there. At least I could exact payment from them.

The next day, I met with my parole officer, Mr. Hooley. The first words out of his mouth were about a conversation he'd had recently with the FBI, and how surprised they were to learn that Dick had been paroled before me.

"Are you bitter about what they did to you?" he asked.

I wasn't sure whether he was trying to play games with my head or whether he was simply naïve.

"Do you really think I should be thankful for a parole that wasn't granted until I had less than a year left to serve on a 15-year sentence? Should I be grateful that Dick got out before me when, on top of everything else, he had two escapes and an assault?"

"What about Dick?" he asked in turn. "Are you worried about him being out?"

"It *has* crossed my mind," I answered, deciding to be honest about it. My own thirst for revenge had reminded me that Dick *was* out there somewhere. I was worried he might want to come after me. On the other hand, Dick had sent that "hit man" from Leavenworth to find me at McNeil, and that had amounted to nothing despite my very reasonable paranoia.

Mr. Hooley continued, "Well, he's on my caseload, and he tells me he has no ill feelings towards you."

"What would you expect for him to say to his parole officer?"

Mr. Hooley pulled out a picture of Dick and showed it to Dolores so she would know what he looked like if he approached her or her home unannounced. This precautionary act made me all the more conscious of the threat Dick posed, and it made me feel trapped.

"You don't plan on seeing much of Nancy or of Dolores's ex-husband, do you?"

"No," I replied. The mere mention of them sent a chill running through my body. "Why should I? I want nothing to do with either of them."

"Well, that would certainly be the best course," he said. "As I'm sure you realize, I'll have to investigate any reports of you bothering them."

He advised me to find a better job than the busboy position my sister had arranged for me at the restaurant where she worked then brought our interview to a close. My reentry process into society was complete.

ഗ

Just days into my freedom, Dolores really started getting on my nerves. She wanted me to meet this person and that person, pushing me hard to "assimilate." All *I* wanted to do was relax.

I enrolled at Mt. Hood Community College on a part time basis, hoping to spend the other half doing some writing. Mr.

Hooley advised me to get a part time job in addition to my schooling.

The tension inside in me continued to build. I felt as if I might explode at any moment. I arranged for a dummy job and fake paycheck to show my parole officer. It would cost me about $150 a month to set that up, but at least I'd have some free time to think and put myself back together again.

On my ninth day out, Dolores and I rented a car and drove to Seattle. From there we flew to Las Vegas to meet with Curtis Ray Michelson, who had some bad news. J.B. had been arrested, and Curtis suspected that the police might be able to make a connection to Dolores through J.B.'s girlfriend. Curtis admitted having placed periodic calls to Dolores from the girl's residence.

"Curtis!" I gasped, understanding the possible ramifications. "You know better than that! That's going to bring so much heat on us that I won't be able to move!"

"Hell, they aren't going to be able to prove a thing," he said, brushing aside my concerns. "J.B. will beat that rap, even with a court appointed lawyer. Besides, why worry about a little heat? You aren't planning anything right now, are you?"

It sounded like an invitation. "Well, I do have some personal matters I need to attend to. What do you have in mind?"

"How about the biggest bank robbery ever?"

"How big is that?" I asked.

"Two, maybe three million. The Professor and I have been casing out a place for over two months now. In Reno."

"Two or three million?" I asked, incredulous. I couldn't help but shake my head in disbelief, convinced he was exaggerating. When he spelled out his plan, I was sold. We drove to Reno the next day. When we got there, Curtis pointed out the building. It was the First National Bank of Nevada, which I later learned was in a building owned by and attached to Harrah's.

"*That*, supposedly, is the bank that can't be robbed," he said, chuckling. "There are approximately 30 alarm buttons inside, and there are always one or two Harrah's Club guards on duty, in addition to the bank's dedicated security." There was a hint of a smile on his face as he spoke, as if he was savoring the challenge and risk of such a difficult job.

"But you don't really expect to just walk in there off the street wearing a mask, do you?" I asked. "I mean, just look at that crowd outside. There must be hundreds of people milling around!"

"That's the beauty of it, Frosty. We won't have to come in off the street. There's an entrance in the basement, accessible from Harrah's Club next door."

"Basement?" I asked. "The bank has a basement?"

"That's right," he replied, "the safe deposit vault is downstairs. There are three alarm buttons downstairs as well, so we'll need a fourth man to help gain control and carry money. I want to hear your recommendations. Remember, only a real heavy will do."

Most of the people I knew were *not* heavies—that is, people who would be willing to die, if necessary, and who would never rat if captured. As I reflected on that I wondered, just for a second, what Curtis would think if he knew I'd been an informer.

"I don't know, Curtis. The only two people who I would ever trust on a job like this are both in prison."

"What about that guy who used to work with us in the butcher shop, Big Frank?"

I shook my head and told Curtis about how Frank had ripped me off for $2,000.

"Damn small timers!" he snarled. "They never want to play for the big stakes. Burning their friends is about all they can ever manage. What about you, Frosty? Are you in or out?"

"It *does* look good," I replied. "But I've got some stuff that I need to take care of on my own before I—"

"Wait a minute," he said, interrupting me. "You're not still hung up with that revenge crap, are you? You forget I went to the Board with eight clean years under my belt and a bag full of positive recommendations, and they still gave me a two-year set off without anyone from the outside calling in and begging the Board to keep me locked up. Why can't you just admit you would have ended up serving 99% of your sentence anyway, even if no one ever tried to screw you over? Instead of revenge, you need to concentrate on getting even. It's hard to be angry at the world when you have cool million, free and clear!"

"Do I need to decide now?" I asked.

Curtis frowned. "How long do you need?"

"Give me a couple of weeks," I said. "I'll be able to let you know something by then one way or the other."

We set up a series of dates and times to call from various phone booths and Dolores and I returned to Portland. We were not getting along particularly well. We felt a let-down after the expectations we'd held in the months before my release. We were also under the added pressure of the FBI poking into our lives. I asked an attorney with connections to find out what they were up to. For $500, I learned we were under sporadic surveillance. The house was being checked from time to time for out of state cars, and discreet record checks were being made on all long-distance phone calls originating from or coming to Dolores's phone. The telephone wiretaps, the intrusive calls to relatives and friends, and even unannounced visits to harass Dolores at her job came soon after.

"How can the FBI pull all this stuff?" I complained to my lawyer.

"Things have changed since you went away the last time around," he replied. "Ever since Hoover died, the FBI pretty much does whatever it wants to do."

"Well, I want you to file a civil suit against them. I want you to get them off my back!"

"You are on parole, Floyd, so there's not much I can do for you. Maybe I can do something for Dolores. By the way, what is she going to say at the Grand Jury?"

The FBI had warned Dolores that she would be called before

the Grand Jury in a few weeks and likely lose her job if she didn't "cooperate" with them by pointing them to Curtis Ray Michelson's whereabouts.

"She'll take the fifth," I replied.

"You really *have* been away a long time," he chuckled mirthlessly. "There is no fifth anymore. The first thing they'll do is give her immunity. Then, if she *doesn't* talk, they'll lock her up indefinitely until she agrees to tell them what they want to hear."

I left his office filled with rage and set up a meeting with Curtis to plan out a strategy. I found it hard to accept Curtis's nonchalance about how he had involved Dolores.

"Just make up a story for her," he said almost flippantly. "A story so vague they won't have enough to prove anything, one way or another."

"In other words, you want Dolores to perjure herself for you, right?" I spoke deliberately, evenly, but I was feeling very indignant at the moment. "Man, you've already gotten her way more involved than she should have been in the first place. Now you want her to risk her freedom and her whole career for you?"

"Look, Floyd," he said, remaining calm and collected. "After Reno, I'll have more money than I'll know what to do with. You take care of Dolores's testimony and I'll give you an extra $50,000 from my take. Then if she *does* end up losing her job she won't have to worry about money."

At the mention of such big bucks, I instantly warmed to the idea. Somehow, it seemed too good—and too easy—to pass up. Nevertheless, the tension between us was real. At least for me it was. There was a $5,000 reward out for Curtis, and most cons would turn in their own mothers for that kind of money. Admittedly, I'd given a little thought to the idea of turning him in myself. I wasn't particularly interested in the money, but Dolores and I were now facing considerable danger associating with him. Contrary to what Curtis had expected, the Public Defender's office was *not* able to keep J.B. from being convicted on the second of his two robbery charges. He was acquitted on the first charge but, at his second trial, the FBI produced an amazing new informant to whom J.B. had supposedly confessed. J.B.'s attorney repeatedly pointed out to the jury how this same informant "heard" and "invented" many other jailhouse "confessions" during his frequent stints behind bars. Despite the informant's dubious history, the jury chose to believe him. Now Dolores faced the possibility of being charged with several counts of perjury.

Even if I backed out of the Reno job, I would still have to go back to prison for a parole violation—a seven-year number at the very least. Plus, I was also guilty of conspiracy, which would likely add another five years. I wanted to talk to my parole officer about it, but I no longer felt I could trust him. He had phoned me one afternoon to ask me if I knew anything about an escaped Oregon killer. He *knew* my release orders clearly stated that I was prohibited from acting as a police informant, because of course that meant I was involved in more criminal activity, and that would be cause enough for me to be sent back to prison. Yet he seemed to think it was all right for *him* to put me at such risk by asking me to inform. All these rules and nobody, not even the authorities, seemed to want to honor them. I was feeling more trapped with each passing day, with no one to turn to and nowhere to go.

Chapter Twenty

RENO, NEVADA SEPTEMBER 27, 1974

June, 1974. I was still on the periphery of the Reno heist. One afternoon that month, while I was working on a fake Oregon driver's license for Curtis, I heard a knock at the door. Instinctively, I knew it was the police. Hurriedly I threw the printing paraphernalia into a cupboard and opened the door to two sloppily dressed men. One, a guy in his twenties, had long hair. The older one had a crewcut. The elder cop flashed his badge and announced he and this partner were from the Regional Narcotics Strike Force.

This is it, I thought. Busted for four lousy ounces of marijuana.

"Does a young girl who drives a Volkswagen live here?" he asked, handing me a piece of paper that listed at this address the name, vehicle license number, and registration number of Dolores's daughter, Sylvia.

"Yes, she lives here," I replied. "Has she been in an accident?"

"No. She was observed driving here with a marijuana plant in the back of her car. We want to talk to her and get the plant."

"But I thought marijuana was legal in this state," I said.

"It is legal," said the younger cop. "But possession of a whole plant is a felony. With your permission, we'd like to search the premises."

"Sorry guys, I'm just a guest here, I can't give you permission to come in."

"We can get a warrant, you know!" growled the cop with the crewcut. His anger was matched by my own.

"I suggest you do that!" I replied. "Clearly, you don't have anything better to do than harass college kids!" I slammed the door in their faces. No doubt, the FBI must have seen the plant in Sylvia's car and tipped off the Narcotics boys. Just the day before, Sylvia had moved a load of her personal belongings back home from her college dorm. I searched the entire house but found nothing. I went to a nearby payphone and called Dolores, asking her if she knew of any marijuana plant. She didn't

Quickly, I returned home, gathered up the printing gear and a suitcase full of masks and handcuffs I'd gotten for Curtis, and moved them to a safe place. When Dolores came home, we looked for and found Sylvia's pot plant. It was growing in the backyard garden!

I had seen too many college kids sent to McNeil Island for resisting the draft and for using marijuana, even as Nixon and his attack dog, Attorney General Mitchell, were hiding their own criminal acts from the nation they'd sworn to serve. Now they were threatening to ruin Sylvia's future for being in possession of a single marijuana plant! This made me *so* angry that I resolved to wage war against the FBI. Driven by the mindset that the authorities were not any better or more moral than me, I contacted Curtis and told him to count me in on the robbery. Soon we were sitting together a short distance from the bank in Reno, setting up the score.

He brought me up to speed on all the observations he'd made while casing the bank over the past several months. "That's Ed Walker, the bank's security guard," Curtis pointed. "He always locks the front door first, then the side door. He's ever watchful, the kind of guy who just might try to be a hero. I don't want any shooting, unless it's absolutely necessary. Suggestions?"

"Well," I replied, feeling flattered and proud that Curtis was interested in my opinion, "the quickest and surest way to neutralize anyone is with a blow to the kneecap. No matter how big they are, their knee will snap with just a little pressure."

"Okay," he said, nodding appreciatively. "Walker will be *your* job."

My blood began to race again, filling me with a sense of purpose I'd not felt in a very long time. Why I had ever given a moment's thought to attending school and changing my life was suddenly beyond my power to understand.

"There are four money boxes inside the vault," he continued. "One of them is the Federal Reserve box, mostly new money. Even if we strike on a Friday, it alone contains over a million. On Mondays, it's much, much more. Another is the Merchant's Fund, which never holds less than a quarter million."

"What's in the other two?" I asked.

"So far, we haven't been able to figure that out, but we think it's the reserve from Harrah's. We're told that Harrah's keeps a cash reserve somewhere in the bank."

"Just who is giving you all this information?" I asked, deeply curious.

Curtis gave me a long, hard, glaring look, but offered no answer. I didn't ask again.

"For our getaway," he continued, "we have a cabin at Tahoe and will use the fire trails to get within ten miles of it. Then we'll hike in the rest of the way."

"How's the Old Professor going to do that?" I asked, realizing he could not possibly trek through ten miles of rugged terrain.

"We'll drop him off in town," he replied without hesitation, clearly having given a lot of thought to this very issue. "He'll go to a motel and take the bus to Tahoe. We'll pick him up the next day."

"And he'll trust us with his share?" I asked, remembering how I'd been burned before. Again, his eyes narrowed and locked onto mine, staring hard at me for several seconds before answering my question.

"Look, Frosty. We're all pros here. We have to trust each other to do what is right or we're all doomed."

At last, I thought to myself, I was working with real professionals! With Curtis, I could become what I had always dreamed of being. I could use this cold and calculating brand of evil as a magnificent, creative force. I, Floyd Forsberg, FBI lackey, would be in on the biggest bank heist in American history!

"Okay," Curtis said, "the vice president and operations officer should be leaving right about now. They go out the back door and usually walk across the alley through Harrah's and have a drink at the bar." He pointed. "There they are. Let's follow them, then you can see what they look like."

The "alley," as Curtis called it, had a unique quality: It was covered with red carpet!

ೞ

Life went on while we were making preparations for the robbery.

After a lot of thought, I asked Dolores to marry me. I couldn't deny I still loved Nancy, but there was also a part of me that had come to love Dolores. She wasn't someone I always wanted, but she was someone I needed. In prison or out I could not chase away this woman with my games of self-destruction.

Moreover, I started to feel complete in Dolores. I was still nagged by an anxious uncertainty about life and its purpose—if in fact it held any purpose. Her companionship gave me a sense of security that allowed me to explore myself as I'd never dared to do. This gave me an unwavering stability regarding my own self-worth, which I'd thought to have been blotted out by a lifetime behind bars.

The opportunity to go straight seemed to be forever beyond my grasp, never a real option. Even before I stepped out of prison, I had effectively burned my bridges to a life of normalcy. Now, with the FBI closing in, and knowing that they were capable of resorting to any lie or illegality to lock up anyone who they felt deserved imprisonment, there seemed no other choices left except for those falling under the category of "desperate."

August 16, 1974 was the eighth anniversary of the Big Show that Dick and I had staged for the FBI. That really had been the death of Nancy and me. It just took three years to bury the body. So many "ifs"—*if* I had not been arrested that day, *if* the Bureau of Prisons had let me marry Nancy, *if* the Parole Board had not refused to release me earlier than it did, *if* Nancy had not betrayed me, *if* Dolores's husband had not driven Nancy away. A thousand *ifs* and all had led me to stand before Judge Burke with Dolores at my side to become my wife. The Big Show had set off the chain reaction that culminated in the shared bond of understanding and need that now existed between Dolores and me. We thought it most appropriate to pick this date to become husband and wife.

Judge Burke smiled at us as we stood before him. "Is this a double ring ceremony?"

"Yes," Dolores grinned.

"That's good," the judge chuckled. "I expect you'll need to keep a ring on him!"

His Honor's sense of humor and playful allusion to our age difference set me at ease. With time, perhaps, I would learn to love Dolores with the same passion I'd loved Nancy. If I could love like *that* again, maybe the hate would leave.

After we got married, the FBI informed Dolores's ex-husband about our wedding. We had decided to keep it a secret, knowing he would stir up more trouble for me with my parole officer.

"But how did the FBI find out?" Dolores cried miserably.

"I don't know," I mumbled. The Bureau had just won another round inside my head. An invisible band was being drawn tightly around my skull. The only small, ugly consolation I would derive from all this is I was *certain* Bob would waste no time letting Nancy in on the news. With a certain degree of pleasure, I wondered how much it would hurt her.

ග

Delores and I had planned a few days together at the beach for our honeymoon, but a call from Curtis changed all of that. Instead, we spent our honeymoon looking for a van to steal for the robbery.

We met Curtis in Sacramento, where he was enjoying his own "age-differential" experiment with a much younger mate. Marilyn, his latest girl, was just 19 years old. More shocking to me was that she knew about everything, including Reno.

"Are you *crazy*, Curtis?" I exclaimed when he told me of all he had openly shared with her. "She's a kid!"

"So, what does *that* have to do with anything?" he challenged, his voice heavy with resentment. "You just married a woman old enough to be your mother!"

"What I mean, Curtis, is that she's young and naïve. The FBI will tear her apart if they ever get their hands on her."

"Well, they won't," he replied snidely. "They're *not* going to take me alive, and she's willing to die with me."

He continued on with the shabby clichés of those in love, each one a piercing, painful reminder of what I had felt with Nancy. Like most men who don't fully believe in themselves, Curtis was caught up in the illusion that redemption could be found in the arms of a woman. I wanted to tell him of the unmentionable ugliness that lay at the foundation of love. Normally, it was not my place to say anything of the kind to others. They were free to live their lives without my interference. This was different. If Reno failed and Curtis went down because of his young chickadee, *I* would go down with him, too.

But I chose to maintain my silence, knowing he would not hear me if I spoke my mind. Unhappily, I realized my hero had been as twisted by his years of confinement as I had been by mine. Our one true mistress—self destruction—seemed to always be waiting for us in the shadows.

ෆ

September 27, 1974, the day of the Reno robbery. The late autumn sky was pale, its few scudding clouds reflecting my turbulent thoughts in diverse and tumbled forms between heaven and earth. I was so nervous it was as though I'd never committed a robbery in my life.

As I readied myself for the heist of a lifetime, the streets outside the bank were swollen with tourists and fluttering banners that welcomed the Shriners. Curtis and the Old Professor were already at the garage when Dolores dropped me off.

"Where's Gus, Professor?" I asked.

"He's already in position," Ed replied.

Curtis was checking his AR-15. Since I was assigned to carry the bulk of the money, I was armed with two pistols—a large .38 police special I would carry in my hand, and a snub-nosed five shot .38 I tucked in the small of my back. Along with his AR-15, Curtis was carrying a .357 magnum and a snub-nosed .38 similar to mine. Ed was armed with a silver plated .357 and he also carried several cans of black spray paint. Inside the van, in case we needed them during our getaway, we had a grenade and a fully loaded shotgun with a double-ought.

My job was to subdue or incapacitate Walker, the security guard, and make sure all the employees were handcuffed. Curtis's job was to force Bob Frantz, the operations officer, to open the money vaults. Ed would paint a huge Symbionese seven-headed cobra on the wall, along with the letters "S.L.A." next to the cobra, to throw the FBI off our trail. Gus, armed with another AR-15, was parked near the alley to provide us with cover if we became trapped by the armed security forces and had to shoot our way out.

I was becoming more and more nervous by the second. With my mind racing, I found myself thinking about the FBI. Why had I accepted parole with just ten months to go? If I had refused parole and finished serving out my complete sentence, I would not have been so vulnerable to the FBI's intimidation. Suddenly, the sound of crushing metal brought me back to reality.

"What the hell is the matter with you?" Curtis yelled. I'd been backing the van out of the garage and had plowed into the garage door. Sheepishly, I pulled the van back into the garage and tried again. Meanwhile, Curtis got into our stolen switch car, a shiny new 1975 Buick. He'd been pleased that we'd been able to steal a new model Buick before it had been available for sale to the public. I followed as he made his way downtown. There, he parked the Buick in the second story structure of the hotel directly across from the County Jail, then got in the driver's seat of the van. My hands shaking, I climbed into the back with Ed. Evidently, my nervousness was apparent to Curtis.

"Take it easy, Frosty," he reassured. "This is too well planned to fail."

Perpendicular to the red-carpeted alleyway there ran a regular concrete alley, which we entered from behind the bus depot. Curtis cursed beneath his breath when he saw a white delivery van parked in the very spot where we needed to position *our* vehicle.

"It's only six o'clock, General," Ed called out, his voice calm and collected. "Just circle around a couple of blocks and then come back."

When we returned ten minutes later, the competing van was gone. We parked in the now empty spot, and Ed handed Curtis the duffle bag that contained the AR-15 and other equipment. I could hear drums in the distance. Whether the parade had already passed or had yet to come this way, I couldn't guess. I could see that several kids were sitting on the wide ledges of the bank's windows.

As we elbowed our way through the crowd it struck me that we were all wearing brand new coveralls. We should have gotten used ones, the kind that would look most natural on real working men. It was too late to do anything about that now.

We entered the door that led to the Harrah's Club business elevator. Ed and I boarded the elevator and took it to the second floor. Curtis, meanwhile, used the stairs to get down to the basement, after which he returned to tell us there were still some employees down there. We would have to wait.

We stood there silently. It was 6:20PM. The vault was usually closed between 6:30 and 6:45. We would have to decide one way or the other—go or abort—very soon. Curtis went back downstairs to have another look. He came back quickly. Like a true General, he barked his orders.

"Let's go!"

We got back into the elevator and rode to the basement, slipping our masks over our faces just as Curtis slipped our duplicate key into the lock. The bolt snapped back and we walked through the doorway, entering the basement of the bank. Curtis pointed to the safe deposit vault and I went to check it out. It was empty. We then waited out of sight for the arrival of Bob Frantz and his assistant, Mary Bennett, who always closed the downstairs vault before securing the one upstairs. We heard their voices draw nearer, first coming down the stairs and then directly above the alcove where we were hidden. Curtis stepped out. Mary Bennett screamed.

"Do that again," Curtis warned viciously, "and I'll blow your head off!"

Frantz turned pale when Ed and I stepped out to greet them. Curtis ordered them to lie face down on the floor.

"Watch them while I see what's going on upstairs," he said.

When he returned, we grabbed our hostages and moved quickly up the stairs and into the main part of the bank. Curtis had Mary, I had Frantz, and Ed brought up the rear.

I had forgotten how big the bank was. The vault at the other end of the building seemed like a faraway objective, unreachable, and the room seemed to be full of people. I heard Curtis growling at the bank manager, Herb Brown, telling him to hang up the phone or he'd kill Mary Bennett on the spot. My attention was on trying to locate the security guard, who was nowhere to be found. When I glanced back moments later, I saw Curtis marching Brown, Bennett, and a second woman toward the back. With Ed still traveling beside me, I looked around for Walker, but could not see him. My second objective was to secure the vault and subdue any employees who might still be working inside. There was one male employee there when I stuck my head inside.

"On the floor!" I ordered, pointing my .38 at him. A short while later, Curtis led his four prisoners into the vault, the fourth being Walker, the security guard.

I asked, "Where did you find him, General?"

"Watching the parade through the front window," he laughed.

Ed entered the vault with a prisoner, and I became aware of the music playing as a marching band passed on the street in front of the bank.

Curtis took Mary to the money boxes. I made everyone else lay on the floor, except for Frantz who, without being told, seemed to know his place and walked over to where Curtis and Mary were standing.

"Open that one," Curtis ordered, pointing to Federal Reserve box.

"There's *no way* we can get into those," Frantz replied, officiously mouthing the company line for such circumstances. "We don't have the ability to—"

"Do you *really* think we've come this far without knowing you *can* open these damn boxes?" Curtis growled, his voice full of menace. "If you value your life, open it now!"

"I'll get the keys," Mary spoke up, realizing that Frantz was dangerously close to having his brains blown out. Curtis followed her and returned with the keys. By the time he got back, I had finished securing all the prisoners.

"Did you paint the SLA symbol on the wall, Captain?" I asked, whispering to Ed.

"No, I can't," he replied. "Take a look outside and you'll see why."

I looked and saw a uniformed policeman standing in front of the doorway of the bank, watching the parade go by. Just then, a buzzer sounded, sending shills through my spine.

"What's that?" I cried out.

"It's the back door!" Curtis yelled. He turned toward Ed and ordered him to take Frantz with him at gunpoint and deal with the situation at the back door.

As they walked toward the rear of the bank, I kept my eyes on the cop who had his back to us. Within minutes, Ed returned with Frantz and two more prisoners. With Curtis no longer needing Mary, I told her to lie on the floor, then handcuffed and tied her up as I'd done with the others. When I was done, I glanced up and saw that Frantz was again with Curtis.

"Open that one!" Curtis commanded, pointing to the Merchant's Fund box.

"You already have over $2,000,000," Frantz told him. One oversized duffle bag was completely full. A second bag was more than half filled. And there was *still* a mountain of money in the vault that was already open.

"What about all that cash, General?" I asked, pointing at the pile of money.

"They're nothing but ones, Lieutenant. We don't want them." Glancing at his watch, Curtis motioned toward Frantz and ordered me to tie him up.

As I secured Frantz, I saw Curtis leaning over Mary, asking her if her cuffs were too tight. She said they were. I had in fact used standard police procedure, tightening *everyone's* handcuffs as snugly as they would go. Nevertheless, he looked at Ed and held out his hand, saying, "Give me the cuff keys, Captain."

Hardly believing my eyes, I watched as Ed tossed the keys to Curtis, who then bent down to loosen her cuffs. I holstered my gun and lifted the bag that was completely full of money. It *had* to weigh over 200 pounds! I hadn't lifted weights since I'd been stabbed, so my knees trembled and I was literally staggering as I walked away from the vault.

Now it was up to Gus to provide our way out by having the van positioned exactly where we needed it to be. In Spanish, Curtis radioed that we were ready for the last phase. We left the bank and stood at the bottom of the stairs that led to Harrah's dressing rooms, where we took off our rubber masks. Curtis cracked open his bag. Inside, fully loaded, was the AR-15.

"Here comes the hard part," Curtis said, opening the door that led outside. The van was parked just three feet away. The area was tightly packed with people and security guards. Two "change girls" dressed in black turned to glance at us, and one man seemed to stare too long, but he was dressed much too casually to be a plain clothes security guard so we ignored him. Acting as if we were *supposed* to be there, we climbed into the van with the two duffel bags and pulled away. Seconds later, we disappeared into the maze of traffic on the smaller arterials of the city.

Just minutes after we left the alleyway, Curtis started laughing. "They've got the call!" he said. I'd barely had enough time to change in the back of the van and the robbery had already been reported to the police.

"What's so funny about *that*?" I asked.

"The cop *can't believe* that the dispatcher said Second and Virginia!" he roared with glee. "He keeps asking her to repeat the address. And they're looking for *three* men not four!"

The plan had been to split up at the Buick, then meet again at Curtis's motel in Sparks, where Marilyn was waiting. Now, with the alarm out so soon, Curtis suggested I return to the motel. He would call me as soon as the money was counted.

I rued missing the thrill of seeing all that money in one big pile, but the town was filling with sirens. This was no time to argue. After pulling in behind the Buick, I carried the heavy money bag to the car and left, walking the few blocks to the motel where Dolores was waiting. It was 7:30PM when I arrived.

"How did it go?" she asked anxiously.

"Baby, Curtis is truly the best!" I exclaimed. "Even with the cop standing right in front of the bank watching the parade it was a *perfect* job! The one hiccup was Ed didn't get to paint the S.L.A. Symbol, so the FBI will *know* it's Curtis's robbery just as soon as they hear of it."

"And where are the others?"

"The cops got the alarm sooner than we expected so we split up," I replied. "But Curtis will call me here just as soon as the money is divided."

Feeling elated, I took Dolores in my arms and imagined all the fun we'd soon be enjoying with my share. We made love and then I slept, my mind and body suddenly set free from all the tension of the past several weeks.

It was 9:00PM when I awakened.

"Has Curtis phoned yet?" I called out to Dolores.

"No," she laughed. Teasingly, she said, "You're not worried, are you?"

I didn't answer, but I did wonder how long it really took to divide up a couple hundred pounds of money. Most of it should have been in bundles, making it easy to count.

The next half hour passed more slowly and miserably than any week I'd ever spent languishing in the Hole. I began pacing, wondering to myself, "*What if they burned me?*" I *knew* I had no way of tracking down Ed or Gus. As for Curtis, all I knew was that he was originally from Newport Beach and had a sister who lived somewhere in California. I kept telling myself Curtis was a *pro*. He would *never* burn me as I'd been burned by Dick and Big Frank. But what did I *really* know of Curtis Michelson, except for the image *he* had permitted me to see?

The ringing telephone put an end to all my doubts. It was Curtis. My share of the money—$264,000—was waiting for me at the garage.

When I got there, my eyes fell upon the pile of cash that was now *mine*. I was overcome with emotion, *knowing* all this ill-gotten wealth would help me underwrite my wildest dreams. My imperfections had not defeated or destroyed me. They had not kept me from fulfilling this ultimate criminal fantasy—the *Big Score*. To me, this money *was* power—the power to change my life. We had played the game of *win* or *die*.

And we had *won*.

Chapter Twenty-One

"THEY'RE JUST SOFTENING YOU UP"

Triumphant, we headed for home the next morning. While en route, I stopped in Eugene, Oregon and telephoned my FBI contact, asking him for an update on my status.

"I'm sure you recognize my voice," I said, when my contact answered the phone. "I'd like a new report on my status with the FBI."

"I'll just bet that you do!" he exclaimed, laughing. His tone was sardonic and sent a cold shill down my spine.

"What's *that* supposed to mean?" I asked nervously.

"It means the FBI is looking all over the West Coast for you in connection with the Reno job!"

"What Reno job?" I asked feebly.

"Did you *really* think they wouldn't suspect you?" he asked, sounding as if he were talking to the stupidest man in the world. "Why, shit! They've been waiting for you to do something like this since the day you got out."

My entire body was filled by wave after wave of nausea. When he told me I had so much "heat" on me that he had no choice but to increase his fee for information, I didn't protest. He promised another full report by the following Monday, then we hung up.

Dolores and I had planned to head for the beach to establish some semblance of an alibi. Now the most important thing to do was hide out until we could bury the money. Knowing I was likely to be arrested at any time, I went to see the attorney who had represented Dolores at the Grand Jury investigation of Curtis's two robberies. I didn't tell him what my problem might be, but I gave him a retainer of $5,000, the entire sum in fives.

Early Monday morning, Dolores and I buried the rest of the money in three deep holes that I had dug in a secluded place in the woods. After returning to our motel room, I called Sharon to see whether the FBI had been there yet. She replied they had not, but added my parole officer had called her, looking for me.

Dolores's car started acting up again, which sparked a new idea in my mind. We drove her car to a dealership to have it checked out and repaired. From there, I placed a call to Mr. Hooley. He said he'd been looking for me since Wednesday and demanded an explanation as to where I'd been for the past five days.

"My wife and I have been at the beach. We've been stuck there since last Wednesday with car trouble." I spoke calmly, trying to sound as nonchalant as possible. "What's up, Mr. Hooley? Is there something wrong?"

Hooley replied that the FBI had sent him to my house, and when he didn't find me there, they demanded to know where I'd spent the weekend. Beneath my breath, I cursed the bad luck. I knew the FBI might well have nothing on me, and may just playing the old standard parole pressure games.

I later learned that my P.O. had *not* in fact come to my house on the Wednesday Dolores and I left for Reno. Instead, FBI Agent Charles Rand had simply persuaded Mr. Hooley to lie about it, to try to make me believe—a la "The Big Show"—that they'd been watching my every move before I left for Nevada. In fact, the Bureau had been watching my house only since the robbery.

According to my contact, Curtis Ray Michelson had been

picked out of a photo lineup and identified by two people as being one of the robbers. Somehow the Bureau now knew there had really been four robbers, not three. Thus far, although the FBI was certain of my involvement, no one had identified me. Their immediate plan, since they couldn't charge me, was to keep me under 24-hour surveillance and hopefully give me enough rope to hang myself.

Well, *this* time around, I was determined their game would be played out a little differently. I made it a point to shake every tail, to pull up behind them and chase them, photographing *their* every move so as to compile a set of pictures for a lawsuit. In response, the FBI upped the pressure on relatives, friends, and neighbors, clearly trying to provoke me into running. I knew they had nothing on me, so I simply flashed an obscene one finger gesture at them each time we crossed paths. I was convinced they couldn't touch me, and I was enjoying a measure of revenge for their having turned me into a rat after the "Big Show" in 1966. When I went to see my attorney, he did not approve of my defiant actions, warning me I was playing the game all wrong.

"Are you crazy?" he asked, shaking his head in disbelief. "You aren't showing them any respect, Mr. Forsberg. Even the Mafia lets the FBI follow them around without resorting to such foolish antics! *Let them* follow you. It's just their way of pressuring you with the hope you'll break. Your reactionary response is playing right into their hand."

"I'll *never* let the FBI follow me," I hissed. "It's an old feud. I'll run them off the road every time."

Later, the FBI decided two could play the same game. They upped the ante by making an attempt on my life. Earlier in the day, an FBI agent had tried to run me down as I photographed him. When I told my attorney about it, he was surprised at *my* surprise.

"Why should that shock you?" he asked. "They're just softening you up. You're forgetting that, at any time of their own choosing, they can send you back to prison for seven years on a parole violation. It won't be long before they offer you a deal. In the meantime, you'd best give some serious thought to accepting some kind of bargain."

Well, there's thought, there's introspection, and then there's drugged introspection. I found and ingested some acid. As the hallucinogenic drug worked on my brain and my mind, I realized that even after achieving the ultimate criminal success I had *still* failed at happiness. I had *not* evened the score. I could not forgive them but neither could I truly punish them for what they'd done to me so long ago... or for what they were *still* doing to me, provoking me to further misery.

I began to feel like a walking, talking box of cake mix that God was stirring up for his own entertainment. A chocolate marble cake mix, poured slowly into the darkened base. Dolores and her love were the lighter cake mix that changed the dark batter, me, into a lighter and brighter version of myself. The great philosophers had been right! We really are "one" with each other. The people napalmed in Vietnam really *are* "us," just as we are really them.

I felt sorry for the man who had tried to run me down. What if my quick reflexes had not saved me at the last second? I would have been killed and the agent would almost certainly be feeling bad right now. I began to cry as I realized that he and I were truly "one." I got up and staggered from the living room to the phone in the bedroom.

"Where are you going?" Dolores asked, seemingly from some faraway place.

"To call the FBI," I replied, my voice thick with emotion. "To tell that agent I'm sorry he almost killed me. To tell him that I really love him."

Dolores's face seemed to register understanding, but her eyes still reflected a touch of confusion.

"You *are* joking, aren't you?"

Without answering Dolores, I dialed the number.

"Federal Bureau of Investigation," said the male voice at the other end of the line. "May I help you?"

"Since you guys have my phone tapped, I guess I don't have to tell you who this is."

"Sir," replied the voice, "I don't have the slightest idea who you are." His serious tone agitated me. Didn't he understand that all of this was just a big cosmic joke?

"This is Floyd Forsberg," I said. "I'm sure you've heard of me, as you people have been following me everywhere I go." Dolores, who was standing beside me, started laughing.

"Go ahead," said the agent, his voice bringing my focus back to the phone.

"Well," I giggled, "I just want to leave a message for the agent who tried to run me down with his car earlier today. I—"

"Sir, are you alleging that an agent of the Federal Bureau of Investigation tried to run you down?" His seriousness, not to mention his interrupting me, irritated me.

"'Alleging,' hell!" I snarled. "I got his picture and his license number!"

"That's a serious charge, sir. Do you wish to swear out a warrant?"

The call was beginning to bum me out. Somehow, this perfectly articulate and officious voice could not see we were all "one," that we were all imperfect abstractions of God.

"Man, you're too serious," I groaned. "Do you realize that a hundred years from now all your seriousness and rigidity will be nothing but dust riding on the wind? I'm not going to discuss this with you! Just tell the agent who tried to run me down that from now on he can follow me all he wants, and that I *love* him, I *really* do."

With that, I hung up the phone. The next morning, there were three carloads of FBI agents waiting in front of the house. We reached speeds of 80 miles per hour as I chased them down residential streets. Somehow, all my feelings of brotherly love had not survived beyond yesterday's acid trip.

FBI agents started interviewing inmates at McNeil Island, asking about Curtis and me, trying to dig up whatever they could about our hangouts and possible friends. They also started building a case against me through my parole officer. I was still a parolee, and every word I uttered to him, true or not, was immediately reported to the FBI.

Agents followed me into every store, making a list of all the monies I spent. From the service station where I bought my gas, they learned of trips across the desert. They discovered two small bank accounts I'd opened under an alias. They learned from American Express that I had rented a car in Sacramento that had been left in Reno. The rope that dangled over my head was slowly starting to form a noose. It was just a matter of time.

As I settled back into the everyday routine of being a college student that I had started when I was paroled, I began to wonder why I had enlisted in the robbery. I hadn't really needed the money. Nor had there materialized the pleasure I had expected to feel upon striking back at society for all of my penal despair.

It was no longer fun chasing the FBI and, truth be told, I missed Curtis. There was no way to contact or join him, but I felt I needed him and his advice. In order to keep feeding me more rope, the FBI used its powerful influence to make sure I was not arrested for all the unauthorized trips I'd taken outside the state. I knew they were not above manufacturing false evidence against me if they so chose, and I was growing more and more alarmed about their increasing activity.

ꕤ

On October 23, 1974, Agents Rand and Carlyle approached me in the parking lot at school.

"Get away from me," I growled contemptuously. "I don't have to talk to you people without my attorney present."

"You don't have to talk. Just listen to what I have to say." Agent Rand told me I could "write my own deal" and, at the same time, collect the $50,000 reward money being offered for Curtis Michelson. He finished off his spiel by saying, "You could make a new life for yourself with that kind of money."

The FBI wanted me to help them identify the robbers whose composite sketches had been put together by the witnesses who had picked Curtis out of a photo lineup. One of the sketches lightly resembled Gus, with his dark features, his hair, and his thick neck, but I couldn't understand how they had come up with a composite of him. He'd been outside the bank the whole time. Even *I* hadn't seen him that night. How there could be a composite of him was anyone's guess. Fortunately, none of the composites resembled me.

Agent Rand told me the FBI could arrange for me to leave the state to look for Curtis, and asked me where I thought he might be.

"Why, Newport Beach, of course," I replied, believing I was stating the obvious. "Doesn't a man on the run always return to familiar ground?"

Rand went on and on about how I was "doing the right thing." Casually, he mentioned that I would soon be subpoenaed to the Grand Jury hearing in Reno.

"You're wasting your time with your subpoena," I said at this mention of the Reno Grand Jury. "I *will* take the Fifth."

"You've been in jail way too long, Floyd. You can't take the Fifth anymore. We'll just keep you in jail until you talk."

With the bonds squeezing ever tighter around me, Dolores and I left Portland with 11 suitcases. I told her I was headed for the wilds of Mexico until the statute of limitations expired in five years. To my great surprise, she insisted on going with me, fully prepared to hide out with me, no matter the hardship.

We took $29,000 with us. In a year or so, when the heat was

off, I would sneak back to dig up some more. I called various numbers in Mexico to try to locate Benito. I wanted him to meet us in Nogales and then escort us into the interior of Mexico.

ଓ

November, 1974. Realizing the FBI would assume Dolores and I had gone to Mexico, we decided to change directions and head east to lose ourselves among the anonymous masses of New York City's concrete jungle. We found a nice apartment and, after a couple of weeks, had all the trappings of a well-heeled married couple. Inwardly though, we both wondered what we were doing there. The hollow truth was this: The "Biggest Robbery of Our Time," for me, had solved *nothing*. I could buy anything I wanted, except the thing I wanted most: the past and a return to a life that included Nancy, the innocence of First Love, the image of myself reflected in her love. Why had the system destroyed the one good part of my life? And why, though I was now married to another, did I still feel bonded to Nancy by the invisible but mighty chains of madmen and poets?

As Dolores and I lay in bed one night, news broke over the Late Show that Curtis and Ed had been caught in Newport Beach, California with half a million dollars! I was certain it had to be a trick, that the TV was some kind of FBI play, so I called Kendrick Williams, an ex-L.A. City cop, and asked him to verify whether the capture was in fact true. It was.

Kendrick Williams, former FBI agent and now attorney, informed me—for a price—he could spring Curtis out of any jail in California. I was really starting to feel guilty about tipping off the FBI where he might be found, so I decided to take Williams up on his offer, no matter the cost, and try to help Curtis. My conscience was no doubt still trying to get back the semblance of honor I'd lost the first time I had played the informant's game against Dick. I had pretended through my attorney to make a deal with the FBI. I had told the FBI to look for Curtis in Newport Beach. I had assumed he wouldn't be stupid enough to play the homing pigeon. It was a move that led to the capture of so many criminals. This gave me the idea that I could return to Portland. The double reverse psychology of returning to my familiar territory, after what I'd told Agent Rand about Curtis returning to Newport Beach, was something they probably wouldn't expect. What naiveté. I would soon learn I no longer had a deal *or* an attorney.

The FBI pressured my attorney off the case with threats of disbarment. The Portland Office of the Bureau was requesting I be placed on the Top Ten Most Wanted list. Curtis, who had sworn "never to be taken alive," had been singing literally from the moment he was arrested, fingering *everyone.*

What one of the best bank robbers in the country could hope to achieve by ratting on his compatriots was beyond me. Ken advised me his connections no longer wanted anything to do with Curtis. The escape was off. I knew there was no question of hiding out until the statute of limitations had run out. Once a person was indicted, there was no statute of limitations! We would have to find some hole in the mountains of Oregon or Washington, crawl inside, and pray for Armageddon.

Dolores and I found a cabin in the woods and began our wait. They were tranquil days spent far from the real world. They were marked days as well. The end would probably come soon, for *both* of us. We did not kid ourselves about this inevitable outcome. With Curtis having already implicated me in the Reno heist, he was certain to implicate Dolores for her "part" in watching him pull off Oregon's largest bank robbery. She had watched it at his insistence, but that would never be understood or excused, nor was there any chance she might get off with just probation. Word was already out that they intended to make an example of her.

The thought of killing Dolores seeped into my mind like noble sewage. Noble, because I honestly *did* want to spare her the misery that awaited her. Not for a moment did I believe she could ever adjust to the mindlessness of prison. The thought of taking her life was at first frightening and unreal. As surely as a mouse becomes accustomed to its maze, so did the thought of killing Dolores become less frightening and less despicable as I continued to justify it as an act of mercy. Murderous thoughts took on a certain romantic regality, like a marred gemstone proudly sitting on a mounting of gold.

Preparing to kill her, I would watch Dolores move about the inside of our cabin, her final moments measured by the clock ticking silently inside my skull. Miserably, I would add a few more minutes, then hours, to her life—not from kindness or mercy. It was my indecisiveness that gave rise to these stays of execution.

A flicker of long past rage reflected in the window of my memory. I had once thought that killing would be the ultimate gesture of contempt against another human being. At one point, I had compiled a list of ten people who had tortured my soul and who I considered worthy of the grisliest death I could conceive. Now, as I found myself a split second from ending Dolores' life, I'd see her sitting there writing to her daughters and simply could not act. Her maternal instinct and her untiring devotion to her daughters were parts of her I had *always* respected. I'd often felt envious of her daughters over the love she extended to them. Could I *really* destroy that goodness?

I wondered how Nancy would feel. The fact that Nancy would somehow enter into my internal debate amused me, but really it was inevitable. Hadn't Nancy been a part of everything? I hated to admit so much of what I thought and did was measured by my beliefs about how Nancy would feel or react in response. There was also the reality of having to consider my own feelings for Dolores. When we left Portland, I believed Nancy was forever beyond my grasp. I had even come to call what I had with Dolores love, a term I had always used exclusively in reference to Nancy.

At last the thought of killing Dolores took wings and flew away unfulfilled, undone by the simple and mundane human process of communication. That she could sit there for hours calmly discussing her impending downfall revealed to me a new and deeper aspect of her personality. She was a most extraordinary woman. She even guessed why I had been so silent over the previous few days, urging me to not worry about her when our world finally came crashing down, as it most certainly would.

"I'm a lot stronger that you or anyone else realizes," she said, her voice firm and unwavering.

Her statement reassured me, yet her strength was something I found somewhat intimidating. In the past, I had never perceived or accepted Dolores on my own level as I had Nancy. Dolores was just... well... she was simply Dolores. To me, she was merely another victim who'd been unwittingly and repeatedly pushed into my world, first by an ex-husband who created an opening by taking Nancy away from me, and again by Curtis, who diabolically enticed her deeper into my world of crime.

Dolores had never even had a traffic ticket. Now, because of *me,* we were both fugitives from the law. Long ago I classified her as something different, something much simpler. I was satisfied with the niche I had relegated her to, and had been comfortable leaving her there. I had made the age-old male error of taking my woman for granted virtually every day I'd known her, and it grieved me. I never saw all the gifts she offered me because I had been more caught up in *my* imagined machismo than in *her* goodness.

Finally, I posed to her the question I feared most.

"Why are you here with me?" I asked, my voice heavy with emotion. "Really, why?"

"Why am I here?" Her voice contained a certain elusive rhythm. At first, her words were like self-conscious wisps of air, fragile gemstones that might shatter upon striking against a listening ear.

"Well," she said, "I'm *not* here simply to join one madness with another just to see what the result might be—an opinion my family and the FBI seem to consider number one on the list. Nor is it to live in your Twilight Zone netherworld, somewhere between your spiritual hunger and the impossible dream.

"We are what we are," she continued. "The problem is that we seldom ever see clearly what we really are. We become enamored with our own problems and operate on the false premise that we are our *own norm*, that *we* are the genuine yardstick for our own lives. We *aren't* running the universe, though we might believe otherwise. We aren't quite the masters of our own fate, although we may have a little control over the rudder. As for the tumultuous seas and the swirling storms, those things, my philosopher husband, are *never* ours to rule. Bob could not accept me, could not accept the *real* me. One day, I realized there wasn't going to be anything left for me, except to grow old and die. When you decided you could never forgive Nancy, I saw the course that my life had to take. Yes, I *knew* I was the only game in town, the only other woman available to you, but it didn't matter. Your need became my purpose. In meeting that need, you caused me to feel and think amazing new things. Being your woman was a self-confession of sorts. A facing of all the secret hidden things I had never dared to be."

Somehow all my lies and stories, both to myself and to this woman, had led us to this truth. Perhaps there was still some form of salvation to be found in twilight's ebony hue.

She continued, "I decided it was simply time to take a little more active part in my own drifting. I was a common, barely functioning piece of nothing; a failure to my husband, a failure as a mother, and a hindrance to myself. My days were just folds between the nights, differing only in that some were marked by birthdays and holidays. You have always been in your prison, and I was in mine. I was living on decades old memories of a time when I had felt myself a vital part of Bob's life rather than merely a possession—*his* possession—to be cared for as *he* saw fit. I was a cripple in life. The sad thing is that it had become so normal no one noticed my limp..."

As I listened, I began to have the old feeling of being on the outside looking in. Perhaps there was a part of me that was simply too ashamed to listen to this woman any further. To me, she had always seemed to carry happiness inside of her like a huge bouquet whose fragrance permeated all those whose lives she touched. It was finally hitting home why I'd never really felt completely worthy of her love or her devotion. As the world came apart around us, we discussed things about ourselves that had been hidden for a lifetime. No price could be placed on those days of genuine closeness and happiness.

Chapter Twenty-Two

WE HAD PLAYED THE GAME… AND LOST

January 1, 1975. We had been in hiding for more than a month. We had a new house and, in a way, a new lease on life. To celebrate having remained free to see another New Year, we built a fire in the fireplace and each dropped half a "window pane," our largest dose ever of LSD. Even before it began to work, I sensed that a door long closed was about to open for me. I took a vigilant position, with Dolores in my arms, thinking perhaps I might see God. *Something* would soon be revealed, I was sure of it. As usual, the rough edges of reality smoothed out, and the basic oneness of all things became the new reality.

"Very symmetrical!" Dolores exclaimed.

"What, Darling?" I asked, although it seemed my lips never moved. She didn't answer. The fact that she didn't feel the need to answer me was, in itself, a pleasurable feeling.

That I loved this woman sentimentally was beyond doubt. This brand of love always has built into it a certain self-destructiveness. Why did I label it that way? Why do we label anything? To classify something seemed somehow to lessen the quality of whatever it was we considered. Perhaps it was because this allowed us to spare ourselves our own critical self-censure, that most intolerable condemnation, so we could more quickly judge others instead.

After a decade of intellectually pursuing the Truth, I wondered where I really was. I had started from nowhere. With Walt's encouragement, I had traversed a thousand books, millions of words, countless philosophies, and yet I was still *nowhere*. I had not found the Truth, nor had I found the courage to try cracking the greatest secret of all, the veil that so thinly divides life and death.

How I envied those empty souls, clinging unthinkingly to the branches on the tree of life as the floodwaters rise up to overtake them. After taking apart and reassembling my own soul hundreds of times, all I ever found was the same old picture: Nature's humble yet dogged and ever present will to live.

Tears rolled down my cheeks, the symbol of being out of grace with the cosmos and with myself. It was nighttime now. The afternoon had slipped away into the nothingness of bygone time, of bygone thoughts and actions that once could be touched, experienced, and used, but no more. Suddenly, like an ever-intruding phantom, a jumbling swirling figure appeared on the screen of my imagination, pulsing and throbbing as it began to take human form. It was Nancy, my soulmate, a dream crushed to a sour pulp beneath the rolling wheel of absurdity.

I knew that I could never again love anyone else as I had loved her. I knew I had no choice in the matter. Love could not be commanded, nor could it be passionately imparted from a sheer sense of duty alone. Finally, in a healing burst of freedom, I forgave Nancy. With that, I was instantly released from a burden too long carried. I woke Dolores from her sleep-like trance and told her I had forgiven Nancy. Her face suffused with relief and she started crying. We fell asleep in each other's arms.

January 2, 1975. A day of quiet. I wanted with all my heart to go to Portland, not only to tell Nancy I'd forgiven her, but to give the FBI back all the remaining Reno money. If only I could just return and start my life all over again! But life is not that simple...

January 3, 1975. Dolores and I were arrested, unceremoniously and without incident, outside the Post Office where we had rented a P.O. Box under an alias. We could have tried to outrun them, but I could not chance Dolores being killed in a fusillade. Besides, I had promised her daughter Susan that I would no longer carry a gun, so I was unarmed. We were held there at the Post Office for almost an hour until an FBI agent could arrive at the scene to take credit for the arrest.

I remained silent all the way to the jail, refusing to respond to any of Agent Manning's questions. He gave me a copy of the warrant, which contained a statement by Curtis Michelson implicating me in the Reno robbery. For some reason, Curtis made a point of claiming that he didn't like me, adding that although he felt "very much ashamed" over a great deal of what had happened during the robbery, the entire affair had been *my* doing. What he was referring to, I didn't know. What did it matter now? It was over. We had played the game... and *lost.*

There is a certain saddening mix of relief and joy that comes from looking out through eyes that soon will cease to see at all. The adjustment from freedom to freedom-lost was easier to make than most might realize. In the four hours after my arrest, the necessary pronouncement was passed from my heart to my brain that it was all right. Atonements had all been made.

I debated whether to kill myself now or after my trial. Why wait? I was all too familiar with the treachery of hope that springs forth from inside imprisoned hearts. If I waited through my trial, I would then wait for the appeal and the re-appeal. Almost certainly I would cling onto hopeless hope all the way through to my final parole board hearing, which no doubt would be decades down the road. No. Even the beasts of the jungle eventually come to the awareness, as I had now, when the end was finally upon them. The hunter had become the captured. Better to end it quickly than to suffer years of the cage yet again.

I had no paper or pen with which to write my last will and testament. I had no bedding I could use to send me on my way. In the Hole yet again, I was even without water to quench my thirst. Odd. I'd never thought about dying thirsty. It seemed a most appropriate thing now to never again know the blessed relief of a thirst-quenching drink of water.

Had I a pen, what would I have written, or to whom? A protest against the system would take too long—and was unlikely to be read. A note to Dolores, telling her I was sorry and I loved her would be superfluous, for she knew these things already. Then there was the ever-present Nancy. She could not possibly know I'd forgiven her. I wondered, if she *did* know, would she even care?

A long string of bleak yesterdays for the most part, except for the last few months with Dolores and that brief, magical span of 46 days during which my spirit and soul had experienced the pure rapture of Nancy's embrace and love. Truly, by loving *her*, I had learned to love.

I remembered, too, those happier days when Sharon and I had been children. Memories of our playing cowboys and Indians caused a flicker of warmth to spark inside my heart, comforting me. Remembering our last contact, I was grateful she had finally found her true soulmate. With that sense of gratitude wasn't this the time to think of God and salvation?

If He's really out there, how we must surely annoy God with our last minute graspings for redemption and grace! So many prayers delivered up more as desperate expressions of ransom than expressions of honest surrender. If there really was a God, I imagined He must have a very special holding tank for us suicides, self-deluded charlatans convinced we could appear by His side by the sheer will of our minds, by the energy of our own despair.

Before I got too deep into my own philosophical meanderings, I decided the legal noose around my neck was salvation enough. Shifting gears, I started thinking of the Buddhist monks torching themselves on the streets of Saigon, of the Kamikaze pilots who met death as one would meet a new girl: a little nervously, but with great anticipation.

I had always planned on taking a handful of my enemies with me in one spree-like explosion of targeted rage. I'd wanted to go out like a warrior, vanquished perhaps but not dishonored. I knew it was too late for that; there was no enemy present to go down with me.

My coveralls were short sleeved, so one of the legs would have to be secured to the bars of my cell front, and the other leg tied around my neck. As I tied the right leg of my coveralls to the bars of my cell, I knew what it meant to stand completely alone. Curiously, I wondered what Curtis would think upon learning of my demise. Would my sincerity embarrass him and illuminate his cowardice? I would never know but how soon I would be forgotten!

The jailors had given me no underclothes, so I stood there completely naked as I wrapped the left pant leg around my neck. It felt pleasingly snug. I looped it one more time and tested it a little by letting my body go slightly limp, just enough to make sure it was secure. My Adam's apple felt the pressure and, as if it didn't understand the relief promised from the coming strangulation, it began to twist and turn in protest against the noose's embrace of death.

My head started throbbing, each beat of my heart shuddering across and through my eyes. With perhaps just one last thought to think, what should it be? Nancy? Would I ever be free of her? Would she straddle my mind, like Godiva on her stallion, and ride with me into oblivion?

My head ached terribly from the lack of blood to my brain, but I was proud of my courage. In the midst of my dying, I had no fear. I was approaching the event horizon, that point of no return where one crossed over from life to death. I was almost there. You're either there or you aren't. By the same token, once there, you're there forever.

The man who had taught me the most, my favorite author Alan Watts, once wrote that the moment we die is simply the moment we die. Nothing more and, assuredly, nothing less. I smiled at the thought of blessed nothingness.

"This is it," I said to myself, pulling up my feet up so that my weight was entirely off the floor.

The noose tightened and buried itself deeply around my neck, and a million lights went on in my head. No one ever told me death by hanging would be so pretty! I began drifting upward and back, no longer the heavy, clumsy me who stumbled like a bird. Why had I waited so long?

I saw no scenes from the past, nothing of my life flashing before my eyes, but only lights speeding by, merging into an endless kaleidoscope of color. Then nothing but darkness—and I felt very, very cold.

ꕥ

I realized I was awake and waiting for something to happen. At first, I was encouraged that there was some trace of conscious thought. Then, when nothing happened, I began to panic. What if this was it? What if I was doomed to spend the rest of forever waiting in vain for something to happen? *That* would be as bad as life!

I felt my body bouncing and jerking spasmodically, still strangling. Though I felt no pain, I felt profound disappointment that I was still alive. I cursed the strength of my neck. When one is so unfit to live among normal human beings, his neck should be kept ever ready for death.

A little while later, my body quit jerking and quietness fell upon me. I continued to wait for whatever might happen next. Would I meet someone? A spirit, perhaps? God? Suddenly, the convulsions began anew, and I started swearing angrily inside my head. "Damn! How long is this going to take?"

I was aware I could open my eyes at any time. I chose not to. I wasn't quite ready for what I might see. As cold as it was, it seemed altogether possible that God might turn out to be a polar bear. Wouldn't *that* be something? God a polar bear! We go around shooting them, putting them in zoos, and taking photographs of beautiful—never plain or ugly—young women sprawled naked on their skins. If God turned out to be a polar bear, mankind sure as hell missed the spiritual boat. Thank goodness I never harmed one.

I opened my eyes. I found myself lying on the cement, cold and weak, but still very much alive. It took me a good ten minutes to lift myself up off the floor. There was a bad gash on the tip of my right foot, presumably from kicking the bars during my body's involuntary struggle to free itself. I lay down on the iron bunk, questioning the providence that had returned me again to life, as much a failure at dying as I'd been at living.

I could have tried again, but I found the agony and wretchedness disappeared as quickly as frogs along a river bank vanish upon hearing a sudden, unfamiliar sound.

∽

Two days later, after reasoning the FBI would rather deal with me on one bank robbery than with Curtis on four robbery charges, I asked to see Agent Manning. The FBI *knew* that Curtis was the brains and they surely wanted *him* more than they wanted me. When Agent Manning arrived to speak with me, I presented him with two deals to relay to the U.S. Attorney in Reno.

The next day I was moved from Kelso to Tacoma. This time, it was Dolores who rode with me in the back of the U.S. Marshal's transport van. In Tacoma, our bail was set, mine at $1,000,000, double the amount of Curtis's bond. Dolores's bail was set at a quarter million, a tremendous shock to her daughters, who were in the courtroom expecting to take her home. For months, the Portland Bureau had told them *I* was the only one they really wanted. They had driven to Tacoma believing Dolores would be released into Susan's custody.

Susan, who was a parole officer, had been the weakest link in the chain. She had told her father about a card she had received from Dolores while we were on the run. Predictably, Bob passed the information to the FBI, not realizing or caring about the negative consequences this would bring down on his own daughter. The card was not postmarked, and they told her that unless she divulged exactly how it had come into her possession she would never again work as a parole officer.

This in turn led the FBI to Susan's ex-husband, Mark Shannon, who admitted purchasing a Ford Bronco for us while allowing us to use his cabin in exchange for a share of the $50,000 that Agent Rand had offered me for turning in Curtis Ray Michelson. With the reward money no longer a possibility, Mark sold us out for under $2,000 apiece.

As luck would have it, I didn't have to go to Portland to tell Nancy I'd forgiven her. She came to me the day after my bail was set. The brief touch of her lips on my cheek tore off some old scabs from my soul, but I joyfully allowed all my painful feelings to enter through the open sores. Thoughts of loving her stung terribly, but it was a *good* pain.

I told her of having forgiven her. We cried and spoke of many things, seemingly picking up right where we'd left off. I saw her a total of three times while I was awaiting trial. She still had the ability to lift me up from the shallows of my miserable circumstance to heights of all that I could possibly be. I found myself possessed by the same old need to love her. Surely this must be what a long-cured addict feels when confronted out of the blue with the needle. She still wanted us to have those super babies we had planned on having. "Someday," she said, playing the prophetess. "Someday."

Dolores was transferred to Portland two days after the bail hearing. I remained a week while my Tacoma counsel tried to make a deal. The best they would offer me was 20 years on a maximum of 25. For that five-year sentence reduction, I would have to return all remaining monies and testify against the others.

"I don't believe it!" I cried out indignantly. "If they'll give me only five years off one robbery, what do they plan to offer Curtis on four?"

"I am not representing Mr. Michelson, so I have no idea," my attorney replied soberly. Sheepishly, he expressed his opinion that the FBI seemed bent on making *me* the bad guy on this one.

With negotiations having totally failed, I was again loaded into a Marshal's van, this time headed south. I had been ordered transferred to Reno, so I assumed I was being taken there. To my great surprise, I ended up at the Los Angeles County Jail, placed in Maximum Security with Curtis! He feigned shock at seeing me, but the transparency of being taken a thousand miles out of my way was so obvious I could scarcely contain my disgust.

Curtis denied ever having made the statement that was used against me as the basis of my indictment, saying it was actually Ed who was doing all the talking. After all, he added, how could *he*, as the known leader of the gang, ever hope to reach a deal? And besides, he said, he was already working on an escape plot that would include me.

I did not tell him I had already made arrangements for my own escape plan. As soon as I'd arrived in L.A., I'd called Kendrick Williams, who came to see me. He left with a map that would lead him to $30,000—a down payment toward busting me out of jail. I would pay him the balance of the escape fee after I was free.

When I warned Ken to be on the lookout for any traps, he replied confidently, "You forget I've gone through the same training *they've* been through. I've been in this business all my life. I don't make mistakes."

With Ken knowing that Mark Shannon's tip had led to my arrest, he eagerly offered to have him killed, if I wanted it done. The offer was tempting, but I declined.

"Well, if he gets in the way," he said as he studied my map, which also led to Mark Shannon's cabin, "he's going down, whether you like it or not."

"I understand," I conceded weakly. I knew all of Ken's gang members at McNeil had been killers. Killers in prison somehow seemed less real, simply because they seemed altogether appropriate. To hear the taking of a life being discussed so casually by an *attorney*, a man who had spent most of his previous life as an FBI agent, sent a chill running throughout my body.

The price of my freedom would be $150,000, a staggering sum. I asked Ken if he would be willing to include Curtis in the breakout.

"Are you crazy?" he spat out contemptuously. "Break out a *rat*? From the moment he was arrested, he was running his mouth and singing against every one of you all the way to the jailhouse!"

I had tried to strike a deal with the Feds just three days after my arrest, so I was inwardly quite alarmed at hearing Ken's obvious hatred of informants. What if he were to discover *my* own effort to cut a deal?

"Whether you break out one guy or two, what's the difference?" I asked, hiding my own discomfiture. "As long as you get paid, money is money."

"True enough," Ken replied. "But why trouble yourself by helping Curtis?"

Instead of answering Ken's question directly, I told him I liked his plan, which called for two "soldiers" from back East to fly out to L.A. With credentials identifying them as local attorneys, they would take over the attorney room and secure my freedom. Then, after pointing out that the escape fee—$25,000 for each "soldier" and $100,000 for Ken and his boss—was going to leave me flat broke, I explained why I thought it necessary to spring Curtis out of jail.

"I'll be quite honest with you, Ken," I said. "Curtis Michelson *was* the brains of our robbery team, and I want to break him out so I can *use* him to get enough money to leave the country. I promise you I'll not say one word to him about the escape until it's time to go. He'll *never* know your name or who's behind the breakout."

Over the coming days, each time Curtis and I walked together during our exercise period, it became clear to me his spirit was slowly breaking down. I longed to tell him we would soon be free but, as I did not really believe his claim that Ed was the actual informer, I could not risk my one chance at freedom by telling him about the plan. Moreover, Curtis's girlfriend, Marilyn, had never spent a single night in jail, a fact that gave me further reason for suspicion.

Ken soon returned for more money. After two trips to Mark Shannon's cabin, he finally located the stash, but told me he was able to find only $14,000. I must have mixed up some of the jugs.

The "soldiers" had to be paid at least half their fee in advance, and $14,000 was *not* enough. I drew another map to show Ken where I'd left $70,000 in new hundred-dollar bills. He would also find in the same spot another $4,000 in old five-dollar bills, but I told him *only* about the new hundreds, a little test to see whether he would play it straight with me when he returned with the cash. To my relief, he seemed to take pleasure in telling me about the old five-dollar bills that I must have "forgotten." Unlike Curtis, it seemed that Ken *could* be trusted.

The escape was set for Sunday evening, when the attorney room would not be so crowded. On Saturday, I got a visit from Curtis's sister, Diane, who had come to see me at his request.

She was a charming girl and I really enjoyed myself. After our visit was over, and after waiting more than half an hour for an escort to come and take me back to the maximum-security unit, the visiting room officer wearied of watching me sitting there. He took me next door to the attorney room officer and ordered *him* to watch over me as I continued waiting for an escort.

Approximately 20 minutes later two men entered from the street entrance, selecting one of the private glass enclosed interview rooms. I could tell they were FBI agents, but I gave them no more than passing attention. Shortly after they settled into their chairs, Curtis Michelson arrived in the attorney room area. He saw the agents, then noticed me.

"What do *they* want?" he asked me, thus confirming they were Federal agents.

"I don't know. I'm just waiting for my escort back to max."

The taller agent stepped out of the interview room.

"Over here, Curtis!" His tone was completely casual, as if Curtis was an old friend.

Curtis's face flushed with embarrassment, but he didn't move. The agent began walking toward where he was standing, which was right in front of me.

"What do you want?" Curtis snarled at the agent, whose face registered complete surprise. "I don't want to talk to you!"

For my benefit, Curtis made a pretense of being coaxed into the interview room, all the while cursing at the agents. Minutes later, the agents started looking at me. I had not shaved in months, so I looked nothing like my FBI photos. The tall one came over to me.

"Are you Forsberg?" he asked.

I raised my identification wristband for him to read.

"Come with me," he demanded. "I want to talk to you."

"Sorry, pal but you know the rules."

"*What* rules?" he asked.

"Escobedo," I replied, referring to a Supreme Court decision concerning the rules governing the police questioning of detained suspects. "I don't talk to you without an attorney at my side."

"Get in that damn room!" he growled, obviously not at all concerned about any legal niceties.

"I'm not moving," I said quietly. "And if you put your hands on me, I *will* bust your head."

He turned toward the jailer, practically screaming. "Did you hear that?" he said. "Did you? Dammit, *make* him go in that room!"

The jailer's expression remained emotionless and totally unfazed. "He *is* right, you know. He *doesn't* have to speak to you without an attorney present."

"I will get to the bottom of this!" raged the agent as he and his partner left the jail. The next morning, only 12 hours before the escape attempt was to kick off, I was abruptly moved to Reno.

ᔕ

As soon as I arrived in Nevada, I called Ken. He came to see me and suggested an alternative escape plan.

"Like what?" I asked glumly, frustrated I was still behind bars.

"From all I've been able to learn about your case, despite the FBI having kept your file close to their chests the entire time, it appears that they really don't have much of anything against you or Ed. Curtis might well have beaten the rap, too, but he's given so many statements that he's pretty much convicted himself with his own big mouth. As for Gus, all indications are he fled the country, disappeared without a trace."

"So?" I asked again, *still* not having heard anything in the way of a new plan.

"So," he continued, finally getting to his point, "if we eliminate the weak links, you walk free."

"And just how do we go about doing *that*?" I asked.

Ken smiled at my naiveté.

"Everyone can be had," he said. "*Everyone*. I'll just have one of my boys put a bullet through their heads, and the government will have no case. You guys *did* do a perfect robbery. Unfortunately, you also happened to have a weak-assed punk for a leader."

"'*Their*' heads?" I asked.

"Well, sure. Ed has to go, too. That way it will look as if the other gang members silenced *them* because they were really involved, while leaving you untouched. Your 'innocence' gave them no reason to come after you." He smiled at the light that now shined from my eyes.

"That's quite a plan," I said, nodding approvingly.

"All part of my training!" he roared, filling the entire attorney room with his laughter.

Though I certainly liked the plan, I couldn't help but wonder how such an upstanding citizen, a career law-enforcement officer, an attorney, could be so totally evil. Clearly, he was a man who had long ago lost faith in all the inherent values that bind the majority into a civil and coexisting whole. That he apparently lost it while still a cop really fascinated me. I asked him about it.

"Well…" his first word seemed to stretch endlessly as his mind harkened back to a long forgotten and perhaps unpleasant memory. Once his mind hopped and skipped past its temporary discomfort, he plunged right into the story.

"When I was a young man," he began, "I received the usual education about 'Justice' and the 'American Way,' and I *embraced* it, becoming an idealist of the first order. I studied and followed orders. My diligence was rewarded with regular advancement. The higher I went, the more I was exposed to man's inhumanity to man.

"After every election cycle, we'd be sent to sweep the streets clean of whores and addicts and homosexuals. If our sweeps didn't produce enough human refuse, we'd be ordered to branch out to the schools and bust kids for grass.

"I was taught how to build airtight cases against people where none actually existed. We would only do this to those who we 'knew' but couldn't prove were doing wrong.

"The higher I climbed, the more I realized men are not governed by laws, but that laws are governed by self-serving men guided entirely by self-interest. For a long time, I didn't allow any of that to keep me from being a dutiful order following cop.

"One day, I was ordered to cease my investigation and drop my case against a big-time drug dealer. I was shocked, but the order had come from someone even higher up than my own bosses, and there was nothing I could do about it. After that, I woke up and started seeing other examples of institutional hypocrisy. Then I was asked to 'fix' a case of a defendant who was an undercover FBI operative who the FBI did not want to send to prison.

"Turning that animal back out into free society really did something to me. I became what is commonly known as a 'rogue cop.' Not only did I start taking money from some really bad guys, but I actually made more arrests at the same time, not hesitating to jail anyone unwilling or unable to line my pockets. I worked my way up to Captain, attended FBI school, and became one of the 'Fed's people,' which gave me more actual power than my boss.

"More and more, I saw that crime was a business. I submitted false 'Crime Increase Reports' that the FBI needed to justify its requests for greater budgets. The more well connected I became with the 'big boys,' the more money came rolling my way. Then I became 'political,' which is to say I started targeting anyone who the power structure wanted out, and discredited and destroyed them.

"Never once did I look back. It was only natural I would progress into murder, as homicide represents the ultimate rejection of human value."

Frosty started to stir within. No doubt about it, he *liked* what he was hearing.

"Would you believe that the first murder I was ever responsible for was actually ordered by the FBI? They call it an 'over-arrest.' I was told simply that 'the fugitive should be given the chance to resist,' and it was understood by all that the suspect's resistance was to be met with deadly force. There's a lot more of that going on than you perhaps realize."

"Eventually, though, I made a tactical error and was caught in an embarrassing situation. Thanks to a lot of friends in all the right places, I was allowed to retire, and everything was swept under the rug. I went back to school and became a lawyer. The perfect front!"

He continued, but I had pushed Frosty back into his cave and become weary of listening. When he finally finished talking, I okayed the murder of Curtis and Ed, then went back, alone, to the Hole. I felt bad about Ed. I believed he was hanging tough. He was just collateral damage.

The next day, my court appointed attorney from the Reno Public Defender's Office informed me that he knew about Ken's visits. Since another attorney was visiting me, he would have to tell the judge I apparently had the funds to hire my own counsel. I had no choice but to let the public defender go, or else Ken would not have been allowed to remain on my case or to visit me. Before I dismissed the public defender, he did tell me that my plea bargain with Agent Manning which, as a plea bargain, should have been legally considered confidential, was now being considered a confession. With this "confession" *and* Curtis's statement stacked against me, there was no way I could go it alone. I hired an additional lawyer, a man named David Hamilton. He was young but had already made a name for himself as a defense attorney.

Hamilton instilled in me $10,000 worth of hope, which was the amount of the fee he was requesting. He felt certain he could get the plea bargain "confession" thrown out. After that, with Curtis's testimony my only obstacle, we could almost certainly win an acquittal. In the meantime, he believed he could get my bail reduced to $50,000 or less. When Ken came to see me the next day, I instructed him to deliver the $10,000 fee to Hamilton.

"Floyd," he said, shaking his head, "I thought you were smarter than that! That's just the usual attorney line he's giving you. When he sees how easily he gets that $10,000 from you, he'll try to milk you for more. Yes, he'll get your bail reduced. But you're a parolee. They'll *never* let you out the door on bail no matter how low it is. Moreover, here in Nevada, you're up against a powerful club. I know. I've seen them in action. Even if they have to bribe every witness to change his story to nail you, you'll get 25 years. You're wasting $10,000." He shrugged. "What the heck. It's your money. I'd still rather you let me get you out and send you to South America."

"South America?" I asked. The thought of freedom and travel sent an almost orgasmic shudder of excitement through my loins.

"Sure," he said. "If I get you out, I don't simply intend to give you a ride out of town and drop you off in the desert. If you pay us off by doing an added favor, we'll get you all the way to Santiago."

"*What* favor?"

"There's a real special contract that needs to be taken care of, and we don't want to use any of the regulars. Get it done and afterward we'll get you to Chile, and you can work for us there."

"Doing what?" I asked.

"What's the difference?" he replied. "Would you rather be

making license plates in some Federal penitentiary for the next 20-plus years?"

"What's the contract?"

"You'll enjoy it," he replied, a cold smile on his face. "It's a woman."

"Who is she?"

"You'll be given that information when the time comes for you to do the job. The people here in Vegas want her taken out, which means we'll need to get you out of jail *soon*."

I still believed that Hamilton might be able to do me some good, so I insisted that Ken deliver to him the requested fee. I also sent word to Sharon to hand over to him the $5,000 in gold I had entrusted her to keep for Dolores. I had bought the gold coins in New York. I also had $5,000 in new sequential fives, but they were useless to me because I had reason to believe they were trackable.

Despite Agent Manning's testimony that my plea bargain request had been a confidential statement I'd wanted it forwarded to the U.S. Attorney, the court ruled that my attempt at a deal was tantamount to a confession and *could* be used against me. I immediately instructed Hamilton to try for a ten deal, which would include my revealing all I knew of the bank jobs pulled off by Curtis and Ed. When he returned, he advised me that the Feds had no deals to offer me, and that he was also in need of more money.

Ken, meanwhile, went full speed ahead with preparations for an escape attempt, even after I told him I'd had a change of heart about having Curtis and Ed killed. I wasn't quite sure why I had changed my mind. After all, I was not much different than them. Curtis was going to testify against me—and not the other way around—only because the FBI ultimately preferred to deal with *him* instead of me. I still did not know what he'd been promised. I just hoped he wouldn't sell me out cheaply, as in the case of the mere five years off *I* had been offered.

Chapter Twenty-Three

THIS TIME WOULD BE DIFFERENT

April, 1975. Dolores finally succeeded in getting her bond reduced to $50,000 and her ex-husband, Bob, bailed her out. Her freedom presented me with the problem of whether or not she should flee with me. If she didn't, her bond would surely be revoked when I disappeared. If she *did* flee with me, Bob would end up losing the $50,000 tab when Dolores later failed to show up for her court proceedings. I decided she should go with me.

Ken's easy and relatively deep access into the FBI files was making me extremely uncomfortable. If he ever learned I had tried to hatch a deal I'd be finished. Somehow it seemed he had discovered all the pertinent information on me *except* that. The most startling discovery he made about our robbery team was that Curtis had been a professional FBI informant all of his life.

"That's impossible!" I yelled when Ken divulged this to me.

He smiled then continued. "In 1967 or '68, he testified against an attorney with some heavy connections."

"But he never got any parole consideration or anything!" I said, recalling his McNeil experience.

"Perhaps not, but by then he had already robbed more banks than you can count, and they dropped *all* the charges except one. I wouldn't touch him with a ten-foot pole. He's the type of guy that the FBI will allow to get away with *everything* because they know he'll give up anything or any person they ask for whenever they want it. They *like* this type. Crooks like Curtis *know* the FBI will always be ready with a deal, so they involve more and more people in their misdeeds, even people who otherwise would never have committed a crime in the first place. The authorities end up getting more convictions and better crime statistics. Simple."

His parting advice was to remember "you can't beat them in the courts." Then, just before he got up to leave, he gifted me with 75 hits of mescaline.

ᔓ

The plan called for us to cut our way into the ventilation system and escape from the roof. The first vent was in the ceiling, 12 feet above the first tier. A huge black man would lift Spider and Danny above his head, actually "bench pressing" them up to the vent. Once the welds were cut, the vent would be held in place by strips of towel during the 20 hours each day we were otherwise locked up in our cells.

The trip through the ventilation shafts took longer and longer as the escape route neared the roof. Our work time was severely limited. All we had were two two-hour exercise periods and the time allotted to us for showering. Of the four and half hours we were not locked up, only one hour was spent in actual work. Still, minutes at a time, we inched our way to freedom.

A stupid mistake nearly brought disaster. Once, we had forgotten that the afternoon pill cart had not yet arrived, and we were already working. Spider was already up inside the vents when the nurse arrived with his pill. To our horror, the guard called out for him to come get it.

"He's asleep," I lied, trying to sound casual.

"Wake him up!" he demanded.

I walked down to his cell, number eight, and called to the phantom prisoner.

"Hey, Spider! Spider! Wake up, man!"

I then mumbled a reply, trying to sound as black and as tired as I could.

"Because your pill is here, that's why!" I yelled, continuing the charade.

I emitted a second mumble, then turned to holler to the deputy.

"He says he doesn't want it," I yelled, muttering a desperate prayer beneath my breath, hoping the turnkey didn't come down to Spider's cell. To my immense relief, the guard shrugged his shoulders and walked away.

Finally, after a few more days of work, only the air conditioner stood between us and freedom. We had cut through the first vent, removed the crossbars behind it, and passed through the first air shaft into a crawl space used by the maintenance crew. From there, we entered the main air shaft that led to the roof. I went to the roof once, just to make sure I could fit through the opening. The air conditioner was fastened in place from the outside. A big problem. That's where Ken came in.

"Just as soon as you're ready on the inside," he said, "I'll send Harris to take care of the air conditioner for you."

I knew Harris, but had never liked him. His full name was Rudy Valentino Harris, and we'd done time together at McNeil, where he often bragged on and on about a cop who he had killed during a drug bust. I knew he'd been in Ken's gang as a freelancer for many years.

"Why Harris?" I asked.

"Why *not* Harris?" Ken replied. "He needs the money and, just like you, he needs to get out of the country. He's jumped a couple of bonds and is wanted on several drug cases and an attempted murder. I'm presently working on getting fake papers for all four of you."

"What do you mean, 'all four of you'?"

"Well, there's you and Dolores, and then there's Rudy and *his* woman. He even has a bank picked out for you to rob. It's all set up."

Ken went on to explain there was no practical way off the third story roof of the jail. We would instead have to climb up the side of the adjoining six story courthouse building. Once on top of the courthouse, we would be even with the roof of the Riverside Casino and Hotel next door, where Rudy would be waiting with an extension ladder, three pairs of coveralls, a gun, and some ammunition.

"Oh, and one other thing," he said. "Don't be surprised if you see a blonde girl watching you while you're on the roof. Harris has one of his girls driving for him. His current picture I.D. is hot now, and he won't have another usable one for several days, so he *cannot* be behind the wheel."

"He's got *his woman* with him?" I asked incredulously.

"No, she's just a drug runner," he replied. "Don't worry, she's okay. She's made more than a few runs for us to Mexico."

It all sounded so easy. An escape from a maximum-security lockup, from a jail without any windows and surrounded by towering hotels all looking down onto the roof.

When I wondered aloud whether we might be seen by the surrounding hotel guests, he chortled, "Don't worry about *that! No one* looks out of their hotel windows in Reno. They're either gambling or sleeping. If they're awake, they're certainly not interested in the view!"

"Okay," I said, excited that my freedom seemed so near. "I guess this is it. Let's do it!" I shook his hand and returned to my cell. He had instructed me to compose two letters, one to Hamilton and one to him, apologizing for the escape. I spent the evening doing that, then tossed and turned the rest of the night, unable to sleep. I would be burning the last bridge. If I didn't go through with it, I wouldn't get out of prison until I was 48 years old—or older. Kendrick Williams was opening a door for me that I'd thought forever closed. The noose had fallen away. I was alive. Tomorrow, I would be free.

The air conditioner weighed a good 500 pounds. At my peak, I could quarter squat a thousand, but that was when I was at McNeil—and much of my muscle mass had long since withered away. Outside, one does not have time to lift weights three hours a day, or to fantasize about stunning criminal victories. When one was out, the real world pressed you down, just as the air conditioner was pressing down on me right now.

Years before, half a dozen inmates had escaped through the same main shaft from the regular part of the jail. Afterwards, huge iron bars had been installed to prevent the same thing from happening again. I smiled inwardly at the realization that, had the FBI not placed me in the Hole, the opportunity I had now to make an escape would never have presented itself. Fortuitously, the bars were approximately five feet below the air conditioner, a perfect distance for me to stand and raise my upper body to lift the unit's massive weight. A blanket on my shoulders helped ease the pain caused by the metal digging into my body. As I slowly straightened my legs, our last hindrance began to rise.

There was an eerie silence to the entire scene. The steady pulsating hum of the fan was still for the first time in two months. By standing upright, I'd lifted the air conditioner to create an opening of a little more than a foot, just enough space for Danny to crawl through.

What if, once on the roof, he panicked and ran, leaving me behind? Already, Spider had decided at the last minute that he would not go, a decision that left me feeling vulnerable and ill at ease. He had done more work than *any* of us! I half expected the FBI to start blasting away at us at any second. My 9mm

Browning and single box of ammo would be worthless in an ambush.

Such anxious thoughts broke my concentration, causing me to relax just enough to let the weight of the unit to push me down a few inches. Danny, only halfway free, cried out as his stomach was squeezed beneath the weight that had shifted onto him. I took a deep breath and straightened up again, and he pulled himself through with lizard-like agility and speed. Quickly, he stood up on the roof and struggled to topple the air conditioner as I continued lifting from the inside. Suddenly, the weight shifted and it tilted, falling into the shaft itself, allowing me to climb out.

"Somebody's watching us!" Danny whispered.

I turned and saw Rudy standing in a room on the sixth floor, looking down on us, smiling and taking pictures.

"You're late!" he hollered.

He was right. We were running 30 minutes behind schedule, our plans thrown into confusion by Spider's last-minute decision to stay put. I'd suspected a hint of treachery, but was relieved to find Rudy waiting. Besides, we were too far along into the plan to back out now. The panic alarms—installed for the benefit of weaker inmates against the advances of the stronger, predatory types—had already been disconnected, leaving just the air conditioner. Not knowing precisely which wire had to be cut, we simply built a small fire under all of them. The air conditioner belched and sighed and groaned to a stop. If anything else was rendered inoperable by the melting of the wires, I did not know, but I could still hear the Saturday morning cartoon show drifting up from the main jail. I'd locked a new man in his cell and had done the same with a mental case whose behavior was unpredictable. That left Spider and two others who could sound a verbal alarm, but Spider had assured me he would control things until the 11:00AM lockup. However, if Spider decided at the last minute to betray us, who could stop him?

As had so often been the case in my life, I was once again at a point of no return, with only a narrow path forward, like a tightrope suspended above my fears. As we swung the extension ladder into place, I realized it was probably a good thing that fear had become such a drug to me, something my body had learned to need and thrive on.

"Here, you hold this end, and I'll go first," I said to Danny, remembering it could well have been Curtis Michelson holding the ladder for me. He, too, had been transferred to Reno, but we had avoided each other since our arrival. His treachery had at last caused him to turn inward against himself. He had slashed his wrists, totally broken. His world was now bare, while mine was filled with visions of criminal glory.

The tension was all consuming now as we raced across the hotel roof to the fire escape and descended onto the carpeted sixth floor from the trap door that lay open for us. We were met with a questioning stare from a hotel maid, but then Rudy appeared to rescue us.

"Over here, Frosty!"

A big mirror on the wall explained the maid's curiosity. Danny and I were not only still in prison garb, we were completely covered with black soot! While Danny and I washed up, Rudy went to retrieve the coveralls we had failed to pick up on the roof. There was a complete set of clothes for me to change into. Danny, on the other hand, slipped a pair of coveralls over his prison clothes. I gave him $200. Rudy gave him another $50 and the leather jacket he was wearing. Then we were off.

"We'll use the stairway," Rudy announced, leading us from the room. I glanced down to the jailhouse roof. The air conditioner was still resting in its own hole, with no living soul there to see the damage. So far, so good.

As we made our way down the narrow stairwell, my heart pounded inside my chest, though less from the adventure of the moment than from the general loss of conditioning my body had experienced after six months in the Hole. We raced down the stairwell until we ran out of stairs and discovered we'd gone too far, ending up in the basement boiler room. We turned and backtracked a single flight of stairs, but found we were *still* underground. We didn't know it, but we had descended eight floors from the sixth.

"Didn't you case this place *beforehand*?" I asked, my voice a frustrated snarl.

Rudy didn't answer. We raced upward again. At last, we opened a door into a hallway with room numbers that began with "2." We were on the second floor. We walked briskly down the hall. Maids and cleaning people seemed to sense our panic. There was something out of place about us. Leaving them to wonder, we found another stairwell, which led us to the ground floor and out onto the street.

"Good luck!" I said to Danny as he left Rudy and me and started for the bridge across the Truckee River, bound for Sacramento. All of his after-escape plans had involved teaming up with Spider, and now he was entirely on his own. Since it had never been our intention to include him in the bank robbery Rudy already had lined up, Danny would have to go it alone.

A Mercedes pulled up silently beside us on the street. Rudy slipped in front. I climbed into the backseat area and lay down, out of sight as we drove by Second and Virginia Streets, right past the "bank that couldn't be robbed." Now, seven months after proving that it *could*, most of my share of the loot it coughed up was gone—spent on this exercise to win my freedom. Curtis Michelson, on the other hand, remained in the Hole, betraying everyone as he had done all of life. Ed, too, was in jail, as much a victim of Curtis as I was. And Gus was believed to be somewhere in Mexico. I had begun to wonder whether Gus had even participated in the robbery at all.

Chapter Twenty-Four

WHAT DOES ONE THINK ABOUT ON THE WAY TO A MURDER?

With Reno fading fast behind us, I began to relax. The remaining concern for me was the California border inspection station. Spider had done his job well and we weren't stopped. After that I finally took the time to notice Denise Caitlin, the long-haired blonde who was driving. She had both the freshness of youth and the temper of experience. She drove well and smiled in a friendly fashion when I cautioned her to keep it under the speed limit.

Rudy and I began to talk about the people we knew. He was surprised Curtis had given up the War and turned in all of his loot.

"Hell!" he exclaimed. "For that kind of money, I'd even bust a rat out of jail!"

As we left Highway 80 and started heading south on secondary roads, the car began misfiring. Finally, at around 2:30PM, it gave out completely on a long, steep upward grade. While Rudy worked on the Mercedes, I hid in the brush about 50 yards from the road, beneath a scraggly tree, gun in hand. No hick sheriff would ever again hold me and wait for a Federal agent to arrive on the scene to take credit for my arrest. This time, there were no promises about not carrying a gun. I didn't like Rudy, but it was clear he took great pride in being a criminal. He was no paper tiger like Curtis. Certainly, this time would be different.

Within an hour, we were back on the road and on our way again. Later, we found a pay phone in front of a small country store. From there, I called Dolores at the Flamingo Motel in Portland where she was hiding. Williams had said the FBI would have Dolores's bond revoked the minute my escape became known so he had told her to disappear the day before the breakout. Her voice was full of dread and misgiving, lacking its usual warmth. My reaction was one of anger. I slammed the receiver down hard, sending a reverberating crash into her ear.

We arrived in Merced, California late in the afternoon, rented a motel room where I gave myself a much-needed shave, then went to another motel. We decided I would stay at this second motel with Denise, while Rudy drove on to Portland to collect Dolores.

Denise had the kind of closed mouth demeanor that came either from being a veteran in the drug business or from having too many emotional scars. In her case, I suspected that both were the case. As she dyed my hair blond over the bathroom sink, I tried unsuccessfully to get her to talk. Before she could say anything more, the TV in the next room announced the news about the escape. Danny had been caught within hours.

Denise stared giggling, although not over the news of the escape. Her finger was pointing at the mirror over the sink. Looking at my reflection, I saw that, instead of blond, my hair had turned an awful turnip red color that I had never before seen on anything but a Kewpie Doll. Denise and I were still laughing when Dolores arrived. When Delores saw my hair, she really howled. My anger toward her over the phone when we'd last spoken disappeared, and I realized just how much I loved her. We had our own roots now, intertwined and embedded in the earth of our own making, far removed from any part of Nancy or anyone else I had ever known.

Rudy had called upon Paul Jackson to help him with the driving when he went north to get Dolores. Paul was another member of the gang, but wasn't yet high enough in the organization to work directly for Ken, so he worked for Rudy. On the morning after Dolores arrived, Rudy, Denise, Dolores, and I all left Merced for Santa Cruz, then to a mountain resort on Boulder Creek where Paul had a secluded cabin. Dolores and I decided we wanted a little privacy, so we rented a cabin a few miles away, at Timberline Lodge.

A week after the escape, as Dolores and I were relaxing at our rented cabin, I got stoned and loose lipped enough to tell her the FBI knew a lot about the Kendrick Williams organization, all because of the information Curtis had provided them in his attempt to arrange a deal.

"Floyd!" she cried out in horror. "Do you realize the position we're in?"

"Yeah, like a couple of cats locked inside a dog kennel. Which means, somewhere along the line, we've got to get away from them." With that, I began to spell out my idea. I didn't get very far.

A few moments later, Denise burst into the room without knocking, a panicked wild-eyed expression on her face.

"Come on!" she yelled. "The FBI's everywhere! There's no time to grab anything!"

Instantly, the euphoria induced by the grass was gone, and we were speeding away in the car that Denise had waiting. The FBI had descended on Paul's cabin in force. Rudy had escaped; all the others at the cabin had been caught. Denise had been questioned, but since they had nothing on her was released. She had risked plenty by coming to our cabin to warn us and spirit us away.

She drove us into Santa Cruz, where Jackie, another of Rudy's girls, had a room waiting. Not long after, a third girl named Kelly came and tried to persuade Denise to leave with her. Kelly had been through the same romantic routine with

Rudy that Denise was presently experiencing. She was determined to help spare her friend the same heartbreak and grief she had suffered as "Rudy's girl."

"Don't you realize he's just using you, Denise? Everyone knows that *Bobette* is his woman right now. He doesn't really care about you, no matter what he says otherwise."

Fatefully, Denise refused to take Kelly's warning seriously and decided to stay. Kelly bade her friend a heartfelt farewell and turned to leave.

"Please be careful," she said, offering Denise one last warning. "You don't know him like I do."

Two days later, we were still waiting for Rudy to arrive. I was uneasy knowing that there were several people in town who were aware of our exact location. I sent Dolores and Denise out to find a used car to carry us to where the last of my money was still buried. We were just about to leave when, out of the blue, Rudy showed up with a pickup and camper. Dolores and I went with Rudy. Denise followed behind in Jackie's car. As we drove north to Mendocino, Rudy filled us in on what he had learned in the days since the raid on Paul's cabin.

The FBI was aware that Rudy had helped me break out of the Reno jail, and they also somehow learned he was staying at Paul's cabin. They had assumed, incorrectly, that Dolores and I would also be there when they conducted their raid. All of this heat had to be coming from Seattle, Rudy reasoned. The order had come down we were to kill Harry, a member of the Williams organization in charge of the Seattle end of the business, who was presumed to be the person doing all the talking. It was also believed Denise would talk if she was pressured by the Feds. The word came down we were to kill her too before she fell into the hands of the authorities.

Rudy's attitude toward the "weak links" was equal in contempt to Ken's. I wondered how long after the pending bank robbery he would wait before trying to eliminate Dolores and me. Almost certainly the idea of being able to keep the robbery money for himself would be enough of a reason to see us dead.

We drove all day before finally reaching Portland. We set the women up in a motel across the river in Vancouver and headed off to the canyon where the money was hidden. After recovering the last two containers, we returned to the motel to clean up and count the cash. Incredibly, there was only $45,000 remaining in the last two jugs! I had figured on there being no less than $65,000, perhaps even more. Since Ken had found only $14,000 where I'd been certain there would be $10,000 to $20,000 *more,* I had assumed the difference would eventually materialize in the last of my stash. How wrong I was. I simply couldn't believe I was so broke. I still owed Rudy $20,000 for breaking me out of jail, plus an additional $10,000 for his expenses. And, according to Ken's figures, I still owed *him* $42,000.

Convinced I must have missed something, we drove back to the canyon to look again, but there was no more money to be found. So bleak was my financial picture that there was no way I could proceed with my intention to sit idle and wait six months before robbing again. The conversation now turned to my waiting just a single month before hitting a bank. We would strike fast and leave the country immediately afterwards. Rudy was wanted for at least six felonies *he* was aware of. Neither of us had much hope of living our lives in peace—even if we were capable—if we remained in the United States and in the crosshairs of the FBI.

We rented a cabin just north of Fort Bragg. Denise, Dolores, and I would remain there during the month leading up to our planned robbery, while Rudy would return to Southern California to rent a house near the targeted bank.

Our days at the cabin were pleasant. Being with Dolores made my thoughts of Nancy less idealized and more objective for the first time. For too long, I had felt the need to invent reasons—or excuses, if you will—for loving Dolores, as if she'd never been worthy of a freely given love that was *real.* Now I had come to the painful recognition that it was *Nancy* who'd never been real. Like the sculptor of the myth, Pygmalion, I had simply fallen in love with my own creation. *Anyone* who might have come knocking on my door that night would have fallen victim to my chisel, my need to love. Then Dolores had leapt blindly into the fire and had all but been consumed. She believed that somewhere inside of me was a worthwhile human being. She had extended her patience along with her faith. That she had become a casualty in my losing the War with myself and against the FBI was sad, but she didn't sit around counting her miseries. Instead, the here and now of what we had together was more than enough for her. I would forever curse my birth, but I would *never* regret having loved Dolores.

Delores and I tried to pretend that the threat against Denise was nothing more than a nightmare that would soon pass. Because Rudy was late, having been gone 14 days, it made Denise's appointed fate less real.

As Denise's final days ticked by, my mind was preparing the antidote for the poisoning of my soul that would surely come with her death. I told myself that when she was killed it would be because of the madness of *others*, not my own. Whenever I looked at her, I was stricken by a terrible urgency to tell her that Rudy did *not* love her, that he in fact intended to sacrifice her very existence upon his self-serving altar of expediency. When my conscience nagged at me, pointing an accusing finger of guilt for maintaining my silence at Denise's expense, I simply lied to myself, wanting to believe her destruction would never really come to pass.

With Rudy so late in returning, my passive silence took a big step closer toward active responsibility. We had run out of food —Rudy had left us with just enough for two weeks—and Denise had begun hitchhiking to town to buy whatever groceries she could carry in her backpack. During each trip to the market she called people in Rudy's narcotics ring, trying to find out what was happening and when he would be back. During one of those calls, she was told he had been seen arm in arm with another blonde. Denise guessed this was probably Bobette. That was enough for Denise, and she decided it was time for her to go.

Rudy had left orders that Denise should not be allowed to leave. Not wanting to hold her captive against her will until he returned, I lied to her, assuring her she was Rudy's "number one woman," adding that if she really loved him, she would trust him and wait for him, give him a chance to explain. I said to her that I'd bet anything the blonde in Rudy's company was simply another of his many drug runners.

After several hours of persuasion on my part, Denise decided to give Rudy the benefit of the doubt and stay until he returned. Two days later she was sexually violated in the back of a pickup truck as she hitched a ride back to the cabin from one of her shopping trips. When she staggered into the cabin and collapsed onto the floor in a sobbing heap, she never seemed more human. My heart broke for her. I knew then I *had* to talk Rudy out of sending her to Mexico to be killed. After the attack, Denise spoke of nothing else but of how she could hardly wait for Rudy's return so that he could track down the pervert who had violated her body. She knew of Rudy's reputation and was certain he would avenge her. In the meantime, she agreed with my suggestion that Dolores should accompany her on any further trips she made into town.

At last Rudy returned. As he and I walked along the beach, I couldn't help but notice that all of the surrounding coastal beauty seemed cold and indifferent to his presence. During similar walks with Dolores, the beach had always exuded a certain welcoming warmth. Now, with Rudy around, the cove that had provided so many wonderful memories over the past month seemed dark and gloomy, no matter that it was actually bright and sunny outside.

I quickly got to the point, offering to let Denise have

$10,000 of my money from the upcoming robbery as hush money if he would let her go with a warning that she never show her face again.

"It's not that easy anymore," Rudy replied. "Her fate is not up to you or me. The Boss wants her taken out."

"Why?" I asked.

"Someone is talking, and the Boss is convinced she's the one."

"Someone's talking?" I asked nervously.

"Yeah," Rudy replied, his voice edged with contempt. "Two days after the escape, the Feds were at Hannibal's house in Florida. How could they have known who handled the Florida operation unless we had a snitch in the group?"

A cold shiver ran up my spine. *I* had been the one who'd told FBI Agent Thomas about Hannibal. I just hoped my eyes didn't give me away as I beat down the dread and panic swirling inside my heart.

"Also," said Rudy, "They showed up at Paul's house and nearly busted me. Who else could have let on that he and I were there?"

That really puzzled me. Figuring Paul was too small time to offer up to the FBI, I'd never mentioned his name. Maybe it wasn't my information the FBI was using.

"That's why I'm sending her to Mexico. They'll take care of her down there," he concluded nonchalantly. "Oh, by the way, we'll also have to get rid of Jackson."

"Jackson?" I exclaimed. "Why *him*? He won't talk!"

"He messed up. Ken and I used his place as a message relay point during the days leading up to your escape. The damn fool left a written message right there on a pad by the phone! Ken's contacts informed him that the FBI found the message when they searched Jackson's place, so Ken wants him eliminated."

"But, but—"

"Forget the 'buts,'" he hissed, cutting me off. "When you are in with us, there's only one rule that matters: Protect the old man. Above all else, we keep Ken safe."

The bank they wanted me to rob was in Riverside, California, so we made our way south to our new hideaway. It had been obtained for us by Ken's number one enforcer, a thug named George, the most feared man in the whole family. About a week later, he came pounding on my door at one in the morning. Just to be safe, I slipped a gun into the pocket of my bathrobe before responding to his knock.

Apparently, the Reno FBI had coerced Spider into telling them *I* had told him Ken had arranged the escape. I had done no such thing. Ken understood how such things went with the FBI; Spider's motives for lying were easily explained by the fact that the Feds were squashing his two parole violations. Between Spider's damning statement *and* the message Paul Jackson failed to destroy before the FBI searched his home, Ken was in a difficult position and definitely on the defensive. This explains why Ken's goon woke me at one o'clock in the morning.

With the whole house having been awakened by George, I opened the door and let him inside. Leaving Dolores and Denise in the living room, he ordered Rudy and me to follow him into the bedroom, then closed the door.

"You all have to clear out of this place *today*," he growled.

"But we've only been here a week and I haven't even begun to get ready for the Riverside job," I protested.

"Forget the Riverside bank!" he replied. "Move on to those two other banks you've lined up in Oregon. You've got to go to Seattle, anyway."

"Why Seattle?" asked Rudy.

"Because the Feds are bothering people they shouldn't be bothering," he replied. "This means there's people up there who are talking and who need to be eliminated. The order is for you two to go up there and tie up loose ends."

"How many?" Rudy asked, sounding as if were just another day at the office.

"You've got five hits to take care of, including the two broads out there," he said, motioning toward the living room.

I spoke without thinking. "That's my *wife* you're talking about not some damn drug runner!"

"Look, pal, that's just the way it goes." George said, his glare as menacing as his tone. "Someone is talking and the Boss is scared. You know they've got a new immunity law that precludes their taking the Fifth, so they've got to die. It looks like I'll have to eliminate my girl, Joanne, too because she's a link to the house. If I can kill my woman, you can do the same.

"And for your information," he continued, pointing his finger at me, "we talked about killing you, too. You owe us, and you are quickly becoming a liability. Don't push your luck!"

Rudy suggested George could take Denise with him and send her off to Mexico. He declined. When the three of us went outside, George instructed me on how to send him Ken's money after I pulled off the Oregon robberies, then he spoke privately in low tones to Rudy out by the road. Five minutes later, a car approached, blinking its lights twice, and he was gone.

Later, as I lay in bed wondering how to get us out of the quicksand swallowing us up, Dolores spoke, her words splitting the darkness with a simple intensity that seemed to light up the room.

"What are you going to do about me, Floyd?"

I feigned ignorance.

"I was listening at the door," she said. "I heard George's order to kill us."

She was asking whether I intended to kill her just as simply as she might ask what I wanted for breakfast. I pulled her into my arms and kissed her.

"I decided long before George's edict that I could never do that to you," I said. "Nothing has changed. You're not worried, are you?"

"No," she replied.

"Why not?" I asked.

She smiled softly. "I gave myself to you a long time ago, Floyd. I know you love me, and whatever you wish to do, I accept. Even if that means you taking my life. If you do find it necessary to kill me, please remember how important it is to the next incarnation that the last seven minutes of my life be happy for me. No fear, no pain, no regrets. You won't forget that, will you?"

I held Dolores in my arms the rest of the night, thinking of all the happiness I'd not been able to buy with all the money I'd taken. The only thing that the money had brought me was misery.

I talked to Rudy the next morning and persuaded him to let Dolores live until after the bank robberies. He kidded me about not being able to live without a woman, and I let him think that a convenient lay was my sole reason for wanting to delay her elimination. He didn't seem to comprehend or suspect I'd kill *him* before I'd ever hurt Dolores. He suggested waiting until our arrival in Oregon before killing Denise as well.

"Why?" I laughed, trying to mirror his own cold-blooded callousness. "Because you can't live without a soft, willing female beside you every night either?"

"Nah," he replied dismissively. "It's just the percentages. Oregon doesn't have a death penalty and you never know what might happen. Better to kill her there, where we won't fry if something goes wrong."

☙

June 27, 1975. What does one think about on the way to a murder? Rudy was driving, with Denise unaware she had but minutes left to live. For two whole days—while Rudy and I were casing the bank manager's home and while we set about to dig a grave to bury Denise's body—he and I had argued back and forth over just who would actually do the hands on killing. We were both furious that George hadn't agreed to take Denise with him to Mexico, that he burdened us with her extermination at a time when we were trying to focus on planning a bank job. Once again, I suggested providing Denise money from my share, which she could use to simply disappear, after which we could claim to Ken our assignment to kill her had been carried out.

"And what would happen if she later showed up, revealing to Ken we had lied to him?" Rudy asked. "With you and me down in Chile, you know what he'd do. He'd just send word down there and have us both knocked off, no questions asked!"

Rudy was right. With Ken now wanting her dead, there was no simple or foolproof way of getting around his order to kill Denise. I could also understand Rudy's insistence that I should have a direct hand in her murder. Both he and Ken needed the assurance of knowing I was too involved in her death to ever become an informant against them.

Rudy even appealed to the basest desire of my youth, to rape and kill a woman. He spoke of the thrill he had more than once derived from seeing a hapless victim crying and begging to live.

"Especially when it's a woman," he laughed, clearly enjoying his sadistic memories. "Even the most modest and timid female will plead and beg, offering to do anything in exchange for her life."

Denise was not the total stranger who I'd long ago fantasized pulling into the shadows to vent my rage. She was not some stray goat for the Tiger. She was a known quantity, a human being I considered a friend. Lest Rudy decided to brutalize or rape her in her final moments, it was to spare Denise the humiliating plunder of her soul that I agreed to be the instrument of her demise. I figured I owed it to her to be the one, if only because I would be sure to take her out cleanly.

There were only four roads leading out of Bend, all of which could be easily sealed off by the Highway Patrol. We had purchased some camping gear, planning to spend several days in the woods, exiting at the small town of Sisters in time to lose ourselves in the Fourth of July weekend traffic.

Among the camping items we'd purchased were another pack and a length of rope—the latter of which Rudy used to show me how to strangle a person most expeditiously. Then we returned to the motel and picked up Denise.

Driving out to the gravesite, I sat in the back, behind Denise. Somewhere between the highway and the spot where Rudy and I had dug the grave—which was several miles off the paved road—I would loop the rope around Denise's neck and strangle her, using my strength and the back of the driver's seat for leverage. I had wanted to use a gun, but neither of us wanted to get rid of our weapon after killing her. So, we had decided in favor of strangulation.

As we bounced along the dirt road, my mind replayed over and over my persistent fantasy of being a warrior, the all-American penal cowboy outracing the posse. In prison, there was nothing else to cling to, nothing else I could claim any identity in. Now the warrior and self-imagined outlaw cowboy simply could not muster up the wherewithal to lift the rope from his lap.

The hole in which we planned to bury Denise was 50 yards off an unpaved fire road. Rudy pulled off the dusty trail, his anger building over my not having acted. He got out, slammed the door, and went to sit on a fallen tree. Sensing his anger, Denise turned to me, giving me a questioning look. She couldn't see the rope, which I'd already tucked between my legs.

"Doesn't he trust me to handle this?" she asked. She had no idea that she'd been brought here to die. Instead, Rudy had told her this was the spot where she and Dolores were to wait and pick us up after the robbery.

"He's just got a lot on his mind," I replied.

Rudy returned to the car and we all drove back to the motel. When we got there, he took me for a stroll in the park next door, all the while calling me a coward, a charge that required me to explain a personal part of me that I resented sharing with a brutish piece of human scum like him: my belief that it was critically important for a soul to die happy, to experience no last minute panic or pain. Had she been strangled, Denise would have *known* that she was being murdered, and thus would have known the absolute terror of impending death. A rope was simply not quick enough. I could *not* have her knowing she was a victim of deliberate murder during her final conscious moments on earth.

"I'll *do* it," I said, "but you'll *have* to let me use my gun."

"Man, you prison intellectuals make me sick to my stomach!" he said, adding that he thought I was crazy and my Eastern religion was nothing but a crock full of fecal matter.

"The only real religion," he continued, "is to always figure out the odds and get away with whatever you can. It's eat or be eaten. That's the only way to survive. Denise is a threat, so she has to die! It's as simple as that. You get one more chance. Don't blow it!"

∽

June 28, 1975. This time we all rode in front. Denise was driving. Rudy sat in the middle. The backseat was folded down to accommodate the trail bike we had purchased earlier. Rudy's calm shamed my nervousness, but he was at least fulfilling his part of the agreement that we had reached before setting out to end Denise's life.

At first, he scorned my request that, on this last trip, he should buoy Denise's spirits by telling her how much she meant to him and of how happy the two of them would be as they shared their lives together in Chile. Now, as we neared our turnoff, he was clearly getting a big kick out of the charade, knowing he would never have to deliver on any of the vows of happiness he was pouring out to Denise. I hoped that my consideration for her last moments would somehow balance the bad karma that would arise from this most profane act. Would she someday thank me for arranging such a clean death? For allowing her soul such an unobstructed passage to the other side?

Admittedly, my motives at this point were not entirely altruistic. There was something almost sexual about murder, a powerful swelling of sorts, a growing feeling of strength. I knew now with astonishing clarity that murder, like suicide, had *always* been inside of me.

I glanced over at Denise. She was really loaded and seemed altogether giddy over the rare display of affection being lavished upon her by Rudy. I searched inside for Frosty, but he was not there. He had never failed me before, though he sometimes liked to tease me by hiding, only to reappear at the last minute to help me accomplish my less than savory acts. Surely, they were no more than that. Amoral. Neither black nor white.

Yet I still felt some conflict, a moral uncertainty. Rudy had assured me that he had felt the same moral conflict before his first killing.

We left the highway. For Denise, only a couple of miles of life remained. I was just a couple of miles before my first murder, the next milestone in my criminal career. Mr. Tennison had been right. He had told me that, under the right circumstances, I would kill. I had thought he'd meant in a shootout with the FBI or some unfortunate bank guard. It never occurred to me he meant this.

I had already told Rudy that if Denise suddenly discovered our real intentions, I would not go through with it—*he* would have to kill her. He laughed but agreed. My plan was to casually position myself behind her and then shoot her through the head. Such would be a high form of death, a Zen death. Alive and happy one moment and dead the next. No pain. No desperate clinging to life as death claimed the soul. It was the way *I* had always hoped to go.

Denise pulled off the road. She had needed just two reminders from Rudy to find her way back to the spot we'd visited the day before. I began to envy her. In a few moments, without any pain, in one unmeasurable instant, a mere pinpoint of time, she would be gone. Her essence, in a flash, would be gone. No more illusions. Only her body would remain.

As Rudy and Denise sat there talking, I pulled the gun out of my jacket pocket, slipped the safety off, and got out of the car. I wondered what his last whispers to her might be. Was he assuring her yet again of the nights they would spend making love on a Chilean beach? I hoped he wasn't spoiling the happiness that his previous words, false though they were, had created during the long drive into the woods.

The 8-track was playing some romantic music. That was good; she liked that kind of music. Now that I realized this was it, that there was nothing left for me to do but kill her, I became impatient as they continued chatting inside the car.

I looked out at our surroundings, forcing myself to think, telling myself we had picked a perfect place to kill someone. Only the rocks and trees would hear any noise made by my gun. If by chance the echo of my discharging weapon fell on distant ears, it would be upon the ears of hunters who themselves were out blowing away squirrels or chipmunks for their evening stew. To them, my gun's report would be the most perfectly natural sound to hear this deep in the woods.

Something broke my wandering thoughts. I glanced through the back window and saw Rudy was still sitting inside, half behind the wheel, facing out the driver's side door. Denise was no longer beside him. I had not heard her get out of the car. Where was she?

I spun around quickly, holding my Browning at my side, and found she was standing only six feet away, facing in the other direction. Her long blonde hair seemed to shimmer softly in the muted sunlight, an effect I found altogether mesmerizing. I glanced at Rudy, who was now standing by the open door. He smiled and nodded approvingly, his signal to get on with the deed. I hesitated, standing there with my insides swirling in philosophical revolt.

My whole life, I had been a time bomb waiting to explode. Unrelenting thoughts of murder and mayhem had kept me afloat in the cesspools of prison. Now that the moment had arrived, why was I waiting?

I glanced again in Rudy's direction, and he motioned for me to go ahead. Right at that moment, Denise began to turn toward me, and I realized she was about to see the gun I was holding at my side. I'd just started to jerk and hide my weapon behind my back when *BOOM!* The blast of Rudy's gun reverberated through my soul.

For a fleeting second, I thought he'd missed, that the noise had merely frightened Denise, for her body seemed to stand tall and motionless for an imperceptible period of time, as if she'd been untouched by the projectile that had hurtled out the barrel of Rudy's handgun. That standstill effect was just an illusion. In the next millisecond, her head started to spin away, even as her body began to crumple beneath her.

"Tragedy" is the term we usually apply to an event after carefully processing it through our own sense of madness, after rejecting all other terms in favor of that label. If a defining term had been forthcoming as I watched Denise totter and then hit the ground like a felled tree, "instantaneous tragedy" would have been more appropriate. As it turned out, there was no need for labeling. It was over. Denise was dead.

I'd half expected her to writhe about involuntarily after hitting the ground, as so often depicted in movies. But even as she was falling her eyes had been dull and empty, devoid of all life. She fell gracefully, as if in slow motion. Only when she hit the ground was there an ugly thump as her lungs released their last store of air.

"Now that wasn't so fuckin' bad, was it?" Rudy sneered. "Man, my grandma has more guts than you! How you ever robbed that Reno bank, I'll never understand!"

To see her lying there, lifeless, was to be reminded of my failure to stand for right. Even though I'd not personally pulled the trigger, I was still deeply ashamed of the thoughts I'd embraced to fuel my cold-blooded intent to strike her down. A moment before, she had been alive, a creature full of energy and vitality, and in love. Now, she was entirely devoid of any suppleness or movement, capable of loving no one. A congealed mass of human debris.

"Come on, give me a hand," Rudy muttered coldly.

He was already dragging her through the thick brush by her feet. Her sweater had become tangled in one of those scrubby plants so typical of the high Oregon desert and had pulled up over her head. Already, her skin seemed pale, its natural glow entirely gone.

"Grab her hands, man!" Rudy yelled. "Let's go!"

I grabbed Denise by the wrists. Two steps and her snagged sweater pulled completely off over her head. Her blonde hair was drenched with blood. But even as I felt its wetness slap against my pants as we laid her in her grave, I could not look down.

Rudy told me to go pull the car off the fire road a little more and return with the shovels. The large pool of blood where Denise had fallen really surprised me. With one of the shovels, I scooped up the dark muddy mixture and tossed it into the trees. I then noticed Rudy's empty shell casing and picked it up. Returning to the grave, I was sickened to see him dropping a large rock into the pit, directly on Denise's face. She must still be alive, I thought, and now he was finishing her off by crushing her skull with a heavy stone!

"Is she still alive?" I cried out.

"Hell, no!" he laughed, amused by the disconcerted wide-eyed horror on my face. "She's as dead as a doornail and already stinkin'. I'm just destroying her teeth and bridgework so she can't be identified if her skull ever gets unearthed."

"Man, just bury her, will you?" I choked.

I handed him the larger shovel. I did not want to look down, but somehow my eyes were drawn to her. I was surprised to see she was totally naked now, all of her clothes lying to one side. I wondered if Rudy had some perverted reason for stripping her down.

"Aren't you going to bury her clothes with her?" I asked.

"No," he replied as he started shoveling dirt on her. "They can be used for ID purposes.

Take the other shovel and go bury her clothes over there, on the other side of the fire road."

By the time I returned, he was already jumping up and down on the soft earth, packing it down. At his instruction, I gathered up some dry pine needles and piled them on top of Denise's grave. Then we burned them and spread the ashes over the mound to make it appear as if someone had camped there. We rolled a huge fallen log over the grave and walked back to the car.

After driving just about a mile from Denise's gravesite, Rudy suddenly pulled over and stopped. Suspecting that this unexpected stop might well mean that I was next, my hand slid toward my gun. Ever since George had pulled Rudy aside to speak with him in private, I couldn't be sure whether Rudy had been ordered to eliminate me as well. I assumed, however, that an attempt on my life would occur only after the robbery.

"What are we stopping for?" I asked, trying to keep my voice calm.

"Get out," he replied gruffly. Then, as if realizing what I was thinking, he smiled. "Don't worry, we're just going to bury her jewelry and get rid of the shovels."

We dug a hole for her turquoise, pushed the shovels inside an old rotten log, and returned to the motel. We told Dolores that Denise had gone back to California. But, as we gathered her things, I knew Dolores knew the truth. At about 9:15 that night, Rudy went out to call his other girlfriend, Bobette.

Although Rudy was entirely unaware of it, he had caused me to discover something about myself I had too long feared, something that would forever haunt me. As I'd stood there in the woods, unable to pull the trigger, I realized the formlessness that had always fed upon my guilt—that nameless terror that had so often given me the power to do *anything*—was not the evil I'd always thought it to be.

I had feared that formlessness since it and I had first met when I was 11 years old. A neighbor lady had asked me to drown five sick little kittens. I put them in a gunnysack, carried them to the river and, being careful not to injure them, placed two large rocks in the sack with the kittens. I petted each one goodbye before tying off the top, and then flung the bag into the middle of the river. Although the sack sunk at once, the terrified meows seemed to force their way to the surface, echoing back toward me and straight into my consciousness. It was that precise moment when the formlessness stirred within me for the very first time.

I thought the Devil had entered me. As such, I was somewhat comforted by the idea that it had not been me, personally, who had tossed the kittens to their watery deaths, but rather the formlessness within me. Curiously, the kittens' cries seemed to cease the moment I embraced the notion I'd been inhabited by some diabolically black "other." Thereafter, I would never again feel a single ounce of remorse about anything I did—until Denise Caitlin. Until the day of her death, the formlessness, that unmentionable ugly being within me, had *always* assumed responsibility for everything. No more.

Now it seemed that Denise's final breath had taken direct aim at the formless entity within my being and blown away its underlying pretense. For the first time in my life, I *knew*, without any doubt, that the "formlessness" and I were one. The ugliness was *me*.

Chapter Twenty-Five

"YOU GAVE US A PRETTY GOOD RUN, FLOYD"

The ancient Greeks believed that murder was the one act of man most likely to attract the attention of a passing god. Even though I had not let Rudy humiliate or torture Denise before she died, I guess I shouldn't have been surprised that our retribution was swift in coming. As it turned out, Rudy's call to Bobette had been traced and our location was quickly relayed to the Portland FBI office. Local authorities kept our motel under observation until they arrived.

I was sleeping when they decided to make their move. Rudy and I had already discarded Denise's personal things, cosmetics and such, in the garbage bin downstairs, and we'd also packed up her remaining clothes, intending to drop them off at a Goodwill later on. I'd then returned with Dolores to our room, where I'd laid down, mentally and physically exhausted.

Dolores seemed to sense my detachment and profound weariness, and said nothing, choosing not to intrude upon my tears as they fell onto my pillow. As I wrestled with sleep, I knew all too well there was not a single trace of purity in any of the tears that streamed down my face. There was no salvation in regret.

I finally fell into tortured dreaming, running helplessly from the chasm that was opening up all around me, threatening to swallow me. Then I felt myself being shaken violently. Was it some Greek god trying to wake me up to stand trial before Zeus? No, it couldn't be. The voice crying out my name was a woman's voice. It was *Dolores's* voice. As soon as I recognized it, I released the dream and opened my eyes.

"What's going on?" I asked as she continued tugging and pulling at my arm.

Before she could answer, I heard screams and shouting coming from the adjoining room, then I heard the words "FBI!" being broadcast through the wall. A ridiculous, fleeting hope entered my mind that they were here just to arrest Rudy, after which they would apologize for the intrusion and let Dolores and me go back to sleep. Suddenly, my consciousness was flooded by the realization that the FBI was making sure I had enough time to wake up and reach for my gun.

"Get in the bathroom!" I yelled, convinced we were only seconds away from being executed in a staged shootout. "This is it!"

I was still pushing her off the bed when the door flew open. Two agents rolled into the room and popped up in a kneeling position, their AR-15s poised for action. Two other agents stood in the doorway, one with a shotgun, the other pointing a spotlight directly into my face.

I was ordered to inch my way off the bed, keeping my hands high. As I stood up, my knees buckled and I fell to the floor. An arm on each side of me kept me from pitching forward. A hand grabbed my hair, lifting my head up. It was Agent Rand.

"You gave us a pretty good run, Floyd," he said smugly. "But your running days are all over now."

Within hours of Denise's death, I was locked up. For whatever reason, I had been spared an "over-arrest" at the motel, which is a polite way of saying the FBI didn't feeling like murdering me that day. Once again, I was at the end of my warrior's rope. I had ventured forth, a sheep in a tiger skin suit, to prey upon my fellow sheep, but while smugly devouring others I had succeeded only in consuming myself.

Before I died, I wanted to be forgiven for what I'd allowed to happen to Denise; that was the one thing I wanted for my conscience before I took my own life. If I could see to it that Rudy, was also punished for her death—Rudy, whose guile and pretense of love had killed her just as surely as the bullet that exploded into her brain—then just maybe I could be forgiven. Denise danced like a figurine in my inner vision, in the space just behind my forehead. These thoughts of her would not stop, each one a frozen still life painting in my mind. I thought maybe I'd gone mad, struck by some vengeful God who'd heard her lifeless form crash to the ground in the woods.

When my attorney came to see me, I told him the whole story, that Rudy and I had killed someone on Kendrick Williams' orders. I also made it clear to him that I wanted to plead guilty on the Reno robbery.

"What kind of deal do you want me to make?" he asked, readying his pen to write down my terms. I swept his question aside with a wave of my hand.

"I'm *tired* of all the deals," I said wearily. "Tell them that I want to make sure that everyone who was involved in Denise's murder is punished. I mean *everyone*. Those sons of bitches were even going to kill Dolores!"

I also spoke about the killing with Agent Rand, who seemed genuinely surprised I was so open with him about how the whole thing went down. When I finished, he affected his most soft and understanding tone, and said, "I think you should tell us where the body is and *trust* us to work out the details about Dolores's release later."

"I'm sorry, Mr. Rand, but I trust you people even less than you trust me."

"Well, you'd better take your chances with us," he countered, returning to his usual menacing tone, "or we'll just end up making a sweet little deal with Rudy instead."

"You really think you're gonna reach a deal with *Rudy*?" I laughed. "*He has killed five people* that I know of, and he has felony charges all over the West Coast. What kind of 'deal' are you going to give a guy like *that*?"

Rand smiled an inscrutable smile, as if he was the one holding all the cards. When it became clear that I was not going to give him what he wanted, however, he got up and left.

Later I learned I would not be allowed to plead guilty for the Reno robbery. My attorney advised me that the U.S. Attorney in Reno would not accept such a plea.

"What do you mean, I can't plead guilty?" I asked.

"For some reason," replied my attorney, "he *wants* you to have a trial."

I had my own ideas as to why the Federal Prosecutor wanted to drag me through a trial on the Reno heist. The unofficial story is that he desperately needed and wanted a "show trial" with lots of press coverage, a forum that would give him the opportunity to save face. Ed Malone had been acquitted, causing the U.S. Attorney a *lot* of bad publicity. He figured that *I* was the answer to all of his problems—if he could win a conviction after demonizing me at length in front of a jury and the press.

Mr. Hamilton was given just five days to prepare for the first trial, which was on the escape charge. This was a tactical move. An escape conviction would then become admissible during a subsequent robbery trial as evidence of a "guilty conscience" on my part. Hamilton protested that the shortness of time would not allow him to prepare an adequate defense, but he was overruled. The judge muttered something about Congress wanting defendants to have "speedy trials"—and mine was certainly going to be *that*. After Spider testified for the government in exchange for the reinstatement of his two paroles, it took the jury just 20 minutes to find me guilty as charged.

ᔕ

Day one. On November 2, 1975, my second trial got under way. U.S. Attorney Semanza opened by saying he intended to prove that Curtis, Ed, and I were the men who had robbed the First National Bank of Nevada of $1,044,000. Apparently, the prosecutor simply intended to ignore the fact the Ed had already been acquitted of this criminal claim when Curtis refused to testify against him. I asked my attorney how Semanza could legally prove Ed's criminal participation when a jury had already reached a legal finding of "not guilty." He responded by telling me I had nothing to worry about, that there was *nothing* in the record of Ed's trial that would hurt me in my trial. In fact, he said the Feds had *nothing* they could use against me. His plan was to offer no defense whatsoever. He was convinced no defense would be necessary.

Day two. The parade of government witnesses continued, but still no evidence against me. Several bank employees testified that the tallest of the robbers had stood 6' 2½"—precisely *my* height description from my FBI files. During cross examination, my attorney mocked them about the "remarkable improvement" in their respective memories. Both of them had initially told the FBI that *none* of the robbers had stood taller than 5' 10"! From the snickers I heard coming from the jury box, it was clear they didn't believe these witnesses either.

Day three. A fingerprint expert testified he had found one of my fingerprints on a toaster in the cabin where we had stayed after the robbery. As I listened to his testimony, I recalled a friend from McNeil Island who had been framed by a corrupt fingerprint specialist. He'd been innocent and had won his freedom only after some honest cops discovered the expert producing false evidence in another trial. *This* fingerprint expert did nothing of the kind. His testimony did *not* put any of my fingerprints inside the bank.

Day four. Until 2:00PM, the government still had no solid

evidence against me. Then came the star witnesses, Curtis Ray Michelson and Rudy Harris. Rudy recounted everything about the Reno escape and said I'd told him all about the Reno robbery after he had helped break me out of jail. I had been careful to tell him *nothing* about the robbery. I *had* told him he could read all about the robbery in *True Magazine*. Apparently, he had done exactly that. His testimony was almost a verbatim retelling of the story that had appeared in the article.

He denied he was "getting away with murder" in return for his testimony against me. He also denied that Denise had ever been his girl, or that he owned a gun, and that he certainly was *not* the owner of the murder weapon in the Caitlin case.

Hamilton asked Rudy to read an FBI report, signed by six FBI agents, swearing they had taken the murder weapon, a Luger, from *his* room. He read it aloud and said, "Yes, that's what they *wrote*, but they are now going to say they found it in *Forsberg's* room and simply forgot they had carried it into mine." The FBI agents who were present in the courtroom all shuffled in embarrassment at Rudy's words.

Then Curtis Ray Michelson was called to the stand. As he raised his hand to be sworn in as a witness, my attorney leaned over and whispered in my ear.

"This guy will either make you or break you," he said.

Within minutes, I knew I was doomed. The truth itself would have been bad enough. But, in his zeal to please his handlers, Curtis added lie after lie to close all of the gaps in the government's case.

He also told the jury that he'd never liked me. I thought back over all the years we'd been friends, planning our Wars together. I recalled how funny he had looked on the morning of his escape from McNeil Island, standing there all naked and covered with grease as the air rushed out of his punctured air mattress. I wondered what the FBI had promised him in exchange for testifying against me.

My attention was drawn back to the testimony he was giving

on the stand. He was saying I had stayed at the Peppermill Motel on the night of the robbery. I knew that he could not have forgotten where Dolores and I had really stayed because *he* had chosen the motel and made the reservation. Dolores had been the one who checked us in. I didn't want to be seen by anyone or to sign anything.

The government asked for an immediate recess to get the registration card. Hamilton came and saw me as I waited in the marshal's office.

"If the government finds a registration card putting you at the Peppermill that night," he warned, "it's over."

"I never stayed at the Peppermill Motel," I assured him, "There won't be any card."

I shouldn't have been surprised, however, when they *did* come back to court with a Peppermill registration card, in the name of Jim Ryan, whose signature, the experts testified, "strongly resembles the handwriting of Floyd Forsberg." Ken had been so right! Even if they had to resort to lying or fabricating evidence, the Feds in Reno could *not* be beaten in court.

As I thought of Ken, I wondered whether the FBI would ever dare to move against one of its own. He had once told me he would never spend a day in jail, that the Feds would *kill* him before they would ever allow him to expose the secrets of their power structure.

Hamilton's closing remarks were as precise and splendid as they were thorough. He did a great job of explaining that Rudy's account of the robbery was so entirely different from Curtis's account that one or both of them *had* to be lying—a point that caused several jury members to nod their heads in agreement. Even as he was driving that point home, the judge interrupted him, telling him to hurry up and cut his closing argument short. My attorney became embarrassed, mumbled something about almost being through anyway, and sat down a few seconds later.

The jury was sent away to deliberate. They were gone for most of the day. When they returned with a verdict, they announced that they had found me guilty. Three days later, Curtis's 20-year sentence was reduced to 10, to run concurrently with the 14 years he still owed on the sentence he was serving before his escape from McNeil. He had also received a five-year sentence for holding a gun to an FBI agent's head during his arrest. That sentence, too, was to run concurrently with his remaining 14-year number, as were the 2½ years he was given for his escape. On top of all those breaks, the FBI promised him no further prosecution on any of his other robberies. In return for testifying against me, the net result of his deals with the Feds was that he would not serve a single day of additional time for any of the crimes he committed after his escape from McNeil! At least his testimony had not come cheap.

ᔕ

As for me, I was sentenced in December of 1975. Five years for the Reno escape and 25 for the Reno robbery. I was still so numb from what I'd learned the day before, after a visit from my sister, that I experienced almost no feelings whatsoever when my sentence was announced by the judge. According to Sharon, Mr. Semanza had told her that had I not escaped he could have never convicted me on the Reno heist. From another source, I'd learned that Spider had been an FBI plant who had only *pretended* to be in on the Reno escape plot. Memories of the FBI's "Big Show" in 1966 flashed through my mind at the realization that, once again, I had been set up.

I was sent to Leavenworth. There, members of Ken's gang sought to find out what I intended to say about their Boss at his upcoming trial. One of them, Big John, hand delivered a letter to me from Ken. In the letter, Ken wrote of his being aware that Dolores would be testifying against him in exchange for a reduction on the five-year sentence she was presently serving at Terminal Island on a perjury conviction. He assured me he would *not* hold this against her, as long as *I* did not testify against him. His letter closed by saying that he just needed enough time to get his affairs in order before he jumped bail to avoid prosecution.

Frankly, I would have liked to see Kendrick Williams indicted for murder in the death of Denise Caitlin, but I agreed to lie for him on the Reno escape charge. I did this not so much to help him as to get back at the U.S. Attorney, who was now working with the FBI to cover up Rudy's involvement in Denise's death. I issued a statement denying I had ever sought a deal with the Bureau to entrap Williams. But once I was on the witness stand, the U.S. Attorney showed me a copy of an FBI report detailing my offer to bring down one of their own men. I knew *then* it was just a matter of time before Ken put out a contract on *my* life—if he hadn't done so already.

Another surprise came to light during cross examination when Mr. Semanza let it slip out he *knew* I had actually stayed at the Continental Motor Lodge on the night of the robbery. I started to remark on how he had used a phony Peppermill registration card with a forged signature as "evidence" to win a conviction against me. Quickly realizing a convicted felon challenging the credibility of a U.S. Federal Prosecutor would only be harmful to *my* credibility, I decided to let it go.

Despite my well-rehearsed lies, Ken was convicted. My perjury had not been enough to counter the damning testimony given by Rudy Harris, who had unhesitatingly turned on his old Boss.

The U.S. Attorney made a big deal about sentencing Rudy to 25 years. Soon enough, however, that was reduced to five years, which was then followed by an even earlier release. To boot, when he *did* get out, the FBI released him with a new identity, presumably to hide its own treachery in helping a murderer go free. He ended up serving less than 18 months for his involvement in my escape. All of the many charges that were outstanding against him at the time of his arrest were dropped. Just a few years after he blew Denise's brains out in the woods, I learned that Rudy was living somewhere back East, reportedly in charge of a thriving narcotics business.

There *had* been more compelling evidence to convict Rudy of murdering Denise Caitlin than there had been against me. The FBI had found the murder weapon in *his* room. Denise had been *his* drug runner. Almost as soon as we'd been arrested, I had admitted to Agent Rand that Rudy and I were *both* complicit in her death. Yet, in spite of all that, *I* had been indicted in Denise's murder, not Rudy. I immediately filed for a speedy trial in Oregon. I had hoped that once I was there, I could find a way to expose Rudy and the FBI.

Chapter Twenty-Six

"TIC A FAR, FAR BETTER THING I DO"

Spring, 1976. After a *year* in the Hole, I was transferred to Oregon. By that time, I had documentation that showed I'd been a pawn in a giant conspiratorial FBI game, a new Bureau program designed to control and neutralize targeted criminals. Even before I was released on parole from McNeil Island, FBI Agent Rand had been meeting secretly with my parole officer to plot a strategy for somehow getting me involved with FBI operative Curtis Ray Michelson. As it turned out, the reason I'd been transferred to Los Angeles when I was *supposed* to have been sent to Reno was solely to steer me into the arms of Curtis's organization.

I was bitter. I had wanted to get an education and try to go straight. I would have liked to have been given the opportunity to succeed—by simply being *ignored* by the FBI, rather than being conspired against to fail. Every positive illusion I'd ever had now drifted away from me. True, I might have gravitated back into a life of crime on my own after my release, but I was never given the option. I was left alone with nothing but seething hate in my soul.

One day, as I was festering away in isolation, I was jolted

from a deep and darkly meditative silence by the sound of my name being called out. A woman in white appeared.

"Floyd?" she said. "Are you Floyd?"

I looked at her and recoiled inwardly. She was Salvation Army.

"Get away from me!" I growled, cutting her no slack for being a woman. "I don't want to hear any of your junk!"

"Well, I *do* believe you'll want to hear *this* junk," she said, smiling. "I have a message from your wife."

I jumped off the bed, embarrassed by my rudeness. She gave me Dolores's message and asked if I was doing okay. I assured her I was fine, that I was used to being in the Hole.

A week later, this same lady returned, and I finally took the time to ask her name. She went by the name of "Rusty," she said, and her rank was that of Major. Major Tomlinson. She had come to let me know that Dolores was bearing well. Once again, after relaying Dolores' message, she left without preaching.

On her third visit, Major Tomlinson finally asked if I wanted a Bible.

"I knew it!" I snapped. "You just couldn't leave the Bible out of it, could you?"

She laughed in her friendly way, not at all offended by my words or my tone. "*What else* would you expect from a person who has been in the Salvation Army for over 25 years?"

"Yeah, I guess you're right," I conceded. "As a veteran bible-thumper, what else *would* you know? How about literature?"

"Fine," she replied. "Which would you prefer? American? English?"

I had read many American writers from Poe and Emerson to Steinbeck and Hemingway. From her confident tone, I suspected she might have read them as well, so I chose English.

"Anyone in particular?" she asked.

My guess was that she probably favored the women writers, like Charlotte Bronte and Jane Austen, so I picked a male.

"How about Dickens?"

"Any book in particular?"

"I've always thought 'A Tale of Two Cities' to be his best work. Wouldn't you agree?" I asked, affecting a tone of superiority.

As it turned out, Major Tomlinson had taught school in Africa for 20 years. English literature had been her major. "A Tale of Two Cities" was her all-time favorite book. She had, in fact, used the novel as a teaching tool throughout her decades-long career as a teacher.

After schooling me thoroughly on the novel, she returned to pressing her cause: Jesus.

"In your studies, Floyd, have you ever sought an answer to the most profound philosophical question of all time?"

"And what is that?" I asked, still wondering how I could have been so hapless as to choose the one book in all of human literature that she had used as a textbook for over 20 years.

"Was Jesus who he said he was," she said, "or was he a fake?"

Frankly, I didn't care one way or the other, and I said as much. Nevertheless, she encouraged me to give it some thought, advising me to not jump to conclusions on a purely emotional "anti-God" level, but to reason it out based on an objective and fair evaluation of "the facts."

Ironically, shortly thereafter, I received a letter from Floyd Hamilton, who used to run with Bonnie Parker and Clyde Barrow. I had idolized him back in my Luther Burbank days. When I started reading it, I was certain it had to be some kind of prank, because this person didn't identify himself as the Floyd Hamilton I'd so admired, the bank robber and fugitive from the law, but rather as *Floyd Hamilton, Christian.* He wrote of committing himself daily to helping all the kids who had tried to emulate him. It turned out he had met Major Tomlinson at a chaplain's conference, where *she* had asked him to write to me. I'd thought the FBI had killed all of my gangster idols, including Floyd Hamilton. Although only mildly touched by his professed transformation, I appreciated his sincerity and his willingness to reach out to others. I was genuinely glad to learn that he was still very much alive.

When Rusty came to visit me again, I told her about Denise —about how Rudy and I had killed her and of how badly I felt about her death. I also explained to her my outrage over how the FBI was helping Rudy get away with the crime. She responded by saying that if I really wanted to do the right thing all I had to do was ask Jesus to show me the way. Skeptical though I was, I decided to give prayer a try. But because I didn't hear or feel anything in the way of divine guidance, it seemed that nothing came of it. If anything, I felt like an absolute fool for having cast aside reason and intellect for wishful thinking. But, after speaking with my court appointed lawyer, Max Merrill, I began to think my prayer had been answered or at least that the cosmic scales of karma were beginning to return to an even keel. According to Mr. Merrill, Rudy's latest statement to the FBI was *so* absurd that even the District Attorney, Louis Selkin, couldn't believe or accept it. He let me read the statements for myself.

In his first statement, Rudy said Denise had never even accompanied us to Oregon. In his second statement, she had come to Oregon and then quickly gone back to California. In his third and fourth statements, he had been walking in the woods all day long, and when he returned, I told him she had left. In his fifth statement, his claim was that I "confessed" to him in the back of the Marshal's van that I killed Denise and then told him, in exacting detail, the precise location of her body—in the event he ever wanted to "go visit the burial site."

I laughed repeatedly as I read each statement. Agent Rand, with whom I had discussed the killing, had clearly walked him through the fifth statement, which was a masterpiece of subterfuge. The official FBI version was 46 pages long! Rudy's other statements had been brief, no more than a page or two. Not only did Rudy portray his relationship with Denise as completely platonic, he actually claimed that she was *my* girl, that *I* had hired her, and that I alone had killed her. Realizing all of these lies were laid out in language much too articulate to have been formulated by Rudy, I recalled the inscrutable smile of Agent Rand when he'd threatened to deal with Rudy if I refused to cooperate with him. At the time, I was certain he was merely bluffing. Now I realized that this Federal agent was capable of *anything*, even fabricating an exonerating statement for a murderer.

I was impressed by my attorney from the start.

"This is the most absurd case I've *ever* seen!" he exclaimed, after reviewing all of the statements with me. "The FBI has twisted everything around. Obviously, Rudy Harris is a murderer. I've been to the gravesite and *no one* could have ever led the FBI to that secluded location without having been there beforehand."

"I'm glad you have the courage to admit that," I said. "I want to use my trial as a forum to expose how the FBI arranged my escape, how a graduate of the FBI Academy ordered a murder, and how everyone is now covering up the truth. I know they expect me to keep my mouth shut, but I won't. I want to expose them all!"

When the D.A. discovered that we would have more evidence to present than he had, he realized my intentions and offered a deal of a concurrent sentence. If I would forgo the trial, I would serve no more time for the murder than I would serve for the bank robbery. Moreover, with the D.A. knowing that Dolores had been released from Terminal Island and was now living in Portland, he sought to sweeten the pot by offering to let me serve out my entire sentence in Oregon, which would enable her to visit me on a regular basis.

"No deals!" was my response after my lawyer laid out the D.A.'s offer. "I'm going to expose the escape, Agent Rand's perjury, the whole ball of wax. They made such a big show of busting Kendrick Williams and then giving him 25 years. Just a short time later they reduced it to five years, *ensuring* him an early release. He always bragged about 'knowing too much' to ever be given any serious time, and *that* cannot be allowed to stand. I want him *and* Rudy Harris prosecuted for Denise's death! Maybe *then*, the publicity might prompt someone to look into the FBI."

A week before the trial, Max came to me with another deal from the D.A., which would include the prosecution of Rudy Harris. Max now had a witness who could completely destroy Rudy's alibi, and the D.A. could no longer hide the fact that the FBI had falsified its entire case to protect its image. Now the D.A. wanted my cooperation at the Harris trial. In return, the prosecutor promised to help get a reduction on my 25-year Federal sentence.

"No deal!" I howled yet again. "Those SOBs *never* keep their word!"

Max knew I had been double crossed by the FBI in the past. "Your biggest mistake is that you never got any of it put down in writing. This is different. If they don't keep a written agreement, the entire sentence becomes invalid."

"Are you sure Harris will be prosecuted if I accept?" I asked. I reminded Max that Agent Rand had sworn he'd never allow Rudy to be brought to trial.

Max replied with perfect confidence. "The District Attorney has *assured* me he is not part of any such arrangement with Agent Rand. Rudy Harris *will* go to trial."

With that, I decided to change my plea and accept the D.A.'s offer. Emotionally drained as I was from a year in isolation, I felt myself incapable of speaking clearly in court, so I asked Max to read my statement for me. It said:

"I am not used to speaking before people, and because this matter is too charged with emotion for me to express myself with any semblance of calm, I have asked my attorney to read these words on my behalf.

"The sentence to be rendered in this case is, by law, mandatory. I therefore hope that anyone who hears these words today will appreciate the sincerity of my statement and understand that it is not an attempt to win for myself a less severe punishment by flattering the court.

"There are only three pleas possible for the crime with which I was charged: 'Not Guilty,' 'Guilty,' and 'Not Guilty by Reason of Insanity or other Mental Defects.' After discussing the third of these options with my attorney, and being shown that, under O.R.S. 161.295-2, a 'psychopathic personality' is not a permissible defense, I was left with only the other two from which to choose.

"I believe, as does my attorney, that considering the evidence and related facts in this case, the probable outcome of a trial would have been a favorable result for the defense, this despite all of the hardships imposed upon the defense by the FBI.

"For reasons of which this court may or may not be aware, the defendant is of special interest to the FBI. In this case, six members of the Federal Bureau of Investigation have already falsified evidence that was presented to the U.S. Attorney in Portland for use in my prosecution. It has since been rejected because it was determined to have been obtained by illegal means.

"The FBI has also created a form of de facto incommunicado for the defendant, thus hindering his every attempt to defend himself, not only in this case but in other cases as well. Furthermore, a member of the FBI withheld substantial evidence, both from the Grand Jury which indicted the defendant and from the District Attorney, Mr. Louis Selkin.

"Mr. Selkin, having no personal or vindictive axe to grind, and desiring only that justice be done, has expressed a sincere desire for the truth of this crime to be laid before the bar of justice and before the public, both of which he serves. The truth of this crime is known to the defendant, as well as to persons in high positions of the judiciary. Shortly after his arrest on June 29, 1975, the defendant informed these individuals, through other counsel, about exactly what had transpired just 24 hours earlier, on June 28, 1975, the day Denise Caitlin was murdered. These facts are what the FBI has withheld from Mr. Selkin for its own self-serving ends.

"The defendant, through his counsel, Max Merrill, respectfully asks this honorable court to be allowed to enter a plea of guilty, so that justice, in its most pure essence, may be achieved.

"I know that many people, especially the FBI, have counted upon my remaining silent and taking my chances on running through the judicial gantlet, which probably would have resulted in my escaping any responsibility for this hideous crime. I had, in fact, once entertained the idea of taking that route, waiting to speak out afterwards. But if I ended up losing who would listen?

"Lacking the eloquence to express the many reasons for which I desire to plead guilty, I will simply quote the words of Charles Dickens and say, on behalf of and *for*, Denise Caitlin, 'Tis a far, far better thing I do here today than I have ever done before.'"

Immediately after my attorney finished reading my statement, I was sentenced to serve life in prison and then transported directly to Salem, Oregon. There, at the Oregon State Penitentiary, I settled into a single-man cell, sat down on my bunk, and started trying to stir up hope, while gazing at a future that seemed to offer only bleakness without end.

Chapter Twenty-Seven

"THE TOUGHEST PRISON OF ALL"

The first hint that a State plea bargain carried no more weight than its Federal counterpart came when I was informed that if I didn't stop trying to expose the FBI, and Agent Rand in particular, I would never be allowed to see my wife again. To my good fortune, Max had that base covered. After six months, I was able to get visits from Dolores.

As time passed, however, I began to realize that Rudy Harris would never be brought to trial. The D.A. now took the position that there was "not enough evidence" to convict him. The promise of a ten-year release date for me became, in reality, a 20-year number, and Agent Rand would never be exposed.

I now had affidavits from individuals who the FBI had terrorized in connection with my case. I'd also collected FBI documents disclosing Rand's perjury. I sent them all to the Director of the FBI. Nothing happened. I wrote letters to all the newspapers. I received not a single reply.

There was only one thing left to do: escape. I would escape and kidnap some bank tellers, and I would hold them hostage until the Director of the FBI did something about Agent Rand.

The Oregon State Penitentiary was different from any other prison I'd been held in under the federal system. This was my first time in a truly maximum-security facility, and I quickly realized this prison would not be an easy place to escape from. Inmates without jobs spent 20 hours a day locked in their cells, except during the summer when there was evening yard. Television viewing was allowed only every third evening. Movement inside the institution was tightly controlled.

I was asked to join various escape plots, but I refused. For one thing, I had had to make a deal to stay in Oregon to be near Delores, and part of the deal was that I wouldn't be involved in any escape attempts. Otherwise they would move me out of state. And second, this prison had an informant network surpassing any other in the country. Indeed, the constant presence of its all watching network of informants presented a bigger obstacle to overcome than the 30-foot walls surrounding the prison.

At least initially, I spent my time filing lawsuits against the jailors who had abused my civil rights by beating me on the orders of the Federal Bureau of Investigation. Much to my glee, my jailors openly admitted having acted on the orders of an FBI agent, but they swore they could not remember the agent's name. In addition to these lawsuits, I also had appeals pending on my federal convictions. I decided to just sit back and watch in silence.

During these legal battles, I became friends with a prison legal clerk by the name of Rod Addicks, a former certified public accountant who was doing life for the murder of his business partner. Rod's pretrial confinement had also been rife with flagrant violations of his civil rights. He had, in fact, been framed, and emphatically denied his guilt. I was surprised when he asked me if I was as good at escape as the prison gossip claimed.

"*Any* prison can be beat," I replied, "if you can find enough truly dedicated people. Why do you ask?"

"I want out," he said simply enough.

"But I thought you were innocent."

"I *am* innocent," he said, his voice indignant. "Does *that* preclude me from wanting to escape?"

"I suppose not," I replied. "But you just don't understand what you're up against."

I explained to Rod that it would probably take nine or ten people to pull off an escape. Before we could be ready, one of the ten would surely snitch off the plan—or brag to one of his buddies, who in turn would run straight to the warden's office and tell all.

Without question, Rod was the most educated convict I'd ever met. He not only had an accounting degree, but he had studied psychology and was determined to put that acquired knowledge to good use.

Thanks to my clerical skills, I was able to land a job in the Assistant Superintendent's office, where there were files on each and every inmate inside the institution. These provided me access to names and backgrounds of potential participants in the plan.

We began by working up psychological profiles on all possible recruits for our escape. The first profile Rod suggested we should compile was on his codefendant, James Scarbrough.

"Scar?" I couldn't believe my ears. "He testified *against* you!"

"Yes, I know," he replied. "But he did so *only* because they promised him he'd be free in one year. Besides, he never dreamed they'd convict an innocent man, with or without his testimony."

Scar's plea bargain clearly stated he *should* and *would* be paroled at his first board appearance. He wasn't.

John Akin, the psychologist in charge of all the case workers, frequented the office and examined those same files for more legitimate purposes. He was a man of incredible experience, and I always enjoyed talking with him about "the good old days."

I was particularly fascinated by his keen insight into the criminal mind. He would sit at his desk for hours, carefully paring through the files, looking for men to assign as trustees. Even though most of those inmates, who had less than a year to serve on their sentences and wanted to remain on their best behavior, would be good candidates, he would toss one after another of their files onto a pile of those he considered "too dangerous" to be granted the custody status of a trustee. Others, he'd say, *would* escape, but wouldn't hurt anyone while on the run. The prison was overcrowded, so Akin would send these men out to the camp as trustees, being confident they would harm no one when they ran off. Sure enough, just as he'd expected, the inmate would walk away. His predictions for how long a man would last on parole before reoffending were uncanny. Often, he would even correctly predict what manner of crime the convict would commit while on parole.

In watching him, I quickly realized just why the FBI had been so confident in the use of its psychological games against me. Clearly, by 1976, that kind of thing had become quite a science. Not to worry, I thought to myself. I would soon be in a position to strike back at them.

Before long, Rod and I figured out a way to beat the metal detector in the industrial area and soon had nine weapons collected for our group. At this point, however, we were still in need of three more conspirators. Our plan involved two teams: Rod's, which we called the A-team, and mine, the B-team. As a precaution against informants, neither the A-team nor the B-team knew about the other. Only Rod and I knew everything and everyone involved.

As each psychological profile was completed, either Rod or I would attempt to recruit the man for our team. If he expressed interest, he would be given the details of a plausible sounding escape plan, but not the *real* escape plan. Slowly, he would be told about other members of the team. Even so, we would always make sure to give each new team member a few names of men who were *not* part of the escape plan. Thus, if the man snitched, we would automatically know that *he* was the informant because of the bait names given just to him.

ꟹ

One day, about three months before the target date we'd set for the escape, Dr. Akin asked me a question that caught me completely off guard.

"So, tell me, Floyd," he began, his voice altogether casual, "have you got your escape plan all set up yet?"

Most psychologists stare straight into the face of the person with whom they are speaking while awaiting a response. Like most professional cheats and practiced liars, I had perfected an unflinching poker face that permitted me to look anyone straight in the eye with complete confidence whenever I lied. But in Akin's case, he always posed his questions *only* while looking intently through a file or while writing a report, never so much as glancing at the inmate. Clearly, he understood how easily one could be fooled by the false sincerity of con-wise inmates well versed in eye to eye confrontations. Just as clearly, he understood that such conwise inmates could be better judged by what they *didn't* say.

"Wh-what do y-you m-mean?" I asked, stammering. My heart was beating so loudly I was certain he could hear it pounding inside my chest.

"Have you figured a way out yet?" he repeated, posing his question a little differently this time around. "You've been here at OSP well over a year now. Surely you *must* have found a weakness you think you can use."

I felt trapped. "Did some snitch tell you something he made up?"

Dr. Akin kept his eyes lowered, looking at the index cards that were spread out on his desk. Instantly, I realized I'd made a telling mistake by offering up such a defensive reply. Finally, after allowing me to twist in the wind for a couple of minutes, he spoke.

"No," he said, "no snitch has told me anything I believe. You're way too smart to trust just anyone after what you've been through. I simply assumed that enough time has passed for you to be ready to make your move."

"I'm going to *win* my case on appeal," I said, affecting as positive a tone as I could muster up. "I don't *need* to escape."

Before speaking again, Dr. Akin put down his index cards and looked me straight in the eye. "Have you ever given any thought to breaking out of the toughest prison of all?" he asked.

"This is the toughest one I've ever been in," I laughed. "Maximum security, 30-foot walls, TV cameras everywhere, alarms on the walls, and every third convict a hired snitch working for the warden. What prison could be harder to escape from than this one?"

Without saying a word, he got up, tucked some files under his arm, and headed for the door.

"Aren't you going to answer me?" I asked. "What prison is tougher than *this* one?"

He stopped in the doorway and turned around, grinning as he would often do after setting me up for one of his psychological punchlines.

"I'm referring to the prison you locked yourself into when you first stole a car or snatched a purse," he said. With that, he turned and left the room, closing the door behind him. This was the first of many times he would reveal to me something about myself, as well as about the many other predators with whom I was living.

Every time a child molester arrived, the prison would explode with violence. The latest had been welcomed into the fold by having his cell burned out with a fire-bomb.

"I don't like child molesters," I hissed contemptuously. "They're jackals!"

"Jackals?"

"That's right. They're the lowest form of beast."

"I see the analogy now," he said, smiling as he peered at me over his reading glasses. "And what would you call the confidence man, the check writer, or the Bunco artist?"

"A black panther," I replied without hesitation, instantly liking the game. "Stealthy, sneaky, and cunning."

"Very good. What about the armed robber who hits gasoline stations or all-night markets?"

I thought for a minute before settling on my answer. "A lion. They say that the armed robber is the king of the beasts."

"Excellent!" he said, again smiling agreeably as he spoke. "And now we come to you." He stepped back and sized me up. "You're the cat who stalks a bank for months on end, and then strikes only when everything is ready. The cat who is so smart he hires FBI men to help arrange his escape. The cat who is so fast and sure footed that he runs those same FBI agents right off the road when they attempt to capture him. If you asked me, I guess that would make you a cheetah, the fastest animal of them all. Wouldn't you agree?"

I liked the comparison. I had trained my body long and hard for escape. I could run ten miles in an hour. None of the younger inmates could equal my pace for that distance. I was clever too. Lightning fast and clever. Like a cheetah. The imagery was perfect. My chest swelled with pride.

"Yeah, that's me all right. A cheetah—the fastest of them all!"

Shaking his head slowly from side to side, Dr. Akin smiled his gotcha smile, and I knew he had me yet again.

"There's only one problem with all of these analogies," he said, pausing for a moment before delivering the final blow. "They're all predators, Floyd. That's why we keep *all* of you locked up in cages."

A day later, Dr. Akin brought me the results of a ten-year study of the criminal mind. I couldn't put it down. The most fascinating part revolved around why virtually every criminal is eventually caught. It reminded me of the story in "True Magazine" about the Reno job. It had said that the Reno robbery was the "perfect crime," but that it had been carried out by "imperfect criminals."

It soon crystallized in my mind that Dr. Akin was right. There really wasn't any place for me to escape *to*. I carried my *real* prison inside me. No matter where I went, I'd still be me, and I would *still* be in a prison of my own making.

I resolved then and there to do whatever I could do to escape from the prison of my own criminality—or, as Dr. Akin called it, "the toughest prison of all." But, having made that resolution, I was immediately faced with the question of how to disentangle myself from Rod's escape plan.

The question was rendered moot by the last member of the gang. The man had been serving a double life sentence and had, in fact, already been shot off the wall during an earlier escape attempt. To us, he had seemed the perfect candidate, full of determination, eager to try again. We had misjudged him. He turned out to be a rat. Fortunately, he knew almost nothing about the *real* plan, and five of the names he gave up were innocent dupes, none of them the least bit involved with the escape plot. We were all sent to the Hole, but released the next day. The Chief of Security *knew* he was getting close to something big, so Rod announced we needed to shut things down completely and postpone any escape attempt for at least a year. He got no argument from me. But, just a few days later, he came to me with another scheme he'd evidently given a great deal of thought to.

"I've been thinking," he said. "I believe I have an even better way of escaping."

Not having told him I was no longer interested in any escape plans, I mustered up all the enthusiasm I could and asked him what he had in mind.

"Do you realize how easy it would be for *you* to confess to the murder for which *I* was convicted?" he asked.

Obviously, such a thing had *never* crossed my mind. After all, why would I ever confess to any crime I did not commit? As Rod continued talking, I was truly amazed by the plot he unveiled. Essentially, I would confess to having committed the murder for which he'd been convicted, which in turn would result in his being freed. Civil suits for wrongful imprisonment would follow and leave Rod a very wealthy man—and he would use some of his riches to finance a prison breakout by helicopter to free both Scar and me. As insane as the plan sounded on the surface, I realized it might actually work!

I had in fact lived in Longview, Washington. I could easily have known Scar, who had already confessed, but who would now claim he had implicated the "totally innocent Rodney Addicks" *only* to protect me. Aside from my having lived only 20 blocks from the murder scene, there were so many other "coincidences" it was scary, even as to a plausible motive. Rod's accounting firm had prepared income taxes for many of the FBI agents whose names he had seen in my legal work. We decided that, for my motive, I had killed Rod's partner after he discovered me rifling through their business files looking for addresses of FBI personnel.

Through my entire first year in Oregon I had been unable to interest even a single reporter in the FBI cover up of Denise Caitlin's murder. Now they flocked to the prison in response to the affidavit I filed in court stating I had committed the murder for which Rod stood convicted. Story after story appeared on TV and in the newspapers about the "innocent man" who had been "wrongly convicted" and was now "languishing in prison" for a crime "he didn't commit." Rod filed millions of dollars in civil suits against various agencies for their involvement in framing him. Investigators were sent out to look into Scar's and my statements. All of our stories checked out, even our having been in the same reform school.

I used every opportunity to expose Agent Rand. I showed reporters the FBI reports that revealed him to be a perjurer. As each story was printed, I photocopied it, then sent the whole lot of them to every member of Congress and the top FBI officials, asking them how long it was going to take before they stopped ignoring the cover up. Yet for all my efforts nothing changed.

When I wasn't talking to reporters, I was concentrating on breaking out of my real prison—my own criminal mentality. Most importantly, I learned to hear the truth when someone spoke. I became honest with myself and began to communicate honestly, really honestly, with Dolores for the first time in our relationship. I had always loved her as best I could. But, as a predator, I had also used her and taken unfair advantage of her love—and I admitted as much.

Still, something was missing. I would spend a week thinking *good* thoughts, *right* thoughts, and then I would suddenly become all enthused about Rod's plan to break Scar and me out of prison in a hijacked helicopter after the courts overturned his conviction and ordered his release.

From past experience, I knew there was little chance he would ever keep his word but I continued on with the entire "innocent man" hoax. It *would* eventually prove to be a *real* hoax, for I would later learn he really *had* killed his business partner. It was ironic that the police had lacked the evidence necessary to win a legitimate conviction, so they chose to concoct the evidence they used to convict him. But, at the time, the hoax was *vital* to me, not just because I wanted to believe in Rod, but because it got the reporters to listen to my story.

In truth, Rod was my last attempt to find that mythical "solid" criminal partner that all convicts look for. Every Butch Cassidy wants his Sundance Kid. I was no exception. Every predator I ever befriended had burned me in the end, from Dick Hedges, who had simply skimmed $1,000 off the top, to Curtis Ray Michelson, who with great forethought had created a nonexistent "fourth member" of our Reno robbery team so he could help himself to an extra 25% of our takings. Rod was so new to prison, with a seemingly loftier set of values, that I genuinely believed he would be different. Moreover, he was aware of all the inner conflict and shame I felt over having worked with the FBI. He *accepted* me. He told me repeatedly the only thing that really mattered was our loyalty to one another.

The State delayed taking action for 18 months. They checked and rechecked our story, but they could not break it. If I was willing to take on another life sentence, there was little they could do but stall and hope something would happen to trip us up or cause us to turn on each other. Virtually every investigator who questioned me also gave me the following advice: "Whatever the hell Rodney Addicks is promising you, you'd better get it in advance!"

I knew they would resort to the strategy of divide and conquer. It was equally true I honestly no longer wanted what Rod had been promising. I no longer wanted to escape, be it by helicopter or otherwise. The bottom line is that whether he intended to burn me or not, I was *still* going to be stuck with another life sentence. If only a more reasonable solution would appear!

ᔕ

On one of the infinite, nameless days at OSP I was stretched out on my bunk reading the newspaper. My eyes were drawn to the picture of a cute little five-year-old girl. The story was about a man with a long history of pedophilia who was being sentenced for child molestation. After his previous convictions—of which there had reportedly been several—he had always received probation rather than prison time. His lawyer had argued this pedophile was merely "sick" and didn't really belong in prison. Instead, he "just shouldn't be around children." I wryly thought to myself the same rationale could be applied to bank robbers: We were merely "sick" and, rather than be imprisoned, we should simply "not be permitted to be around banks."

In any case, according to the article, this molester had actually been set free to prowl the playgrounds again after his previous conviction, which is exactly what he did. After the most recent arrest, the judge couldn't let him off with another conditional probation. This time, a search of his home had turned up the skull of a young girl. He insisted he had found the skull while picking through a garbage dump. There was no evidence to contradict his story or to charge him with the girl's murder. He was sentenced to a prison term of just eight years for the child molestation charge, which was completely unrelated to the murder.

The story so enraged me that my first reaction was to have the man beaten as soon as he arrived. Then I realized that there were many other inmates reading the very same newspaper, and one or more of those readers would surely take care of him without any involvement on my part. But then, as I thought of all the hell this molester was soon to experience upon arrival in prison, it occurred to me that his grief could work to my benefit. I knew I'd now reached such a level in the study of the criminal mind that I could, in time, get this child molester to tell me where the rest of the little girl's body was located.

By this time the press had wearied of my campaign to free an innocent man and expose official corruption. But if I could solve this murder, I could *demand* a television spot—and thousands of people would watch and learn the truth. Rod listened to my plan incredulously and then offered his feedback.

"Do you honestly believe you can walk up to a man who has only an eight-year sentence and just *talk* him into accepting a life sentence for *murder*?"

"Man, let me tell you something," I replied. "I stood up to some pretty heavy psychological games with the FBI, challenging them every step of the way, and I *still* broke. Even though I'm one tough son of a bitch, I eventually crumbled. As for this child molester, don't forget that he's always been given probation and has *never* been in prison before. When he gets here, they're gonna tear him apart. That's when *we'll* step in and become his friends. He'll turn to *us*, just like I turned to Curtis when *I* needed someone to trust."

Soon, the molester arrived. I began to wonder whether he'd even survive the two-week administration and orientation process. He was repeatedly spat upon, chased out of the chow hall, and relentlessly abused, both physically and verbally.

When he was finally assigned to the regular prison population, I had him moved close to my cell so that I could begin to draw him out. I started calling upon the FBI techniques I had learned so well. When I first approached him, I found him a complete emotional wreck. He was so physically small that virtually *everyone* had taken to punching him, even other sex offenders. Since he could no longer endure the beatings he received every time he left his cell, he had stopped going to the chow hall and had not eaten for days.

The first time I spoke to "Bud," as he was known, he literally jumped at the sound of my voice, his whole body shaking like a leaf. When I offered to be his friend, he broke down and sobbed like a child. I arranged it so Bud could eat his meals ahead of the main line with Rod and me, and we put out the word that I was protecting him.

I spent hours in front of his cell, probing his mind, just as FBI operatives had done with me. Like all criminals, Bud believed he had gotten a raw deal from the system. He said if only he had been granted probation, he could and *would* have made it. He believed he was "sick" and thus more worthy of treatment in a State Hospital setting than of punishment by incarceration in a State Prison.

Playing that angle, I led him to believe that I had enough pull through my position in the Assistant Superintendent's Office to possibly get him transferred to the State Hospital. There, I said, he would receive the treatment he wanted and needed, and he would almost certainly be paroled much sooner. At my urging, after claiming it would help expedite the transfer,

Bud agreed to fill out a "psychological questionnaire" that Rod and I concocted for the purpose of teasing out some usable information. We advised him that a transfer would require his answering all of the questions honestly. Although we included several questions about Andrea Tolentino—the five-year-old girl he was suspected of killing—he stuck to his story about having found her skull in a local garbage dump. We advised him that he could not be transferred until a certain "memorandum of suspicion"—which, of course, did *not* exist—was removed from his file. In order to do that, we said, we would need for him to share with us all of the evidence the police were claiming to have against him so Rod could then prepare a writ to have the memo removed.

Bud told us the police had little evidence against him outside of the skull that had been found in his home, but he did admit to being in the area where the little girl had been kidnapped. At this point, I became convinced that he had murdered Andrea Tolentino. We tried hard to break his story, but he would not change a word of it.

"He's not going to break," Rod said, clearly frustrated.

"Don't give up yet," I replied, trying to sound encouraging. "It's time for us to move to 'Phase B.' I told you that I learned a lot from the FBI. I'm going to send the D.A. an affidavit saying that Bud has confessed and I know the location of the girl's body."

"What if they call your bluff?" Rod asked, looking at me like I'd lost my mind.

"Oh, you can be sure they will call my bluff!" I replied, smiling. "And that's the whole purpose. They are going to think they are interrogating *me*. Instead, they'll be telling *me* all the information we need to break Bud's story wide open."

The D.A. sent a state policeman and one of his own investigators. Before I would talk to them about Andrea, I made them listen to all the evidence against Rudy Harris in the death of Denise Caitlin. Both agreed there existed an airtight case against him and that he was worthy of being brought before a jury. Believing that they were honorable men, I told them what I wanted in return for leading them to the girl's body: I wanted several reporters, all of my choosing, to be there when I led them to the girl's remains. I also wanted their guarantee of a television show wherein I could expose the FBI. After promising to speak to their superiors about meeting my demands they questioned me about my affidavit.

After the men left, Rod was eager to find out what I had learned. The cop and investigator had played it close to the vest with what they knew of the case, but the few confidential details they unwittingly revealed provided me all the information I needed to get inside Bud's head and produce results. Within minutes of speaking with him again, Bud dissolved into tears and confessed to the killing, telling us he had returned to the body to take the girl's skull home to use as a candleholder. I put my arm around him and assured him everything was going to be okay. Calmly, I asked him where he had left the girl's body.

Bud stiffened. His eyes darted toward my face, then toward Rod's face, then back to mine. Clearly, he realized he had said too much. He was not about to give up such damning information as the location of the young girl's remains.

"Wh-why would you g-guys p-possibly want to k-know th-that?" he stammered.

"So that I can take the State Police to the body, of course," I replied.

"That's not funny!" His face turned white.

"Who said I was trying to be funny? Do you think we've been feeding you and protecting you all this time without a reason?"

I looked him right in the eye as I spoke, just as FBI operative Curtis Ray Michelson had looked me straight in the eye while telling me he'd wanted me in his gang *only* so he could deal me off to the FBI if something later went wrong. Like Agent Rand had looked me straight in the eye while lying through his teeth as he assured me I could write my own deal. I'd learned about predators and their prey the *hard* way!

"Do you really expect me to tell you where the body is after telling me you were tricking me the whole time?" he asked.

"Sure I do," I said, my voice now hard and cold. "You don't seem to understand your position, Bud. The beatings stopped because Rod and I spoke to a lot of people to get them off your back. We've taken a *lot* of crap for being your friend. If you don't tell us where the body is, we will withdraw our protection and the beatings will start all over again. If you cooperate, you'll be out by Christmas. I think that's called a 'deal you can't refuse.'"

At that last line, I laughed, and Rod joined me. Even Bud smiled at the false hope I tossed out for him. Or perhaps he was smiling as a means of denying the hopelessness of his position without us and our protection. In any case, Rod and I would certainly testify against him, with or without the body. But *with* the body I would at least get a television audience to generate public support for my own cause. I was relieved when Bud, feeling he had no other alternative, divulged to us the precise location of Andrea Tolentino's remains.

Eventually the FBI got wind of my negotiations with the State Police and tried to get them to betray me, to somehow persuade me to provide the location of the girl's body *up front* and then burn me. Fortunately for me, the State Police were made of more honorable stuff than the FBI. They didn't tell the FBI to get lost. Neither did they succumb to the FBI's demands to deal with me treacherously.

After the State Police allowed me to record my grievance in front of a television camera, two FBI agents went to the studio and demanded to see the tape before it was aired. In it, I asked FBI Director Webster to look into the Caitlin murder and I asked State authorities to look into Rod's case. The footage also showed me leading the State Police to the body of the little girl.

Unfortunately, we had completely misjudged the public's potential interest in our scheme. Fifty thousand people watched the broadcast but only one viewer wrote to offer any supportive feedback. The publicity was intense for a few weeks, but then nothing ever came of it, and things soon returned to normal.

Well, slightly *worse* than normal. My fellow inmates were enraged that I'd helped the police solve a murder, and that I had been, by my own admission, an FBI informant. I was ostracized. But, because of my reputation, and because Superintendent Hoyt Cupp had never surrendered control of his prison to inmate gangs, no one tried to kill me.

Rod soon came up with another scheme, a scheme in which Bud would be needed to play a central part. We had to make sure no one tried to harm him.

"I don't know, Rod," I said, after he explained his new idea. "What happens if they call our bluff this time?"

"It won't matter," he replied. "*This* time we collect and get everything we want up front. We were fools to solve a murder and only ask for a TV show. *This* time, we demand a new trial for me, and they pay in advance. By the time they realize they've been burnt, it'll be too late."

The plan was simple. Bud was suspected of several other sex crimes. We had him write out confessions to several more unsolved murders that Rod and I gleaned from newspaper articles and which we fleshed out with details that came straight from our imagination.

Once again, the newspapers went wild and sent their reporters to sit at our feet. In one interview, I offered Agent Rand the solution to six murders—*if* he would answer six questions on a polygraph.

We cautioned Bud that the authorities might try to pressure him into accepting a separate deal rather than taking the risk of letting Rod go free. Then, after telling him the best he could expect from the authorities was life, we assured him his best option was to hold his ground and count on *us* to use our influence and get him transferred to the State Hospital. Soon, even *I* was being approached with a deal: Sell out Rod and the State would fulfill my plea bargain. I laughed in their faces. Their offer made me realize just how close we were to getting Rod out of prison—and just how soon *I* would be serving *his* life sentence.

I still hadn't told Rod I was no longer interested in escaping, that my criminal mindset was the only prison from which I needed to escape. When I finally told him, he was understandably surprised, especially when I said I wanted to rewrite our deal.

"Listen, Rod," I said reassuringly, "as an innocent man, you're going to collect a lot of money from all the civil suits you're going to win. I'm not going to back out of my commitment to take on your life sentence. Instead of repaying me by breaking me out of prison, I'd like to settle instead for one third of all you get."

"But what if I end up winning only $100,000?" he asked. "When all is said and done, I don't think you'll be happy if you end up with only $33,000."

"You're right about that," I replied. "I wouldn't be happy with only $33,000. But considering you could just as easily win a million, I'm willing to take my chances. The bottom line is that I don't have any money left, and I'd like to come up with some cash for my wife. If I end up with enough, I might be able to hire a good appeals attorney. The government made significant errors in my case. With a bit of money, anything is possible.

"Before you answer me, Rod, don't say 'yes' just because you don't think you have any other choice in the matter. You are free to say 'no' if you wish. But, if you *are* okay with my proposition of giving me a third of all you win, I simply want *your* word you'll take care of your end of the bargain. I want you to *mean* it, Rod, just as you've sworn time and again that you *would* arrange to break me out with a hijacked helicopter."

"Don't you worry about a thing," Rod said, a wide smile on his face. "You'll get a third of all I get. You have my word on that!"

"A *third*, no matter how much you win, right?" I asked. "If you win $30,000,000, I get $10,000,000, right?"

"I'm a CPA, remember? I *know* what 33⅓ percent means. I'm just having a hard time believing you don't want to escape. Surely you *must* want out of prison."

"I'm just thinking of Dolores," I said. "I want her to have some money. Her career was ruined by being sent to prison because of me. She doesn't have a thing. Besides, I've spent my whole life in prison. I can bite the bullet if I have to."

"Okay," Rod sighed. "But let's keep the escape plan as an option, in case you change your mind. In the meantime, I agree to abide by whatever you choose. As you'll see, my word is my bond."

No long after this, Bud turned on Rod and me, and our house of cards—built on fabricated confessions—collapsed and came tumbling down. I'll never know whether the FBI got its hand on Bud and convinced him to turn against us. A deal was offered and he followed his lawyer's advice to reveal Rod's and my machinations. We had produced all of these plausible but false confessions and then held them hostage to our own advantage, milking them as long as we could. But Rod and I had finally met our match. Although Bud *did* receive a sentence of one day to life for the murder of Andrea Tolentino, all the kidnapping and sex charges Rod and I concocted and pinned on him were dropped. Presumably, as his reward for turning on us, he was legally granted a new name and transferred to a new prison, with the promise he would receive medical help for his "problem."

Shortly after that disastrous turn of events, the first crack in Rod's personality presented itself. He and I had often discussed the topic of the criminal mind, and we'd both laughed about how pathetically some convicts spent so much time and energy writing to women, desperately trying to "catch" them. Not that this kind of pursuit wasn't a normal activity on the outside but, for predators, we both recognized the motivation was different, more a lovesick game of manipulation than genuine courtship.

Rod had sworn repeatedly he would never act like such a fool over a woman. I, too, had once made the same declaration. But, after four years of loving Nancy and 15 years with Dolores, I was old enough to understand "skirt chasing" meant something altogether different than "relationship" to a predator.

It was with that thought in mind that I became disturbed at Rod's behavior when he began writing to a young woman who contacted us after the televised airing of our grievances.

Almost immediately, Rod was strutting about like a rutting buck, consumed by his desire for the little hotty, all of which made me wonder whether he and I would fall apart as Curtis and I had. While he wasted no time in proposing to and then marrying the girl, he assured me he was not like all the others.

Not long after Rod's marriage, the first of his many civil suits went to trial. From the witness stand, I testified for hours as to why I had killed Rod's partner. The jury *believed* my pack of lies and awarded him $125,000 from the city and $5,000 from the county. Although this sum was substantial, even *bigger* lawsuits were yet to be heard. Even so, I was *elated* at the prospect of finally receiving my third of this monetary victory.

Predictably, the city appealed the $125,000 judgment. The county had already spent tens of thousands of dollars fighting against Rod's suit, so it quickly decided not to spend many thousands more to appeal the loss of a mere $5,000.

"What's a third of $5,000?" I asked Rod when the news came through that the county would not challenge his smaller award. I already knew the answer to my question, but now that there was some real money to divvy up between us, I wanted to see how he would respond. Because I was the reason for his newfound wealth, I fully expected him to answer me enthusiastically and with the sincerest expressions of gratitude. What I did not expect was for him to walk away without answering me.

Throughout the following month, while waiting for the

check to arrive, I made it a point to mention what I intended to do with my share of the award. Rod continued to ignore my comments about what I had coming and I began to panic. Surely, Rod wouldn't burn me *now*, not after I had remained loyal to him by refusing the State's offer to have my plea bargain fulfilled if I would turn against him. I had stuck by Rod even when the Parole Board warned me they would add another ten years to my current possible release date if I continued to maintain that Rod was innocent. But, as David Hume stated in his *Law of Probability*, "the more times a thing has happened in the past, the more probable it will reoccur in the future." *No* past partner or friend had *ever* treated me fairly when it came to dividing our spoils. Not one. Why should I have expected it to be any different this time?

The showdown came when Rod cashed the check and I asked directly for my percentage.

"You want a share of the $5,000?" he asked, sounding as if I'd just presented him with the most unreasonable request he'd ever heard in his life. Clearly, he was *angry* I had at last forced the issue. "You *actually* want a share of the $5,000?"

"That *was* the deal, wasn't it?" I said, as if he needed any reminding. "My take was to be one third of *everything*, right?"

I could see his eyes narrow as he struggled to control himself, his mind racing as he tried to come up with something. Like a trapped monkey with its fist stuck inside a gourd, its hand unwilling to open and let go of the goodies so he can slide it out and go free, Rod would *not* let go. Predators always wanted it all!

"Sure, we agreed to a third," he finally said. "But I thought you meant a third of the *big* stuff. This amount is just peanuts. *Peanuts*! It's not even worth bothering about. I never dreamed you would be so petty over a third of a mere $5,000!"

I'd heard this "I'm gonna make you feel small time" guilt trip a thousand times during my years in prison. Usually it was heard when someone was trying to slow pay a *small* debt of a carton or two of cigarettes.

"Well," I said, looking him straight in the eye, "$1,600 might be 'peanuts' to you, but it doesn't even begin to make up for all the money Dolores has spent out of her own pocket on all of our schemes."

We had sent thousands of letters during our campaign to create public support for "Rod Addicks, the Innocent Man." We'd also established a newsletter, and each printing and mailing ended up costing at least several hundred dollars. Neither of us clever Big Shot convicts had any money of our own, so I imposed on Dolores to spend a couple thousand dollars of her money over the years. I knew that my reminding Rod of this would put an end to this ridiculous "don't bother me with your petty bullshit" routine. At my mention of Dolores's spending losses, his face flushed. Just for an instant, he lost control over his tongue.

"Well, I'm *not* giving it to you!" His eyes were ablaze with rage. "I have a young wife to take care of now!"

As soon as the words were out of his mouth, like arrows never to return, horror crossed his face at the realization of what he had just revealed about himself and his intentions.

"Wh-what…what I m-mean," he stammered, his face white as his mind scrambled to repair the unrepairable. "What I m-mean is that I'll give you the money after I'm out. That won't be much longer. The judge has deliberated over a year now, and he'll *have* to make a decision soon. I'll be true to my word, you'll see!"

That was the end of it. I returned to my cell and cried. All my life, I had turned to men in search of some quality I could respect. But, from the beginning, placing my trust in them had been a foolish exercise. Why did it always surprise me that the friends I made in prison always ended up betraying me?

I had no choice but to write off Rod, then find some way to pay him back. With the elections approaching, I thought I saw an opportunity. I might even be able to get my plea bargain fulfilled in the process.

Six Oregon State policemen had agreed there was something wrong about Rudy Harris not having been prosecuted simply to protect the image of the Federal Bureau of Investigation. They also agreed that nothing could be done about it without having the *right* man in the Attorney General's Office.

One contender in the race for the next Attorney General was the District Attorney who once had issued a press release stating that Agent Rand had never known me—a deliberate bold-faced lie meant to protect Rand *and* attack my credibility. Obviously that D.A. was not the *right* man. Just three days before the election, I called a press conference.

My first order of business was to expose Rod's plot to defraud the state of millions of dollars in false imprisonment suits. In explicit detail, I explained how Rod originally conceived the cunningly elaborate scheme, as well as how my own frustration over the justice denied in the Caitlin murder case had compelled me to participate in the media attracting plot. I also pointed out the losses the State had incurred thus far, a total of $130,000, would *never* have happened *if* the District Attorney now running for Attorney General had honored the plea bargains he had made with Scar. This was the D.A. who had convicted Rod by promising Scar freedom for his testimony against him.

My own payoff, I admitted, had initially been a shot at freedom by way of an escape plot to be financed by Rod after he was released. I then explained how I eventually changed my mind and settled upon accepting a third of all monies that Rod ended up winning through his "false imprisonment" suits. Lastly, I led the cameras to our cache of weapons and to four hidden sections of a 30-foot ladder.

Whether any of these actions had any actual influence in the race for Attorney General, I'll never know. The fact of the matter is that the "right man" won the election. Almost immediately afterward, however, a new nightmare began. I was placed in isolation and deprived of access to any and all law books. My visits were restricted. Then, despite the plea bargain that promised my serving the whole of my sentence *in Oregon*, I was advised I would soon be transferred to a federal prison.

The fact of the matter is that I could not survive in any other prison. A transfer, I knew, would mean certain death. My attorney filed a motion for a hearing. Not only was the motion denied out of hand, but the judge wouldn't even allow me to say a single word. As for the government's attorney, he pointedly stated that my "days of trying to expose the FBI" were over. At long last and much too late I realized I had simply pushed them too far.

I could not honestly blame the FBI for my plight. I could have run away from every FBI operative who tried to enlist my involvement in further criminal acts. I could have run from Rod Addicks. Instead, I chose to partner with every one of them, in spite of my knowing full well the nefarious nature of their schemes. John Akin was right. Criminals are like the crabs inside those big uncovered baskets used to trap them. There's no need for a lid to keep them in. Every time one starts to climb out toward freedom, another one grabs him and pulls him down.

Upon realizing Rod was simply going to throw me away after using me, I could have quietly informed the authorities, and he would have been transferred out. Instead of following that wiser and less sensationalistic course, I jumped into the middle of an election and stepped on toes that were attached to some very big feet. I would probably be transferred to some prison where killings were the norm and I would be murdered. It would all be perfectly legal, and no one would lift a finger to help me.

I thought of suicide. It was one way, perhaps the only way, to cheat certain assassination. I had plenty of bedding available this time around, and I could make a proper and fail-proof noose if I chose to go that route. There were a hundred reasons to die—and none to live. I had done what I could to fulfill my promise to the memory of Denise Caitlin. Having failed, I truly felt I had no right to die in peace.

Death was imminent and I knew it. There was nowhere to turn. Nietzsche and Sartre could not help me; they were dead. So where, at this darkest hour, could I possible turn?

When help came, it came from the most unexpected quarter...

Chapter Twenty-Eight

"YOU ARE ADDICTED TO CRIMINAL THINKING"

When help appeared, it came in the form of one of the few corrections officials for whom I held any genuine respect: Dr. John Akin. Dr. Akin had retired several years earlier from his position as Chief Psychologist at the Oregon State Penitentiary. Every so often he would return to visit the prison where he'd spent most of his adult life trying to bring reason and compassion to a system that, because it despised reason and compassion, was counterproductive to the goals it claimed to expound. It was during one of these visits, which occurred at one of the lowest points of my misdirected life, that he sought me out, making his way to my isolation cell for the purpose of having a heart to heart with me.

"So," he began, after entering my cell and sitting down on the edge of my bunk, "perhaps now is the time to start getting serious about your quest to escape the toughest prison of them all."

At the sound of his words, a dark, half-hearted laugh escaped my lips. I instantly regretted it, for this was a man who genuinely cared, a man who had never bought into the culture of negativity and ugly inertia that ensured the prison system would never *improve* upon its 75% recidivism rate—a failure rate that would *never* be tolerated in any other organization.

"Floyd," he said, his voice a mixture of sternness and compassion, "do you think it odd or insane that some part of you truly *yearns* to turn his life around? Deep down inside, all of you do! Only a mentally ill person would consciously choose or *want* to spend the greater part of his life in such a negative, soul deadening system as the penal system. Yet, for all the many inmates who really want to break free, *few* ever do.

"Believe me, Floyd, I *know* all about the entrenched interests that keep the system in a perpetual state of failure. The bottom line is that each and every inmate must somehow resolve to *make* the change, no matter that the odds are stacked entirely against him.

"There's no denying that turning your life around will be tough when the system itself is structured to make such positive change extremely difficult at best. In the more than 30 years I've spent in this business, I've known just a handful who were able to make the change. Any words of wisdom I've shared with you will have no meaning until you actualize them in your own experience, in your own daily existence. Simply 'wanting' a new life is easy but, as Benjamin Franklin once said, '*Well done* is better than *well said*.' It's the *doing*, Floyd, that really matters. That's what is going to make it possible. But you've got to start *somewhere*. Why not start *now*? Once you get back into general population, be it here or elsewhere, move *forward*. Start by pursuing some educational goals."

As Dr. Akin spoke there was no escaping the reality that he *believed* in me. For the life of me, I had no idea *why*, especially after all of the scheming machinations I'd involved myself in over the past few years. I was deeply moved by his unselfishly having come to see me and by his real concern for me.

Five months later, I was shackled and led out of the isolation unit, then transferred to the California corrections system. Almost immediately, I realized that every negative thing I'd ever heard about California was true. After the years I'd spent in the well managed Oregon system, it was a real shock to experience firsthand the culture of terror and violence in a California prison. Guards lived in constant fear for their lives, as did most inmates. Armed guards on catwalks supervised every meal line and shower period.

My counselor at Vacaville threw up his hands when I walked into his office for the first time. "Good heavens!" he exclaimed. "What are *you* doing here?"

He and I had never met, but after all the widespread publicity that followed my having solved the murder of Andrea Tolentino, I was well known throughout prison circles as an informant. For my own safety, my counselor had me transferred out of Vacaville to Folsom, but I was no safer there. Just days after I arrived, I was stabbed in my midsection with a homemade 12-inch knife, its blade just missing my heart. After two weeks in the hospital and six months in Folsom's isolation unit, I was transferred back to Oregon.

My return to the Oregon State Penitentiary was stressful, to say the least. I was completely ostracized. No one spoke to me. No one would eat at the same table with me. After a week of this silent treatment I was struck in the head and knocked unconscious with a pipe. When I woke up, I found myself in the prison infirmary, my lacerated scalp sewn back together with 70-plus stitches.

The prison administration wanted to isolate me in the psychiatric ward when I was well enough to be released from the infirmary. With a life sentence yet to serve, I insisted my only hope at living a relatively normal prison existence was in my being allowed to return to the general population. To my considerable relief, they permitted me to do exactly that.

The man who attacked me had once been a friend. When I was questioned by the State Police, I refused to finger him, insisting they suspected and were intending to charge the *wrong* man for assaulting me.

"I *saw* the man who hit me," I said, "and the guy who hit me was someone I'd never seen before in all my life. I *know* the man you suspect, and it *wasn't him* who hit me."

Ironically, Rod Addicks—of all people!—had witnessed the assault and was the one who provided the State Police with a statement fingering my former friend. In return for playing the informer, Rod finagled a transfer to Walla Walla Prison where he could enjoy regular conjugal visits with the young woman he'd married before burning me for my share of his "false imprisonment" monies.

As for the man who attacked me, he soon sent out word from the Hole, thanking me for not having fingered him. He ended up being sanctioned by the prison to one full year in the Disciplinary Segregation Unit after he was found guilty of assault, based on Rod Addicks' statement alone. If *I* had provided a second statement against him, he *would* have been formally charged with a new crime and prosecuted in a criminal court. When the word got around that I'd spared my attacker an additional criminal conviction and more prison time by keeping my mouth shut, it helped to ease at least *some* of the pressure from the ostracism I'd been experiencing.

ᨐ

Another important turning point came by way of my meeting an inmate by the name of Manolo. I was, as usual, sitting by myself at a four-man table in the chow hall when a young Mexican set down his lunch tray and sat across from me. I realized he *had* to be new and simply did not know he was sitting with the "infamous OSP informant" who had put a fellow inmate away for life—notwithstanding that the "fellow inmate" was a notorious child molester and killer. As Manolo started chatting away, I knew it was only a matter of time before someone pulled him aside and brought him up to speed about me, whether here in the chow hall or when he returned to his housing unit. Sure enough, within a couple of minutes, the leader of the Chicano gang approached our table. He gave me a menacing look as he leaned over to speak into Manolo's ear. I had become fluent in Spanish years before, so I understood every word he spoke.

"Hey, brother," said the leader, "you've got enough problems of your own without sitting with this rat! Get up and leave."

"Listen," Manolo replied without hesitation, "why don't you mind your own business?"

The gang leaders inside most prisons, like the heavy who approached Manolo at my table, use the mythical "convict code" to manipulate and control all the less violent, less hard-core inmates as they enter into the system. Although most gang leaders have no scruples about twisting or breaking the "code" whenever it suits their selfish needs, they inevitably demand newly arrived first timers to abide by the "code" as if it were some sacred scripture. I was quite surprised by Manolo's defiant reply. Clearly, Manolo was not yet given over to a "convict mindset" with all of its knee jerk posturing.

As it turned out, Manolo was not only a first timer, but one of the most intelligent first or *any* timers I'd ever met, educated at one of the finest private universities in California. Remembering John Akin's advice about furthering my education, and with Manolo's encouragement, I decided to enroll in college.

On several different levels, college turned out to be another rebirth for me. The classes were held on the third floor of an administrative office-like building, still inside the prison walls but behind some thick iron doors instead of oppressive metal bars. While it was still a prison setting in that a uniformed guard checked you onto the education floor and from time to time walked the hallway, keeping an eye on all the classrooms, it was nevertheless a different world up there. In this setting, my fellow inmates and I intuitively understood our purpose for being there and we treated each other as equals. The "convict code" was left back in the prison proper, and not once was I called a *rat* by any of my classmates. No doubt about it, this made my time there feel like daily furloughs from the intensely stressful, hate filled environment that was the norm downstairs in the housing units and on the yard.

The teachers were all great, as dedicated to their craft as they were non-judgmental towards the felons who filled their classrooms. The one teacher who contributed most to my breaking totally free from the real and "toughest" prison I was trying to escape from was a lady by the name of Jane Fields.

In addition to having taught at some prestigious universities across the country, she was also a Unitarian Minister who involved herself deeply in the Civil Rights movement and other humanitarian causes. When I asked her who or what Unitarians believe in, she looked at me with a Buddha-like smile and replied very simply, "Anything they can!"

Although Jane was a diminutive woman, I was moved by her big heart and undeniable courage to take as many of her classes as I could. It was during one of these classes that she encouraged me to study epistemology, which she said was "the foundation of it all."

"The study of why we know what we know and why we believe what we believe," she said, "is the foundation of all knowledge and wisdom. What knowledge it is," she said, "that sustains and guides us."

That is what I began to question my own thought life. Even as I began to understand more about the hows and whys of my criminal thinking, I was still missing one small but important facet in my pursuit of self-awareness.

One afternoon, I was called to the office of my case manager for my yearly program interview, during which she noted I had no record of any group or individual counseling in my file. After explaining to her I did not believe in such "nonsense," she made it clear to me that if I was ever to have *any* hope of making parole on my life sentence, *some* history of counseling on my prison record would be imperative. Reluctantly, I agreed to her booking me an appointment with a Dr. Rex Newton.

When I met the man a couple of weeks later, I asked him to share with me his background and area of expertise. His schooling was impressive, but I couldn't help rolling my eyes dismissively when he mentioned his specialty was in the area of addiction.

"Well, that's that," I said, intent on bringing the conversation to a quick end so I could leave. "I don't think I would ever get anything out of your groups. I don't use drugs."

"Oh, yes you do," he replied, looking me square in the eye. "You're one of the worst addicts I've ever seen!"

Instantly angered by Dr. Newton's assertion, I tried to slap it down by pointing out that, since my teens, I had trained myself to be a professional bank robber—a self-disciplined *pro* who *never* allowed myself to become addicted to using hard drugs. Then, after puffing out my chest with shameless bravado and pride, I challenged him to go through my thick prison file—which presently was resting on his lap—and find even one single mention of drug abuse on its pages.

In response to my challenge, he flipped leisurely through just a part of my file, pausing a handful of times to read a paragraph or two here and there. Then, as if to convey that he had seen more than enough to make his case, he closed the file as leisurely as he had opened it and looked up at me, smiling.

"It seems clear from your file," he said, "that you are addicted to *criminal thinking*!"

His words were an epiphany to me. Never had I thought of criminal thinking as an addiction. But, as Dr. Newton would drive home repeatedly to me over the coming years, an addiction is "any *thing*, any *one*, or any *thought* from which we cannot break free on our own, despite all the evidence that *that* thing is *not good* for us."

Over the ensuring years of instruction I received through the college courses offered at the prison, through my classes with Jane Fields and my counseling sessions with Dr. Rex Newton, I gradually came to see the insidious, ugly, and self-serving lie that was the "convict code." I also came to recognize the sheer badness behind all the poor and self-destructive choices I had made throughout my life. Looking to such people as Mrs. Fields and Dr. Newton as models of right thinking, I began to embrace a value system that rejected taking from or using others for my personal gain. At long last I began to understand and feel something that was altogether natural to people who lived their daily lives in peace *outside* of a prison setting: There is *virtue* in being a decent, honest, rule-following human being.

As I continued to examine my heart, trying to change for the better, I began to notice the prison system itself was changing, mostly for the worse. With politicians trying to outdo each other at being "tough on crime," laws were passed that forced judges to mete out mandatory sentences for first time drug users and for petty crimes, which led to prison overcrowding. The administration had to start housing two men in the tiny cells designed for just one person. They were also forced to convert the gym and one of the prison factory buildings into dormitories crammed with metal bunk beds. With the wholesale warehousing of increased numbers apparently destined to be the "new normal," the construction of new prisons was also well underway, with the first of these due to be up and running within a year.

ග

Not long after the overcrowding crisis reached a peak at OSP, Dr. John Akin came to visit me. Although retired for almost ten years by this time, Dr. Akin still interacted with both retired and active corrections staff, always keeping his ear to the ground to remain current on the changes taking place in the system. After the usual chit chat about health and the weather, he finally asked, "Tell me, Floyd, how many sentences do you have left to your name?"

He knew I had spent years filing various appeals. Unlike many who worked in the justice system, Dr. Akin firmly believed the law should be applied to, and obeyed by, the *keepers* as well as the *kept*. He always encouraged me to pursue all legal remedies wherever it was truly appropriate.

"Well," I said, "I'm now down to the life sentence for the State of Oregon, and 30 years for the Feds."

"Great!" he replied, smiling. "You won a couple of your appeals."

"Yeah, I did. I was able to get a seven-year sentence thrown out by showing that the Feds waited over five years to serve the warrant. After sending a copy of my college degree to another judge as proof of my efforts to change, he agreed with me that *if* I was made to serve an additional five years *after* being paroled from my life sentence, it *would* be excessively punitive and therefore wrong. I was surprised and relieved to see that *some* judges still believe in the professed purpose behind prisons and imprisonment: *rehabilitation*."

"Amen to that," Dr. Akin said. "I'm glad you stumbled across one of the few judges who apparently *does* believe in rehabilitation. Unfortunately, the legislature doesn't share the same belief. All of its new, heavy handed mandatory sentences have about broken the system."

Although I had a life sentence, mine was not a mandatory—natural life—sentence. I was one of just three prisoners left in the Oregon system with a "discretionary" life sentence, meaning the Board could legally parole me after serving one day or 50 years behind bars. Just a year or two after I was sentenced, the Oregon legislature had passed laws that required mandatory minimums of 25 or 30 years attached to life sentences.

I didn't quite understand where John Akin's conversation was going. The Parole Board would see every new lifer within a couple of months of his arrival and would set a "release consideration date." In my case, they deemed that I would have to serve 20 years before being given "serious consideration" for release. In the meantime, the Parole Board was required to see all lifers at least once every two years to determine whether these men were trying to rehabilitate themselves. In some cases, extraordinary progress would prompt the Parole Board to reduce or lower a lifer's "release consideration date."

I had a 30-year sentence for the Feds, so I had always waived my two-year reviews with the Oregon Parole Board. I *knew* I would probably be made to serve no more than 20 years on my Oregon life sentence, meaning my 30-year Federal sentence would almost certainly be longer than the life sentence. Why should I have bothered going to my Oregon review hearings every two years when a realistic shot at parole was still ten years down the road?

To my surprise, Dr. Akin brought this up as well. After looking around to make sure we could not be overheard, he leaned forward and softly asked, "Floyd, when are you scheduled for your next two-year review?"

"In a couple of months," I replied. "Why do you ask?"

"*Go* see the Parole Board," he said, "and you *will* be paroled."

I sat there, stunned, unable to believe what I'd just heard. I felt certain I must have heard him wrong.

"Wh-what d-did you s-say?" I asked, barely able to get my words out.

"The overcrowding here is now reaching the point where the Federal boys will have no choice but to shut down the Oregon system. The Oregon government doesn't want to be responsible for the backlash from federally mandated large-scale releases to cut down the prison population. The Parole Board is going to parole every inmate who has an out of state or federal detainer in his file. *Anyone* who owes time to the Feds or another state *will* be pushed out of the Oregon prison system in order to ease the overcrowding problem. Admittedly, the Oregon Parole Board would *never* parole you right now if it meant your being released directly to the streets, but by paroling you *now* to another prison sentence and into the federal prison system, they'll essentially be covering their butts against any political blowback while at the same time dealing with the overcrowding problem."

If John Akin was right, I was lucky indeed to have a shot at being paroled from my life sentence *far earlier* than I could have ever dreamed possible!

But what would I say to the Parole Board? As John Akin had noted, the Oregon Board knew that even if they paroled me, I still had a 30-year sentence to complete in the federal system. I would *still* have to convince them I was no longer a threat to society. By definition, a lifer cannot be released *except* by parole. When a released lifer hits the streets only to commit a new crime, the media and the public inevitably go into a hysterical frenzy—screaming for the heads of the Parole Board's members. I wasn't completely sold on the idea, as Dr. Akin apparently was, that parole would be easy. In their business, self-preservation—or more bluntly, cover your own ass—was the number one priority behind every decision the Parole Board made.

Even so, I felt good about myself and was confident my personal growth would be apparent to all who sat on the Board. Previously, my life had been a lie. Having embraced a value system based on respect for others as well as for myself, I could no longer stomach lying. No matter what, there would be no more lies. If my being forthright with the Parole Board turned out *not* to be good enough for them, so be it.

When the day of my hearing finally arrived, the Chairwoman of the Parole Board looked at me and said, "Well, Mr. Forsberg, what changes have you made? Are you here to tell us you've found Jesus?" Her second question was delivered in a somewhat mocking tone, as if she'd heard one too many tales of an alleged jailhouse conversion to Christianity.

"No, ma'am," I replied simply. "No Jesus. I *have* had a spiritual awakening of sorts."

"Really?" she said, a touch of sarcasm in her voice. "And what was *that*?"

"Time."

"Time?" she asked.

"Yes, ma'am, *time*," I said, placing great emphasis on the word. "And I'm not referring to the over 30 years I've already been in prison, nor to the many years I will still have to serve in a federal prison even if you end up granting me parole here in Oregon. The 'time' I refer to is the time I realistically have left to live."

"But can you at least say you regret robbing the banks that you robbed, Mr. Forsberg?"

"Well, Madam Chairwoman, I regret *getting caught*," I replied forthrightly, believing there was no point in trying to pull the wool over their eyes. "Admittedly, it was exciting to me, the planning and carrying out of those robberies, and then having all that money afterwards."

She seemed puzzled by my words. The other four members of the Board also had questioning expressions on their faces, looking at me as if I somehow lost sight of where I was or *why* I was sitting before them.

"If all you say is true," the Chairwoman finally said, "what assurance can you give us that you won't just rob another bank?"

"Madam Chairwoman, since I was a teenager, I've been released from prison twice—once for 141 days and the second for ten months. Plus, I escaped on one occasion and was out for another two months. That makes for a total of merely 16 months of freedom since I was first locked up as a teenager. Even if you were to grant me a parole today, I'll be 52 years old before the Feds will even consider my earliest possible release date from their system—and *that* is many years in the future.

"Simply put, I am running out of time, Madam Chairwoman. My future is shrinking with each passing day. With what little time I have left in that future, I want to live like a *normal* person. I want to have a job. I want to pay bills. I want to mow my own lawn. I want to own and hold a cat. I want to be free. As the record will reflect, I've already done all I could possibly do to free myself from the criminal thinking that has ruled my life since my teens. *That* is history. Now that I'm free from that prison, I think it appropriate to be freed from my *physical* prison."

After hearing me out and dismissing me from the room, the Board deliberated for over an hour before I was called back inside to hear its decision. To my immense relief, each member voiced aloud and repeatedly this would be the "last chance" I would ever be given to live "as a free member of our society." Finally, the Chairwoman announced I had been granted immediate parole from my life sentence.

Not surprisingly, once the news hit the newspapers and the airwaves the FBI immediately wrote letters to the Board asking —*demanding*, actually—that my parole be rescinded. They had neither forgotten nor forgiven my campaign to expose the criminal agents still among their ranks who I had once blamed for my own poor choices. Fortunately, and perhaps because cosmic karma had somehow recognized I'd finally taken personal responsibility for my past misdeeds, the FBI's shrieks of indignation came to nothing. The Federal prison system could hold me only a finite number of years. After that, I *would* be free.

As for the Oregon prison system, it had changed dramatically over the years and was almost unrecognizable by the time I left it behind in 1990. The mission statement of the Oregon State Legislature pretty much dictated that there would be no more rehabilitation. No more college. No more vocational training programs. Mandatory sentences for petty crimes were now the norm. The overcrowding problem had been dealt with successfully, but only because many new prisons had been built to warehouse a burgeoning state prison population that had grown to at least ten times the size it had been when I'd first entered its bowels.

The sad fact is that prisons had become a growth industry in Oregon. Empty prison beds meant lost revenue and fewer jobs, so the legislature continued to pass laws that guaranteed a steady influx of new prison inmates. In effect, they created a whole new sub-segment of society, consisting mostly of first-time-ever-in-prison convicted felons who were now treated like the "untouchables" were in India's caste system.

I feel fortunate to have been freed from Oregon's prison system before it reached its grinding, unfeeling, and soul-killing worst.

Epilogue

NANCY, 37 YEARS LATER

My release from the Federal prison system came in August, 1992. I've never taken for granted a single moment of my liberty. I was somewhat surprised to find that, just as the penal system in our country is designed to ensure a high rate of failure among the incarcerated, the same was true on the outside concerning society's treatment of *ex*-convicts as a whole.

On a number of occasions since my release, after speaking to groups of college students about the criminal justice system, I've been saddened by the questions raised by some of the young people in attendance who, in their own pasts, had run afoul of the law. After admitting to some youthful indiscretion—a car theft or a drug possession conviction—they wanted to know how long they must wait before they can have the felony conviction removed from their record. I found no pleasure in delivering the straightforward answer to their question: They could *never* get a felony conviction removed from their record. Only through a Presidential Pardon could any person's criminal record be entirely wiped clean.

In my case, of course, I received no such pardon. I was fortunate enough to have gotten some lucky breaks over my past two decades as a free man.

My first and biggest break was that, after sticking with me through my years of imprisonment, Dolores was there for me when I got out. Not only did she have a nice home ready and waiting for me upon my release, she provided me with nonstop support and encouragement during those early years of freedom as I strove to regain a sense of normalcy and reintegrate into free society. I cherish the memory of the ten happy years we shared together before her true and faithful heart stopped beating forever in 2002.

Another lucky break was my being assigned to a decent Parole Officer after my release. In addition to being honest and fair, he took the time to explain to me just how much things had changed in the free world during the many years I'd spent locked up behind bars. Among the things he emphasized were the realities of the modern computer age, and the ease with which prospective employers could use the Internet to find out about an ex-convict's criminal record.

"Don't even think of lying about your past when you fill out a job application," he said to me during our first post release meeting. "If you lie, and the employer finds out about it, you probably won't be hired. Worse yet, if you lie and do get hired, you'll almost certainly get fired when they eventually uncover the truth."

Fortunately, my first employer was not averse to hiring ex-convicts, provided they had no drug offenses or sex crimes on their record. I earned my commercial driver's license, opening up virtually unlimited job opportunities for me as a truck driver. I roamed the network of highways that connected all the Western states, hauling cargo containers from one far-flung city to another. After decades of staring at nothing but steel bars and grey prison walls, my trips through some of the country's most wondrous landscapes—especially in Idaho, Washington,

Oregon, and Montana—were among the most awe-inspiring and fulfilling experiences in my life.

Incredibly, after Dolores passed away, my life was touched yet again by great fortune. Almost 37 years after she first came knocking upon my apartment door, Nancy, my first true love, reentered my life and stole my heart anew. When she'd first come into my life all those years before, it was *Nancy* who had sparked my earliest yearnings for normalcy, for the wholeness and fulfillment that is possible *only* through truly loving another human being *more* than one's self. She had loved me without condition—and I had so wanted to do the same for her—but one bad decision after another on my part had killed our love while it was still in the womb. Years of dismal failure were followed by my decision to change and then years of growth. Though she never left my heart, never could I have imagined that Nancy would return to embrace me again. And yet she *did* —and we married very shortly thereafter.

As Nancy gave me stability and fulfillment in my personal life, so did my many hours on the road provide me with stability and a sense of fulfillment as a contributing member of society—a worker.

As the years passed, I started noticing the introduction of this new law or that new regulation, each one meant to target an increasingly larger segment of the ex-convict population after their return to free society. From the start, it struck me that these changes didn't really mean a damn thing to the average American citizen at large—those with no criminal record. They simply could not see that millions of their fellow Americans were being denied or had severely limited employment opportunities for misdeeds committed in their distant pasts.

Then came the horrific tragedy of 9/11. As most Americans saw firsthand through the increased airport security measures that quickly followed, our country was changed forever by that terrible event. Among the many changes that occurred under the banner of "National Security" was the proliferation of new laws targeting ex-felons.

In 2008, the Department of Homeland Security decreed that convicted felons could no longer enter the nation's ports. Had I been convicted of treason, espionage, or terrorism, or any crime against my country or government, I could have understood the ban. However, the disqualifying list of crimes compiled by Homeland Security included virtually *every* criminal act or statute on the books—forgery, burglary, car theft, and so on—which immediately put at risk the job of every American citizen with a criminal past who was employed as a truck driver inside our nation's borders.

I was extremely fortunate to have accumulated 15 years of no criminal activity on my record at the time Homeland Security imposed this new restriction. This permitted me to be grandfathered onto the list of truck drivers who could work at our nation's ports, and I was able to hold on to my job. If an ex-con truck driver had nine years or less of clean time on his record, however, he was out of luck and out of a job.

I realize that most of free society thinks it's just fine that we have the largest prison population in the world. "Once sinned, never forgiven," society often says about imprisoned felons, adding "we should lock them up and throw away the key!" What many fail to realize is that more and more people are being imprisoned *only* because the slightest moral or behavioral infractions are now being criminalized, thus creating a vastly larger pool of human beings to arrest, convict, and lock up behind bars, all in the name of the "prison growth industry." Then, by deliberately deemphasizing rehabilitation, these convicted felons are being characterized and treated as "untouchables" in this new de facto American caste system, thereby justifying *keeping* them imprisoned for *as long as possible.*

Slowly but surely, however, reasonable minds are beginning to realize that we simply *cannot afford* the huge costs that come with having the largest prison population in the world. One can only hope that cold, hard economics compels the resurgence of a prison system based on *rehabilitation* rather than one based on locking up ever increasing numbers of offenders with little or nothing offered to change or better their lives.

As for the gang that pulled off America's first bank robbery of over $1,000,000, Ed is the only one no longer alive. Although our leader, Curtis Michelson, pled guilty on the Reno heist, he ended up returning the share of the money he still had in his possession at the time of his arrest. Moreover, he gave the FBI directions to the spot where Ed's share of the money had been buried. Although he confessed to committing Oregon's largest ever bank robbery—the same robbery he asked Dolores to watch from across the street, and about which she later committed perjury at his request—Curtis was never charged with that crime. Dolores ended up serving a five-year sentence for lying to protect Curtis, whereas he went unpunished.

The most appalling revelation during my years as a criminal was the FBI's cynical and shameless use of agent provocateurs to further their careers. As Curtis himself testified during one of his trials, he made it a point to involve as many people as possible in his elaborate crimes *knowing* that, if he were caught, the FBI would gladly reward him with generous deals when he turned on —and turned in—his crime partners. Oftentimes, the most publicized cases are the direct result of this kind of FBI duplicity, as when the FBI allowed TV news to follow and film the 1966 robbery in which I was involved.

I *do*, however, believe in karma. I imagine that, even in the case of corrupt FBI agents, every man eventually gets his just desserts, in one form or another. As for Curtis Michelson, he got his after he broke his own cardinal rule of involving as many crime partners as possible in his heists. Upon completing his federal sentence, he went to Florida and robbed a bank all by himself. When he was caught, he had no human fodder for his FBI friends, so he was tried in State Court and given a life sentence. Nevertheless, even with that, he was given a new identity to protect him and keep him alive so he could *continue* serving the pleasure of the FBI as an informant just as he'd done *all* of his life.

As for the final member of the robbery gang—*me*—it is noteworthy that, during my first ten years of freedom, I earned more money before taxes than I garnered from what was the Biggest Bank Robbery of my time. Proof positive, I will be the first to admit, that there is no honor among thieves and only a fool believes crime pays.

I hope that some of you who read this book will undertake the enormous task of escaping the prison you find yourself in. To escape, you must realize that this prison is self-imposed, that only you can escape from it.

If it was easy, everyone would do it.

Afterword

BY GARY YORK

Retired Senior Prison Investigator and Author

Floyd Forsberg spent over a decade trying to expose the corruption of law enforcement officers, FBI agents, parole officers, and prison officials. Before you dismiss his accusations as attempts to exonerate himself from his crimes, let me tell you the kind of corruption he reports is real.

On many occasions I have sat in prison interview rooms, four walls, no window, one desk, two chairs, my burgundy briefcase on the floor and a tape recorder right in the middle of the desk conducting interviews with inmates just like Floyd C. Forsberg. Inmates who had complaints against prison staff or public officials, hoping that someone, anyone, would take them seriously. My job as a prison investigator was to listen to each allegation with an open mind, giving no indication with facial expressions or words how I felt about the allegations. One thing I knew for sure that the inmates did not know was the fact that I conducted all my investigations objectively by developing the evidence, and whatever the evidence indicated, that is how I would proceed. I never conducted an investigation to prove guilt. I am also a strong believer that a person who works in any capacity as a public official, entrusted with the public safety, the safety of their fellow staff members, and the safety of the inmates must be held accountable for their malfeasance. Corruption is harmful to everyone. Inmates like Floyd made their own dumb mistakes and are paying for them with prison time. Many of the inmates I spoke with were swallowed up by a prison industry that makes money from the inmates and their families through the phone system, inmate canteens, and work-release centers. This is not to say the inmates shouldn't have to pay back the community or get a free ride, but public officials should not be lining their pockets with money made from selling services to a literally "captive" market.

Let me give you an example of what I mean about officials lining their pockets. In my books (*Corruption Behind Bars* and *Inside the Inner Circle: More Stories of Crime and Corruption in Our American Prison System*), I have many stories of public officials I investigated for corruption. The majority of these cases started out with an inmate making an allegation against a staff member of the prison. Had I ignored these allegations and said, "I don't believe anything these inmates say," these men and women would have continued abusing their power and stealing money from the inmates and the state.

The number of allegations reported to me by inmates over the years amounts to over 1100 documented cases, not including honest staff members reporting prison corruption and citizen reports. We cannot ignore inmate allegations of corruption. I simply could not ignore what the inmates were reporting. I have been threatened and cursed at by corrupt staff members and their families. I have been thanked by honest staff members who still keep in touch with me to this day, and that's the way I like it. I want nothing to do with corrupt people.

Inmates and staff members who report corruption take a huge risk. Most inmates have to stay in prison twenty-four hours a day, and cannot escape reprisals from the corrupt men and women they expose. The least we can do is hear them out and take them seriously because, in my experience, more often than not the allegations turned out to be true.

I would like to thank those officers and public officials who stay strong and do not give in to the temptation of corruption. For those prison officers, parole officers, and probation officers who provide proper care, custody, and control of inmates without violating laws, general orders, policies, and procedures, keep up the good work! You may help an inmate to turn their life around for the better. Remember, our goal is to see inmates become productive citizens not repeat offenders.

Gary York
June, 2015
Florida

Gary York began his career in 1987 with the Florida Department of Corrections as a Corrections Officer after serving as a Staff Sergeant in the Army Military Police Corps. He has been a probation officer and retired as a senior prison inspector. For 12 years, he conducted criminal, civil, and administrative investigations in many state prisons. Gary was also assigned to the Inspector General Drug Interdiction Team conducting searches of staff and visitors entering the prisons for contraband during weekend prison visitations. Gary is the author of two books, *Corruption Behind Bars* and *Inside the Inner Circle: More Stories of Crime and Corruption in Our American Prison System.* Each is a collection of stories from his investigations of corruption in the Florida State prison system.

Timeline

Timeline of Events

1941: Floyd was born in Ridgefield, Washington.

1952: Floyd's father, a commercial fisherman, drowns in a fishing accident.

1953: Floyd's criminal career begins with shoplifting and burglary. Eva takes her two children, Floyd and Sharon, to Arizona to begin a new life.

1955: Floyd is arrested for burglary in Tucson, Arizona. Eva reports Floyd to the police after she finds guns under his bed. He receives probation. After two more arrests, Eva moves them back to Ridgefield to be closer to family.

1956: Floyd is arrested for purse snatching. He runs away, is caught, and is sentenced to one year at Luther Burbank School for Boys. He escapes once and is later released after nine months.

1958: Floyd is arrested for car theft and burglary. He is sentenced to one year at Washington State Training School at Chehalis. He escapes twice, then is released to join the Army.

1959: After completing boot camp, Floyd goes AWOL and plans a robbery. He is sentenced to one year at the US Disciplinary Barracks at Fort Leavenworth, Kansas.

1960: Upon release from Leavenworth, Floyd, his sister, and another woman, go on a nationwide spree cashing stolen postal money orders. They were arrested in Florida and sentenced to five years at the Federal Corrections Institution in Lompoc, California.

1963: Floyd is convicted for attempted murder while still in prison, and is transferred to McNeil Island Federal Penitentiary in Washington to serve an additional five years.

1966: Floyd is paroled and meets Nancy, the love of his life. 46 days later, he is arrested for bank robbery. He receives another sentence of five years at McNeil.

1974: After being paroled again, Floyd plans and executes the largest bank robbery in US history at the First National Bank of Reno, Nevada. Under surveillance by the FBI, he goes on the run.

1975: Floyd is caught in January, escaped in April, and is recaptured in June. Sentenced to 25 years for bank robbery and five years for escape. Seven more years added to fulfill the remainder of the 13 years received in 1966.

1976: Floyd is convicted of murdering Denise Caitlin the previous year. He is sentenced to life and sent to Oregon State Penitentiary.

1979: While in prison, Floyd convinced another inmate to tell him where to find the body of a murder victim as part of a larger plan to get publicity about a corrupt FBI agent. While he solves the murder, his plan to escape and expose the FBI agent goes nowhere.

1980: Floyd is stabbed and almost killed.

1990: Requests a parole hearing on his life sentence. It is reduced to 30 years.

1992: Floyd is finally released from prison and gets a job as a truck driver.

Photos

THESE ARE PHOTOGRAPHS FROM FLOYD'S LIFE.

Floyd's Childhood

Floyd Sr. and Eva

Eva and Floyd Sr.

Floyd and Unidentified Man

Luther Burbank School for Boys, c. 1940 (above and below)

"Frosty" (right) in 1959 at Washington State Training School in Chehalis

Floyd during his brief stint in the Army

AUG 59

AUG 59

Floyd's First Spiritual Leader: Walt

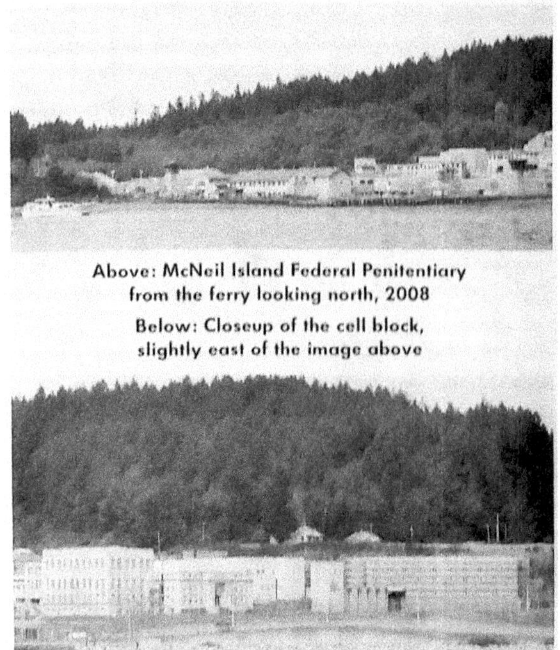

Above: McNeil Island Federal Penitentiary
from the ferry looking north, 2008

Below: Closeup of the cell block,
slightly east of the image above

Dear Mom,

PICTORIAL FEATURE - by JOHN CHING

This is where you can find me during the next few years. McNeil Island looks tranquil, doesn't it

Coming over on the **James V. Bennett** *was depressing because I knew the return trip was about five years-miles in the future.*

18 Island Lantern

My fr... in th... tion... it's...

Most fish (new men) are assigned to work in the dining room, but . . .

draw... room...

Island Lantern

Kitchen at McNeil Island, June 1965

Slaughterhouse at McNeil Island (1)

Slaughterhouse at McNeil Island (2)

Prison Friends

Floyd with Unknown Inmate

Floyd with Unknown Inmate

Floyd's FBI Wanted poster, 1974

Floyd (center) escorted by smiling FBI Agents after the "Big Show," August 16, 1966

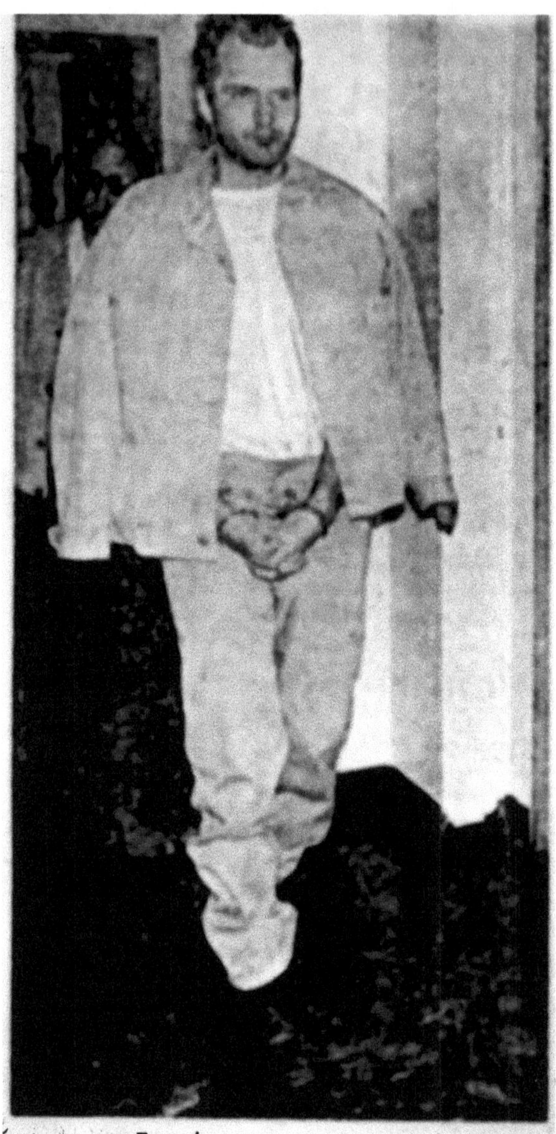

Forsberg arraigned

Wearing handcuffs and leg irons, Floyd Clayton Forsberg, 33, this morning entered Deschutes County Circuit Court for his arraignment. Forsberg, who is charged with shooting Denise Catlin in [illegible] John M. Copenhaver. The judge continued his arraignment to allow Forsberg time to talk to his Bend attorney, Max Merrill, whom Forsberg met for the first time today. (Bulletin photo by Dave Swan)

Dennis Cartwright, Floyd Forsberg, Rod Addicks

Dr. John Akin

July 4th Footraces at OSP

Visiting Room at OSP

Floyd in front of his truck, after getting out of prison

A Message to Readers

Floyd is working on a new book, tentatively titled "Predator and Prey," a fictional story of a psychiatrist on the trail of a murderer.

If you enjoyed this memoir, the author would like to encourage you to share what you liked about it with your friends and others who might be interested. Telling others of your enthusiasm for this memoir means more to us than leaving reviews (which we would appreciate as well).

Please visit www.FloydForsberg.net for more information about the author, or email him at floyd@floydforsberg.net.

You can also check out other books by the publisher at www.carlislelegacybooks.com.

About the Author

After spending most of his life in and out of penal institutions, Floyd now works as a truck driver in the Pacific Northwest.

Learn more at his website:
https://www.floydforsberg.net

www.ingramcontent.com/pod-product-compliance
Lightning Source LLC
Chambersburg PA
CBHW070051030426
42335CB00016B/1852

* 9 7 8 1 9 5 2 0 4 3 1 2 3 *